Me After
YOU

Me After YOU

A True Story About Love, Loss and Other Disasters

LUCIE BROWNLEE

2 4 6 8 10 9 7 5 3 1

First published in 2014 by Virgin Books, an imprint of Ebury Publishing

A Random House Group Company

Copyright © Lucie Brownlee 2014

Lucie Brownlee has asserted her right under the Copyright, Designs and Patents Act 1988 to be identified as the author of this work.

Addresses for companies within The Random House Group Limited can be found at www.randomhouse.co.uk/offices.htm

The Random House Group Limited Reg. No. 954009

A CIP catalogue record for this book is available from the British Library

The Random House Group Limited supports the Forest Stewardship Council® (FSC®), the leading international forest-certification organisation. Our books carrying the FSC label are printed on FSC®-certified paper. FSC is the only forest-certification scheme supported by the leading environmental organisations, including Greenpeace. Our paper procurement policy can be found at www.randomhouse.co.uk/environment

Printed and bound by CPI Group (UK) Ltd, Croydon, CR0 4YY

ISBN: 9780753555835

To buy books by your favourite authors and register for offers, visit www.randomhouse.co.uk

For Mark, wherever He is.

Contents

Prologue   9

STAGE ONE: Famous Last Words   11

STAGE TWO: Well-Placed Protection   59

STAGE THREE: The Shared Experience   127

STAGE FOUR: Just Keep Going   177

STAGE FIVE: A Final Resting Place?   257

Epilogue   309

Acknowledgements   319

Prologue

Bad news travels through letterboxes and under doors like a noxious gas. By lunchtime on the day after my husband, Mark, dropped dead aged thirty-seven, there were at least three casseroles on the doorstep and a dozen sympathy cards on the mat. Representatives from both sides of the family who never met except for on 'occasions' had gathered in Mother's hot little living room.

My brother, Dan, had turned up first. At 8.30 in the morning, he screeched up to the house an hour after receiving the news, having driven sixty miles cross-country. He walked through the front door and held his arms out to me. It was a long time before he spoke.

Everyone was looking at each other, or me, or staring out of the window, and all the while I tried to justify to myself and to them why I wasn't crying. I tried to summon up the feelings I thought I was supposed to have. I repeated the mantra, Mark is dead, over and over again and waited for the moment when I would collapse, distraught, in a heap on the carpet. Nothing.

Meanwhile, our three-year-old daughter B played the bossa nova demo on her Bontempi keyboard to this new captive and catatonic audience, and guzzled the sweets they'd brought her. She asked once where her daddy was and I told her he was at work. She knew I was bullshitting but she had Haribo so she let it slide.

So while they nursed their coffee and their grief and listened to the bossa nova on a loop, I sat in the centre of the blast and calmly opened the Rioja.

Famous Last Words

DAY 1: SATURDAY 11 FEBRUARY 2012, 8.13 P.M.

I knew He was dead. His pupils were shot, and fixed on a point beyond me. He had no pulse. His face was pinkish-grey and doughy. But as the paramedics pounded up the stairs into the bedroom where He lay, I honestly believed they would bring my husband round. I had been doing CPR for twenty minutes on a dead man, but didn't allow myself to believe it was the end.

We'd been in the middle of making love – in my mother's bed. We were there for the weekend for the funeral of my grandma, who, in an unfortunate twist of fate and tragi-comic timing, had died five days before Mark. We were making love in Mother's bed because we were trying to conceive (she was out at the time, I hasten to add).

Those who become embroiled in the complicated world of conception know that there is a 'moment' during the month in which all systems must absolutely go – you have a thirty-second window before the egg explodes and the sperm shrivels or something – so needless to say this wasn't going to be the Barry White of sessions. It was business. We'd lost a baby in September and this was a last-ditch attempt to have another. And besides, *Take Me Out* was starting in ten minutes so we had to be quick.

'You've still got your socks on,' He'd said, climbing on top of me.

Hardly the Humphrey Bogart of last words (*his* were reputedly: 'I should never have switched from Scotch to Martinis'). Seconds later, He crashed on to the pillow next to me, heavy as a felled oak. I slapped His face and told Him to wake up. He was breathing, heavy, laboured breaths into the pillow. I wondered if I should bother the emergency services with my call. Surely He would come round and I didn't want to cause a scene in the street outside. Our daughter, B, appeared in the doorway, woken up by the screaming – I must have been screaming but I don't remember – and she was crying and peering in. I told her the ultimate adult lie; that everything was all right.

The voice on the phone told me to roll Mark over and begin compressions on His chest. I manoeuvred Him, with difficulty, on to His back and started in time with the voice: 1... and... 2... and... 3... and... 4.

B was by my side now, crying and asking me why Daddy wasn't waking up. I remember feeling conspicuously nude

– except for the socks, of course – and considered where the nearest shroud of decency might be found when the paramedics arrived. (Towel... bathroom.)

His lips were turning blue. I opened one of His eyes and it stared through me. I felt His neck for a pulse. His skin was already beginning to get cold, vital signs shutting down one by one, like lights in an apartment block. A nerve in His left thumb twitched. I wouldn't believe He was dead.

But I would later learn it had been instant. There was nothing anyone could have done.

After the paramedics had arrived, I'd glimpsed Mark one final time. I needed to call Mother but the phone was where I'd left it after making the emergency call, discarded in panic on the set of drawers in the bedroom. I stepped in to get it and my eyes fell to where they'd moved Him on to the floor next to the bed. His arm was propped against the radiator. They'd placed a mask over His face and all I could hear were the faint beeps of machinery.

My call to Mother went something like this; 'Mark's collapsed... the ambulance is here... they're upstairs with Him now... you need to come home...'

She was just around the corner babysitting at my sister Beth's house, and while I didn't really register her response, I knew that she would be arranging care for the kids and with us within minutes.

B and I sat at the kitchen table and waited. B looked at me over the rim of a cup of milk. 'I'm frightened of something,' she said.

'What are you frightened of?'

'I don't know.'

'No need to be frightened, love,' I told her. But a cold shard of terror had lodged in my guts. We listened to the beeps and creaks coming from the room above us; each one part of a last-ditch attempt to save her daddy.

When the paramedics came down the stairs after forty minutes, grim-faced and exhausted, and one of them uttered the words: 'Mark's died', you might forgive me for my response.

'Right,' I said. 'Right.'

I suddenly, inexplicably, felt frightened of the body upstairs. Did I want to see Him? No. I regret that response now. A chance for a last cuddle before He went truly cold.

'But whereabouts have you left Him?' I asked. 'Is He on the floor?'

'Yes. With the blanket over Him. I'll come up with you if you like...'

I shook my head. 'What will happen now?'

The paramedic prodded at his electronic notebook with a stumpy digit. 'The police will be here shortly. Then they'll come and take Mark.'

'Are you leaving now?' I asked, watching as the team filed past carrying their arsenal of life-saving equipment, now redundant, back to the ambulance. 'Please, don't leave.'

'They are,' he said. 'But I'll stay until the police arrive.'

10.05 P.M.

'Was it your... husband?' asked the younger, more ample-eared of the two policemen who were now sitting in Mother's living room drinking tea.

'Yes...'

The other one, clearly an old hand at incidents of sudden death, took notes and handed me a photocopied leaflet, 'Coping with Sudden Death'. 'Have you decided if you want your husband cremated or buried?'

Mark hadn't been dead two hours, yet the policeman seemed surprised that I hadn't considered the options for His disposal.

'Tell me this is a dream,' I pleaded with Mother.

'I'm afraid it's not.'

The Old Hand pressed his fingertips together and brought them up to his mouth. 'We have all night,' he said. 'Take your time.'

Policemen, up close, in your living room, have a kind of other-worldliness about them. On the whole, they're taller than you would imagine, and their uniforms are straight out of the BBC costume department. Never having had a proper encounter with one before, their presence seemed to add to the theatrical quality of the evening.

'Cremated,' I suggested.

I didn't know what the significance of my answer was – I still don't – but I was prepared to agree to anything to avoid all night in the company of these two.

This seemed to have satisfied his line of questioning. For him, the bureaucracy of death was complete. He sipped his tea and reassured me that he wouldn't leave until the undertakers got there. Small-talk doesn't come easily in situations such as this ('Been busy tonight?' 'Is this your first sudden death?') so I stood by the window, willing the undertakers to arrive.

It occurred to me that perhaps I should make some phone calls. But should I wait until morning to launch the grenade, or was it best to do it now, in this cold excess of time between death and undertaker? I asked the Old Hand for his advice. After all, he was the bearer of 'Coping with Sudden Death', which must surely have had a sub-section devoted to 'Telling Family and Friends (about the) Sudden Death'. He brought his fingers to mouth again and paused. Then he said, 'It's entirely up to you.'

I called my dad. He lived half an hour away in North Yorkshire with his wife, Karen.

'He's at the pub I'm afraid – anything I can help with?' Karen asked. I glanced at the hour: 10.30 p.m. Dad's habits hadn't changed in forty years. Two pints of Theakston's and he'd be home.

'It's just... well, there's really no easy way to say this... Mark has died, Karen.' Saying those three words for the first time, I felt like an actor rehearsing a script. They seemed fraudulent, somehow, with no basis in reality.

Karen and Mark were good pals; they enjoyed talking over Sunday morning coffee while the rest of us slumbered upstairs on the weekends we spent at Dad's. Mark had recently been exchanging letters with Karen's dad relating to the war; Mark loved his stories about flying Thunderbolts over Burma, and Karen's dad loved regaling Him with them.

Karen had heard the three words, yet clearly they had no basis in her reality either. She replied with: 'Your dad's only just left the house. I'll call the pub. He'll be with you in half an hour.'

I made one more call. To Mark's sister. Perhaps I should have granted her one last sleep before her life changed for ever, but I figured she'd want to know. 'I can't believe it...' she uttered. 'I just can't believe it.'

I left her with the gruesome task of informing her parents, who were living 11,000 miles away in Australia. I can only imagine the phone call and their subsequent desperation to find a flight back to the UK, where each air mile would only bring them closer to the grievous reality that they had lost their son.

Mother offered to call my sister Beth, who was just about to settle into the second half of a performance by Cirque du Soleil at the Royal Albert Hall. It was rare that she and her husband Will were spared a weekend away together, and this frozen one in February was it. The details of the call and its aftermath were described to me only later, when she and I lay in each other's arms on the bed.

She'd stepped out into the foyer to be told the news, whereupon her legs had given way under her. Despite desperate attempts to get home, she had no choice but to wait until the first train out of King's Cross the following morning. She and Will had drunk whisky in the hotel bar until it permitted them to sleep. They arrived home just before noon the following day, as shell-shocked and disbelieving as the rest of us.

Two men finally came to Mother's door. The first man, a raven-like figure, stood in the puddled gloom of the streetlight, and announced:

'We've come to take Mark.'

Even now I can hear his voice uttering those words.

I don't have any concept of how long it took them to package Him up, manoeuvre Him round the bend in the staircase and out the front door. It could have been five minutes; it could have been half an hour. I had the TV on in the lounge, volume turned up full, with the door shut. All I remember was the silence once they'd gone.

I slept fitfully that night, in the sheets in which He'd died. Then I woke, and He wasn't there.

FOUR YEARS EARLIER: SUNDAY 17 AUGUST 2008

By 9 p.m., I knew there was something amiss. I'd been trying to contact my husband by phone for the last hour, but each time it had rung off. He would have started the hour-long journey to the centre of Cheltenham by now, ready to start His 10 p.m. shift at GCHQ. Three hundred miles away in Mother's kitchen in Newcastle, I waited. There would be an explanation for this. He was never late for a shift. At 10.05, I called the office.

'Has Mark arrived into work?'

'No, He hasn't actually. We were just starting to get a bit worried... who am I talking to?'

'This is His wife...' My throat closed up around the word 'wife'.

'Listen, give me a number where you are and I'll make a few calls.'

Panic had cleared my mind. I couldn't remember Mother's number. 'Who are you going to call?'

'I'll just make a few calls. Don't worry. Are you calling from the number that I can call you back on?'

'Yes.'

I paced the carpet in cold dread. Ten minutes later, a consultant from Cheltenham General Hospital rang. They had Mark in. He'd just managed to call an ambulance before collapsing in the flat around four hours earlier. He was stable and coherent, but they were as yet unable to ascertain what the problem was. There seemed to be an issue with the blood flow in His right leg. If it persisted, and they couldn't find a reason why, they may have to amputate the leg.

'Is it life-threatening?' was all I could think of to ask.

'Not if we get the leg off in time,' the consultant said.

I stared at the muted television, unable to take in the words I had just heard. 'I'm coming down, now.'

'Yes, do so. But please drive carefully.'

Mother, Beth and I gathered and held an eerily calm crisis meeting. I pushed the consultant's words to the back of my mind and focused on the practicalities. Who would look after three-month-old B while I drove to Cheltenham? How would she be fed, given she was currently on the breast? Having no transport of my own, whose car would I drive down in?

I threw clothing items into a suitcase, whatever I could find on the floor. Mother would come with me. Beth would stay with B, using whatever milk I was able to express for the midnight feed, and one of the 'just in case' ready-mixed formula feeds for the next morning.

I hurried Mother out of the door and into her car. We drove as far as Darlington before my phone rang. It was Beth. The consultant had called again and asked that I call him urgently.

'Change of plan,' he told me. 'We're transferring Mark to Oxford. We've discovered it's a problem with His aorta. An aortic dissection, in fact.'

'Is it life-threatening?' was all I could think to ask.

'I can't answer no to that,' the consultant said. Those were the exact words he used.

Mother and I drove for five hours through the black August night, each of us unable to find a single word to say to the other. We stopped once at Woodall services for a toilet break. Coldplay's 'Fix You' was piping through the sound system with ominous prescience as I paid for a bottle of water.

I expressed milk from my swollen breasts and threw it out of the car window on to the motorway. We arrived at

5 a.m. in the desolate car park of Oxford's Radcliffe Hospital. I jumped out of the car while Mother went and parked. I ran down empty corridors, whose polished floors reflected the strip lighting overhead, and found the lift to the cardiac ward.

All I could see were His eyes, peering out from above the plastic oxygen mask that covered His face. Machines beeped through the thick gloom of the ward. He was waiting for me.

'Love...'

His eyes smiled.

'Are you all right?' was the only thing I could think to ask.

'I am now you're here,' he said, reaching for my hand.

He asked me to be waiting with a big bottle of water and a smile when He came out of surgery. I chivvied. He chivvied. But we both knew this was catastrophic.

'Have you had any recent impact to the chest? Car accident? Spontaneous aortic dissection this extensive is most unusual in someone so young...' The straight-talking Scottish surgeon, dragged from his bed in the middle of the night to operate in this most acute of emergencies, looked at Mark.

'No...'

The surgeon glanced at his clipboard. 'You're thirty-three, aren't you, Mark?'

Mark nodded through a tangle of wires and tubes.

The surgeon turned to his registrar, then back to my husband. 'Thing is, Mark, we don't at this point know why this has occurred. But whatever the reason, your aorta has ruptured and our immediate and urgent task is to fix it. We're just assembling the team, then we'll take you down to theatre.'

The lighting was dimmed in the ward, but the glare from an anglepoise lamp reflected in the surgeon's glasses. Life had gone from baby shit and colic to the vocabulary of acute crisis in the space of six hours. My hand gripped the rail on the side of Mark's bed. The registrar, a small, kind-faced man, placed his hand over it. 'You look terrified. Don't worry, Mark's in the best place. Professor Chambers is one of the most respected heart surgeons in the country.'

'What will you do to my husband, though?' I pleaded.

'We need to assess the extent of the damage first, but we're aiming to patch up the aorta, and replace the aortic valve.'

I felt foolish having to ask at this late juncture, but I heard myself say; 'The aorta being...?'

'The main artery to the heart.'

'And what was that about the valve?'

'Mark will be fitted with a mechanical heart valve. It'll mean He has to take pills for the rest of his life, but in someone so young we would always go for this option over a pig-skin valve. Those tend to be the option for older patients; requiring no medication but only lasting ten years or so. Mark can expect a normal lifespan and a mechanical valve will go on for ever. All things being equal.'

I turned to Professor Chambers, one of the most respected heart surgeons in the country, and asked: 'Have you done this many times before?'

Chambers was unfazed by the blundering nature of the question. 'Yes. But it's always more difficult in the acute scenario. Let's go, Mark.'

Mark looked up at me and smiled. 'It's like that Al Green song, pet. "How To Mend A Broken Heart". See you soon. And don't forget that bottle of water.' They wheeled Him into the operating theatre, and I saw a single tear crawl down His cheek.

We left the hospital together three months later. 'I'm granite, me, man,' Mark said. He'd been sliced in half, His lung had been drained, He'd suffered a mild stroke during surgery. Yet here we were, racing along the B-road between Oxford and Cheltenham, the fingers of a brittle autumn sun splaying through the trees on to the road before us. He was three stone lighter, gaunt, shell-shocked, yet He had made it. We had made it. 'We win,' we said – our catchphrase against the world.

He took short, tentative steps into the flat. Each stair left Him breathless. He took His first bath when He got home, the livid wound bisecting His sternum. He was smaller. Depleted. He had been violated in the most savage way imaginable. Surgical fingers had sawn open His ribcage and tampered with His heart. But He never complained, not once. Life was different now, dictated by pills and blood pressure and Warfarin, yet it was there to be lived. He'd been given a second chance and He was going to take it with both hands.

A year later, I wrote the following letter to Chambers:

10th August 2009
Dear Professor Chambers,

I am compelled to write a few words to you as we approach the first anniversary of the 'cardiac event' suffered by my husband, Mark.

Mark was brought into the Radcliffe from Cheltenham on 18 August 2008 with an emergency 'Type A' aortic dissection. By some miracle, he found himself in your care and that of your wonderful colleagues. Despite the odds, you saved his life. Although his troubles were not over – further surgery and a stroke – your intervention on that fateful morning has meant that I still have a husband and our tiny daughter B (just three months old at the time of the incident) will grow up to know her dad.

Mark is making a great recovery – he is an unrelentingly positive soul, which helps enormously. As you can imagine, each milestone is an emotional one. One year on, with the immediate crisis over, we find ourselves in the whirlwind of trying to come to terms with what happened. However, we are totally and utterly indebted to you and the team at the Radcliffe, and each day we are thankful that Mark was lucky enough to have been attended by you.

We intend to make a financial donation to the unit,
but I wanted to write to you personally to express my
gratitude.

On behalf of Mark, B and our entire family and
friends – thank you.

Sincerely

Lucie Brownlee

It took me two years to begin to feel comfortable with our new life, for the anxiety to subside and for the sense of doom to lift. The surgeons and the doctors had spent twenty-four months reassuring us.

'What about, you know, exertion...' I asked Chambers during Mark's first review. 'Can we still have sex?'

'As long as you're not swinging from the chandeliers...' Chambers told us.

'And what about the future...?'

Chambers turned to Mark. 'Listen, you get dealt a hand. You can't do anything about it. You've been lucky, though, you're still here, and despite what you suffered, you can expect a normal lifespan. Now go and enjoy your lives.'

DAY 2: SUNDAY 12 FEBRUARY 2012, 6.30 A.M.

I rolled over and instead of Mark there was Mother, lying awake next to me. We'd tried to sleep downstairs, on the sofa-bed ('the rack' as it had come to be known), but we couldn't settle. In the end we had climbed into the bed He'd died in, pulled up the duvet and fallen into a troubled slumber.

'Where are Mark's things?' I asked. 'His clothes, His backpack? His glasses from beside the bed?'

'I moved them,' Mother replied.

We stared at each other over the undulations of our pillows. 'Moved them where?'

'They're in the wardrobe.'

'Why the hell...?' I threw the duvet back and opened the wardrobe door.

'I didn't want you to have to face them, lovey...' She sat up and watched as I burrowed in the bottom of the wardrobe.

I dragged His suitcase out and opened the zip. His brown Dr Martens boots were crushed up inside with all the other offending items: His mobile phone, His belt, His wash bag, His pill box. Those now defunct remnants of a life, hastily packed away. And finally, His glasses. He'd taken them off seconds before we began making love, and I lifted them out of the case and looked at them. I thought I could discern a fingerprint on one of the lenses. I looked through them in an attempt to see the world as He did.

I packed everything back up and pushed the case back into the dark corner of Mother's wardrobe. I turned to look at Mother.

'You didn't get rid of the Guinness, did you?'

'What?'

'The four-pack of Guinness He'd just bought that were sitting on the bench. You didn't throw them out, did you?'

Mother shook her head. 'They're at the back of the shelf in the porch. I just didn't want...'

I pulled on a dressing gown and walked out of the bedroom.

I peered in at B who was yet to awaken into her first day without her daddy. I was relieved she still slept, for I had no energy to deal with her. Downstairs, I boiled the kettle, then went into the lounge and forgot about it. I felt hungry, but the thought of food made me retch.

I looked out of the window at the trees, skeletal against a white February sky. I had been told my husband was dead, but it felt impossible to me that the world could keep turning without Him in it.

It was almost 7 a.m. He hadn't yet been dead twelve hours and already there was a burning in my heart. How on earth was I going to face a lifetime without Him?

It occurred to me that I ought to let people know. I sat on the settee and contemplated how best to do it. In the post-postmodern age, how do you tell friends that one of their friends has died? By text, of course. But how to put it?

Morning all! Just to let you know, Mark passed away yesterday. Happy Sunday!

After numerous attempts at rephrasing, I ended up sending words to this effect. Minus the salutations. There was no way of dressing up the facts. Their friend had died less than twelve hours earlier and the bringer of this news was in a stupor. People tried to call. My closest friends Kim, Beccy, Nicole and Anna were all desperate to get through. But I let the phone ring. I don't remember listening to the messages that began building up. Maybe I never did. I did make one call – to Mark's best friend John – and asked him to relay the news to the other lads. Tag-team bad news. On reflection it was a crass way to announce it to the people Mark loved. But sudden death is crass. What else could I do?

'Where's Daddy?'

I crawled into the bed next to my daughter and drew her close. Her head was tilted up at mine, framed with a froth of ginger curls. Her eyes were His. A deep, creamy brown.

'At work.'

She considered this for some time. 'At Cheltenham?'

Beat. 'Yes.'

Great sobs convulsed through me and I squeezed her tiny, sparrow-like shoulders with my arms.

'Are you crying?'

'Yes.'

We lay for a moment in silence. I looked at the area of carpet where He had last stood. He was the bearer of bed-time milk. He had handed it over and kissed her goodnight. It was the last time He would ever see His daughter, and the last time she would ever see Him.

Finally I said: 'Do you want some breakfast?'

'Yes, please.'

On the way downstairs, we passed the entrance to my mother's bedroom. B stopped, her hand wrapped around mine, and looked in.

'You tried to wake Daddy in there,' she said. 'You said "and 1... and 2... and 3... and 4".'

'I did.'

'Who came?'

'Doctors.'

'But they couldn't wake Daddy?'

'No.'

She accepted this. Now she wanted Shreddies.

Bereavement professionals call it 'puddle-jumping'. Children hop in and out of grief as if they were splashing in puddles on a rainy day. This was unsettling for me at first. I didn't understand how a complex, potentially upsetting line of questioning could be followed by something as mundane as a request for a biscuit. She never cried for Him. But then she was three years old. She didn't understand 'forever'.

DAY 3: MONDAY 13 FEBRUARY 2012

People came and went. Family members had arrived from Canada for the funeral of my grandmother which was taking place in two days' time. I watched them walk uneasily up the path to my mother's front door. I hadn't seen my Canadian cousin for six years, but I couldn't face her. They came into the house and I went upstairs and lay on the bed in Mother's room, in the same position I'd been in when Mark died on me. I glanced around the room, wondering what the last thing was Mark had seen before His eyes closed for ever. The leather headboard, perhaps? The alarm clock on the cane side table? Or had His last image been of me, lying there in my socks?

A sharp pain skewered my guts. I hadn't eaten much for three days, and my innards were protesting. They didn't want dry toast hastily stuffed into them at 3 a.m., yet food had become an ordeal – the sight of it, the preparation of it, its demands to be chewed and swallowed. I had largely managed to avoid the stuff during the day, but hunger had taken to waking me up in the night when I was sufficiently woozy to ingest food without thinking. I rolled into a tight ball and dry-retched into the pillow. When it had passed, I stayed in the ball and wept until my eyeballs ached.

My oldest friend Kim arrived, unbidden, from Preston.

'You don't have to speak to me,' she said. 'And don't worry, I'm not staying long. I just needed to be here.'

I'd known Kim since high school. She was the most beautiful girl I had ever seen and I instantly wanted to be her best friend for ever. At the time she had layered hair like Debra Winger and the longest legs imaginable. We went through break-ups, make-ups. We lost touch then found each other again. And here we were, twenty-five years later, sitting on Mother's bed not knowing what to say to each other.

The constant stream of visitors was a distraction for B, but I worried about when I should tell her the truth. Mark couldn't be in Cheltenham indefinitely. There would come a time when the visits stopped and His absence would be noted.

I asked Kim to contact another friend, Suzie, who worked for a children's bereavement charity called Winston's Wish. I couldn't face phone calls, but Kim could ask Suzie for some advice on how to deal with my daughter on my behalf.

The advice came back, scrawled on the back of an envelope. We sat on Mother's bed, away from the hoopla downstairs, and we wept as Kim explained what I needed to do. I was to tell B that her daddy had died. I should use direct terminology, no euphemisms, and explain, in simple terms, what it meant. That the doctors had tried to save Daddy, but they had not been able to. Daddy had a problem with His heart and it had stopped. She would never see Daddy again. There were to be no more lies.

I brought B upstairs and the two of us sat on the bed where she had last seen Daddy, lying flat on His back with His eyes open and His arm splayed over the side of the mattress.

'Do you remember what happened here?' I asked, softly.

'You tried to wake Daddy up,' she said. She played with a loose flap of leather on the sole of her shoe.

'I did. But I couldn't wake Him. The doctors couldn't wake Him. Daddy died. Do you understand what that means?'

She looked at me. 'Why did Daddy die?'

'Daddy was very poorly. The doctors tried to save Him, but they couldn't.'

She was distracted, perhaps by the voices of the newly landed visitors, or maybe she just didn't want to hear.

'When somebody dies, it means we won't see them again,' I went on.

She said nothing for a short while, then she said: 'My shoe has broked.'

She'd jumped out of the puddle and I wasn't going to force her back in.

DAY 4: TUESDAY 14 FEBRUARY 2012

Dennis from the funeral director's arrived. The salesman of death. He was a mouse-ish little fella with gingivitis and a terrible bedside manner. He offered no condolences and didn't look me in the eye as he unloaded casket and coffin catalogues on to the table.

'This one is very popular,' he said, flicking through the coffin selection. 'At the end of the day, it's only going to end up being burned so you may as well go for the cheapest one.'

It was prudent economic advice from Dennis, but not what I wanted to hear at that moment in time. In fact, I didn't want to be thinking about coffins for my husband at all. It was Valentine's Day and I had anticipated that we would be holding hands somewhere, eating Cornettos and blowing kisses at each other in the wind.

I didn't know where the hell Mark was. He'd been whisked away in a body bag and I could only imagine Him to be filed in one of those drawers in a morgue somewhere with a name tag hanging from His toe.

Truth be told, Dennis couldn't wait to get out of there. It transpired that he'd already been in Mother's living room, in that very same chair, just a few days before, discussing my grandma's funeral requirements. He probably thought the place was cursed. He clearly wanted the choices to be made so he could be excused from the company of this blighted family and get to his next appointment. This was business – the tragedy that had ripped apart my life three days prior was not his concern.

And frankly, I didn't want condolences from Dennis. Not only was I sick to death of hearing condolences, but this whole thing was becoming more and more surreal as each day went on. I just wanted it to be over. I wanted Mark, like Bobby on *Dallas*, to come walking out of the shower and for it all to have been a dream. I believed He would, too.

I took Dennis's advice and went for the MDF, E-Z burn coffin. Selecting the casket proved more difficult. The vessel in which to burn the body of your beloved husband is one thing – the one in which to preserve their charred remains is quite another.

I was jostled into a decision to have Mark interred at the crematorium in Newcastle. When Dennis asked if I wanted to add the cost of a plot to the bill, naturally I said yes. I figured at least He'd be close by and surrounded by hallowed Geordie soil. I hadn't considered the lunacy of this decision at the time; that I would not be able, even two years later, to commit Him to the ground in any form. That doing so would be an acceptance of His death, the dropping of the final curtain.

However, that afternoon, four days after my husband's death, I understood that this was the course of action I would be taking. And interment meant I couldn't go for the free plastic 'sweetie jar' option to hold His ashes. It needed to be an expensively crafted box, complete with brass plaque and lacquering.

'This is a popular one,' advised Dennis. The benefit of his wisdom was welcome by now, as I had had enough of making decisions about the funeral arrangements of a man whom I still hadn't accepted was dead. 'Simple lines, solid oak.'

He sat, pen poised over his order form. I railed and bucked in my chair like an impatient child.

'I don't want Him in any of those! I don't want Him to be dead!'

Dennis said nothing. Eventually, I nodded. I went for limos, top hats, the works. If Dennis had suggested pole-dancing chipmunks, I would have gone for it.

The final query on Dennis's death list related to my sartorial preferences for Mark's journey into the ever-after. Dennis was keen on a standard-issue shroud. Something akin to the capes one wears at the hairdresser's.

'They come in white or blue satin,' he told me.

'I'd rather He wore His own clothes,' I said.

'The crematorium prefers the shroud. It's all to do with emissions these days, you see...'

34

Dennis, I felt, had had his own way too much during this transaction. I shook my head. 'No. I want Him in clothes of my choosing. He is not being cremated in a satin cape.'

He scrawled a note on his form and left the house with a request for an £800 deposit up front. Presumably in case Mark changed His mind.

No sooner had Dennis left than I had a call from the undertaker. Mark had just arrived at the funeral home from the hospital morgue and – great news! – He looked 'very peaceful'. The funeral director, Lee, was an irritatingly amiable fellow, for whom death was so much part of life he was practically gleeful about it.

'But look at the AGE of my husband!' I wanted to say to him. 'Aren't you shocked, or saddened in the least, Lee?'

But seemingly, Lee was not. 'We're just going to get Mark ready and then you can come in and see Him,' he told me with a chuckle.

I could hear him beaming down the phone. I found myself beaming back. 'Great stuff!' I heard myself respond. 'I'll be down as soon as He's ready, Lee!'

I thought about this exchange with Lee later. Why on earth would Mark be *peaceful* about dying at the age of thirty-seven? Excuse the pun, but it wasn't the sort of thing I imagined He would take lying down. On the contrary, He would be fucking furious. Lee's 'peaceful' was an example of the placatory, euphemistic language we use around death and dying, along with, 'He's in a better place now' and 'Rest in Peace'.

But Lee's upbeat attitude to my husband's sudden death had a curious effect on me. The four preceding Mark-less days had been characterised by people arriving and departing, by weary jags of tears, by emotional and physical sickness, by moments of impotence followed by frenzied decision-making. Talking to Lee on the phone, I felt momentarily relieved of the weight of the tragedy. He was an expert in the field, and his jauntiness seemed to suggest that death, even when it was sudden and involved one so young, wasn't really *all that bad*. And at that point, I was ready to pounce on any opportunity for reprieve.

DAY 5: WEDNESDAY 15 FEBRUARY 2012

I walked into my sister's kitchen where a small gathering of family members and Mother's partner, Jim, were drinking tea and waiting for the hearse containing the body of my grandmother to arrive. The mood was light, and I sensed the weight of my arrival.

Mother and I had had a hostile exchange that morning and we eyed each other warily over the teapot. She had been tearful about the prospect of her mother's despatch, and I had spat: 'I don't care about Grandma's funeral. I don't care about anything any more.'

'Well, I care!' she'd shouted. 'It's my mother!'

She was right, of course, but I was unable to summon any sympathy, even for the grandma I dearly loved. Five days in, and already grief had begun to calcify my emotional response to anything other than my own shattering loss.

Now, my aunt placed her arm around my shoulder. 'You'll come to the pub afterwards, then?'

'I'll see how it goes,' I replied. Dad would stay with me and B while the ceremony took place. Two funerals in one week were too much, even for someone anaesthetised by shock and red wine.

They finished their tea and set off to take their places in the two limos which had rolled up outside. I spotted a piece of paper on which Mother had scrawled a seating plan for the limos a few weeks previously. Older generation in the front one, grandchildren and their partners in the one behind. Beside my name, Mark's. Now crossed out.

I don't remember how Dad, B and I passed the time while my grandmother was being sent off. We may have watched a film, or done a jigsaw, or simply looked at each other through the thick silence. At some point I went upstairs and got myself dressed for the wake. It was the first time I'd worn make-up since Mark had died. The effort of lifting the mascara wand, of squeezing the foundation, of applying the blusher had been too much. Besides, the pallid, tear-paunched face that looked back at me every day through the mirror was an accurate reflection of myself. Why try to cover it up?

I drew my face on, and watched as another person emerged. My bone-white face with its hollow eyes decorated into some semblance of a living human being. I dressed B, and Dad told us we both looked nice.

We set off for the pub and again I sensed the burden my presence would bring to the occasion. While the mourners were relatively few, there were old family friends and neighbours in that room whom I hadn't seen for years. Eyes lifted and dropped again as I walked in. Conversations paused and resumed.

I nibbled a slice of garlic bread – that staple of the funeral after-party – and drained a glass of wine. Somebody told me I would 'be all right'. Another said I was 'doing well'. I sat at a table and spoke to people from behind my veil of despair. I managed to form words, and arrange them into coherent sentences. I asked them about their families, their holidays, their jobs.

I drank three more glasses of wine before I left, and throughout that whole time, no one asked about Mark.

DAY 6: THURSDAY 16 FEBRUARY 2012

Following Lee's invitation, I made an appointment to go and 'view' Mark at the quaintly named 'Chapel of Rest'. Dad and Beth would accompany me, as none of us were sure how the mission would unfold. The thought of seeing my husband again after six long days filled my heart with joy, so much so that I ignored the small fact that He would actually be dead when that time finally came.

Six days was, after all, a long time for us. Only once before had we had that long apart. Shortly before He died, He was asked to go to Australia with work.

'Are you sure you don't mind me going, pet?' He'd asked. 'It's a long old time to be apart.'

'I'll hate every minute, love, but you should go. It's an opportunity not to be missed.'

He was gone two weeks, during which time I'd prowled the house like a demented tigress awaiting the return of her mate. He'd emailed from the departure lounge at Heathrow, then again at Doha.

'Miss you, pet.'

'Me too! You've been away long enough! Home now!'

Two weeks later He stepped off the train at Malton and we ran into each other's arms, the three of us, all beaming like an advert for toothpaste. We loaded up His luggage in the car and drove homeward, vowing never to be apart for that long again.

Back at the Chapel of Rest, there was the anticipation, waiting to go in. Like standing in the wings before the start of the school play, knowing your dad's in the audience with his video-camera. The anxiety was further fomented by the receptionist's insistence that we have a cup of tea. We had accepted, Beth, Dad and I, assuming it would be a matter of filling a cup from a machine.

But the kettle was upstairs, which necessitated her running between it and the phone, which was downstairs at her desk. The phone wouldn't stop ringing. We were becoming increasingly agitated, she increasingly placatory, her lacquered blond curls bouncing as she ran up and down the stairs.

'Why can't we just go in?' we whispered to each other.

But clearly, there was an order which needed to be observed before one could view the body of one's beloved lying in the funeral home, and tea was first. We sipped in silence. I studied the picture on the wall behind the receptionist's desk. A blown-up photograph of an oak tree with the words: *from little acorns...* written across it in a dreamy script.

'I've had a request from the *Echo*,' said the receptionist breathily, peeling a Post-it note from the side of her computer screen. 'They want to know if you would be happy for them to do a piece on Mark. You know, how He was so young and it was so sudden. They asked if you would call them. You've to ask for Andrew.' She held her forefinger up with the Post-it attached to it. 'His number's on here.'

I stared at the yellow slip and the number scrawled across it. 'I have no interest in talking to the *Echo*,' I replied, draining my tea. 'Look, can we go and see my husband yet?'

The room was stage-lit. There was a crucifix on the wall and some silk roses in a vase. The lid of His coffin was propped up in the corner, with a brass plaque across the centre testifying to His identity and date of death. But to me, it all looked like theatre. Theatre of the Absurd, of course, but theatre nonetheless. A macabre stage set where Mark had the starring role.

I saw His hair first. It was exactly as I remembered it from the last time I had seen Him. Somehow I had expected it to have changed, in the same way that my entire life had changed. It was Him, there was no getting away from it. I scrutinised His face. All the features I knew and adored were still there. The half-white eyebrow. The mole on His forehead. The tiny hairs on the end of His nose.

'Where have you been?' I asked Him. 'I've been looking for you.'

He didn't stir, but for a moment I thought He might open His eyes and sit up. I examined every part of Him. I stood at the top end of the coffin and looked down His body, checking the shape matched His.

'You can touch Him, you know,' said the receptionist, moving in alongside me.

'I'm not sure if I want to. Is it... you know... OK?'

She put her hand in the coffin and wrapped her fingers around His. Gently, she stroked His hand. 'Go ahead,' she said. She positioned her head on one side and looked down at Him. 'It's tragic, isn't it?'

I ventured a hand into the box. First I touched His shirt – the blue one I'd selected in lieu of Dennis's shroud. It had been specially ironed by Mother, and was complete with the stain on the collar. Mother had protested – surely we couldn't send Him off in that? – but it was His favourite. And at this point, who the hell cared about a stain? I ran my hand over His jeans. Then I felt His feet through the socks I had just bought Him for Christmas.

I reached for His hand and touched His thumb with my forefinger. The hand that had once held me, caressed me, bore the symbol of our union. It was cold now, and the nails were yellow. I kissed His face and rubbed my nose with His. I smelled His skin but got nothing but embalming fluid. I clipped locks of His hair and placed them carefully in a little plastic box. I lifted His shirt (I wanted to see if He still had fluff in His belly button) but the rough-hewn, hastily sewn track of the pathologist's knife made me drop it.

It was, indisputably, the body of my husband. And I'd seen enough. The familiar sensation of sickness rose in my throat, and I cupped my mouth until it passed. Tears spilled down my cheeks as I said goodbye, knowing that I would never see Him again.

DAY 7: FRIDAY 17 FEBRUARY 2012

A woman named Judith arrived at Mother's door to take notes for the funeral service over which she would officiate. With her shaggy auburn mane and vivid make-up pallette, she resembled a doll that had been defaced by an experimental child. A maelstrom of perfume and stale cigarette smoke whipped up as she moved through the hallway and into the living room.

She arranged herself in the chair, placing her closed notepad on the floor beside her feet. Turns out one of her friends had lost her husband when she was younger, and Judith seemed keen to tell us about it. She accepted Mother's offer of a cup of coffee and began the tale of Barry's demise.

'He was forty-four. Worked for the Council. Housing officer I think he was. Went to work as usual. Suddenly, collapses at his desk. Everyone thought he was messing about. Wake up, Baz! But he'd gone. Just like that.' Judith clicked her fingers to illustrate the point. She took a Bourbon biscuit from the plate Mother had placed on the coffee table. 'Same thing as your Mark. Heart attack.'

I raised a hand: 'With due respect, Judith, I can't listen to any more of this.'

It wasn't just Judith's assumption that Mark had died of a heart attack (He hadn't) which caused my patience to expire. I wasn't interested in the shared experience. In fact, I couldn't have cared less about the death of Judith's friend's husband. Yeah, yeah, it sucked and everything, but nobody could have loved their husband more than me, and therefore my tragedy outweighed everyone else's. Plus, I still didn't quite believe that my husband was dead, so why would I want any allegiance with some widow I didn't even know? I flounced off into the kitchen and waited for her while she finished her story and her Bourbon biscuit in the lounge.

Mark's parents, newly arrived from Australia and in a state of total bewilderment, and His sister had arrived to contribute to Judith's notes. We sat around the kitchen table. Stories from Mark's youth were exchanged. His hobbies, his aptitudes.

'He liked to build model aircraft as a boy... finished them off intricately with Humbrol paint. He was a perfectionist like that,' said my father-in-law.

'When He was little, He refused to eat anything green,' said Mark's sister. 'Even cheese and onion crisps. They were in a green packet, you see.'

Mark's mother stepped in. 'He loved his guitar, didn't He?'

'Yes, He loved his guitar...'

Judith took notes. *MARK* (name circled) = *loved guitar*. She accepted the offer of another Bourbon while nodding sympathetically as we talked. Everyone chuckled dumbly at reminiscences of a man who was not yet laid to rest. Meanwhile, the tinny pulse of the bossa nova demo resounded for the umpteenth time from the lounge.

DAY 8: SATURDAY 18 FEBRUARY 2012

It occurred to me that funerals normally involved flowers. Swathes of them, all over the coffin and in the hearse. Sometimes these flowers were teased into letters spelling out the name of the deceased, or fashioned into a guitar, or a set of golf clubs, or in one case, a bar stool and pint of Theakston's. Mark would not want flowers. Flowers were a nod to tradition, and they bore no relevance to the subject of this particular funeral. I made a firm decision that there would be no flowers.

As the day of the funeral approached, I began to fret about the flowers. People would wonder why there were none. I phoned a local flower shop and explained my predicament.

'Everyone goes through this, love. Come in and have a chat to Xanthe our creative director. She'll come up with something lovely for your husband.'

Xanthe was very thin and very blond and in a rush. She used her long, plum-coloured talons to flick through the catalogue and point out the various features of each bouquet.

'Did Mark have a particular flower that He liked?' she asked, pulling her hair round to one side of her shoulder where it hung like the tail on a coonskin hat. She was the type of woman who would flirt with herself in a mirror and was probably filthy in bed.

'He lived in Japan for a time, and often talked about the cherry blossoms.'

'So, Asian-themed then?' Xanthe flicked through the catalogue. 'Hmmm. I'm thinking pussy willow, cherry blossom, a palm frond here and there...'

'Yes, and how about bamboo?'

Xanthe looked at me as if I'd just shat on the floor. 'Asian themes are all about simplicity.' She closed the catalogue and brought out her purchase ledger. 'I think we can come up with something special here. Leave it with me, it'll be beautiful.'

'I want something from our daughter too. She won't be coming to the funeral so a little bouquet from her might be nice.'

Xanthe opened the catalogue again. 'Does your daughter have a particular flower that she likes?'

'Not really. But she has ginger curly hair. I was wondering if there might be an orange flower that we could use...'

'Gerbera. A posy of orange gerbera, with twists of greenery in between the flowers to signify the curls. I think we can come up with something special here. Leave it with me, it'll be beautiful.' She closed the catalogue again and went to stand up.

'Just before I leave... Would you like to see a picture of my husband?' I asked.

Xanthe's face softened. She lowered herself back into her seat and said, 'I'd love to.'

I pulled out the passport-sized picture of Mark from my wallet and handed it to her. She held it lightly with her plum talons.

'He looks like such a lovely man. Lucie, I'm just so sorry for your loss. But don't worry, we'll sort the flowers.'

Satisfied that the flowers were in expert, perfectly manicured hands, my mind turned to any other aspects of the funeral circus that I might have neglected. Dennis had left me a checklist along with his bill, outlining things I should consider for the day. I had tossed it to one side, believing that if I ignored it the whole thing might just go away. I unearthed it, and discovered that we had no order of service, no provision for charity donations should people wish to make them, no book of condolence. These were the sorts of frills people expected, no matter how untimely the death or how apathetic the shell-shocked spouse felt about them. They were part of the send-off, integral to 'celebrating' the life.

Rather than an order of service, I curated a selection of photographs of Mark spanning almost four decades, and Mother's partner Jim turned them into a four-page booklet for each mourner. On the back, he directed people to a webpage I'd hastily set up with the British Heart Foundation in Mark's name, specifically for research into genetic heart conditions. In the event, I forgot all about the book of condolence, but I figured it was for the best. It wasn't the sort of literature I was in the frame of mind to read.

DAY 12: WEDNESDAY 22 FEBRUARY 2012

Lee loved funerals. You could just tell. He was the sort of man to whom one might refer as a 'fellow', and who pronounced the word 'Hallo' exactly as it is written.

'Hallo,' he said, walking into the reception area of the funeral home, where we had all gathered in advance of the service. 'How are we all today?' Top hat on, he clutched a pair of white gloves in his fist. By now, Lee's relentless jocularity was starting to wear thin. His aim was to elicit a smile from grieving relatives, but I wanted an expression of sadness. All I got was a chuckle from beneath a top hat.

The reception area featured a small cast of mismatched characters. Our respective parents. Siblings. An aunt. My sister's parents-in-law (for reasons that remain unclear to this day). The men told jokes; the women laughed nervously like people queuing up for a Ken Dodd show. I stared at a vase of fake chrysanthemums on the windowsill, and then at the traffic on the road outside. I thought about B. I had made the decision not to bring her to this final farewell. She'd borne witness to her daddy's last moments and I felt that was enough. I'd left her bouncing on the trampoline at a neighbour's house in Mother's village, happily unaware of the grim significance of the day.

'We'll be leaving in five to ten minutes,' said Lee, pulling on his gloves with a smile. 'In current traffic it should take around twenty minutes to get to the crematorium. Would anyone like a final look at Mark before we put Him in the hearse?'

Lee made it sound so commonplace, so in the order of things. I'd already looked. I didn't like it the first time round. I couldn't imagine it would be any easier now. I had, however, taken some time to inspect Xanthe's flowers, which had been delivered that morning and sat in the garage area out the back of the funeral home.

The Asian-themed arrangement for the top of the coffin was as thin as Xanthe herself. Two sprigs of silk cherry blossom nestled unassumingly amid three or four long fingers of pussy willow, which themselves were almost lost in a forest of fern and bracken. As for B's, the orange gerberas were gathered into a posy, but the greenery which I had envisioned spiralling delicately up out of it was in fact a heavy hula-skirt of grass and foliage around the base. I couldn't help but feel disappointed.

On Dennis's recommendation, I had ordered one limo for immediate family. The driver wore a peaked hat three sizes too big for his head. He'd been listening to Smooth FM while he waited for us on the double yellow lines outside, and we were serenaded by 'When The Going Gets Tough' by Billy Ocean until, a hundred yards down the road, Dad shouted: 'Music off!'

The man-child blushed beneath his visor and apologised. We continued the rest of the journey in silence, looking at the Asian-themed box containing my beloved husband through the rear window of the hearse in front. I could just make out the top of Lee's balding pate in the seat beyond.

We passed my old school, then The Three Mile Inn (site of many lost evenings with Mark), and snaked down on to the A1 for a short stretch, a section of motorway well travelled by our family tyres.

We pulled round into the crematorium and suddenly, the hearse stopped and Lee got out, placed his top hat on, and walked slowly ahead of the cortege. I wondered what the hell he was doing. He led us in, past the line of mourners. It seemed everyone Mark and I had ever known was there: faces from our shared past, faces unknown, the face of that bloke Mark hated from work, as well as my oldest friends Kim, Beccy, Nicole and Anna. I watched as their eyes fell on the coffin, looks of revulsion and disbelief etched on their faces.

This was one reason I had wanted to see Him in the funeral home – imagining what lay inside the box would have been too much for an overactive imagination – I needed to know in order to have some kind of peace. And, of course, to believe it was actually Him in there.

I got out of the car and for some inexplicable reason *waved* at the crowd, like someone out of *Celebrity Squares*. I had requested that Mark's three best friends, His brother-in-law, my brother, Dan, and Mark's dad assume the grim task of carrying the coffin from the hearse into the crematorium. They were waiting anxiously by the door, sucking on cigarettes, hunch-shouldered, trying to keep warm. I saw Lee amiably giving them instructions as to the best way to balance their departed friend.

And then came Lee's second offence of the day. I'd requested Neil Young's 'Heart of Gold' be played as people entered the crematorium. It was one of our favourites; we had sung it to each other under the Tyne Bridge on an early date, our voices straining in a parody of Young's. But Lee had downloaded the live version, and frankly, even in a studio Young's voice isn't pretty. And because there were over a hundred people in attendance, we had to listen to it on a loop for ten minutes while they all packed in.

The men carried Mark in through a side door. We watched as they manoeuvred the coffin on to the plinth at the front of the crematorium, then took their seats. Looking at the box, with its gaudy golden handles and wood-effect whorls, it was impossible to believe who lay within it. I looked across at Beth, who was sitting in the row behind me with her head in her hands. I scanned the rest of the congregation, my eyes alighting on grey face after grey face. I turned back to look at the coffin and felt utterly detached from the reality of why we were all here.

Judith took to the lectern and set her face to 'wistful'. I'm not sure whether the lack of note-taking had got her, or perhaps it was the size of the crowd, but she proceeded to mangle facts and vowels with gusto. In fact, you could hear the collective exhalation of breath whenever she stumbled to the end of another paragraph.

'As a boy [verifies name on notes] Mark loved to build *modal* aircrafts...'

Finally, she invited me up to the lectern. It's incredible what post-traumatic shock, a shot of gin and a beta-blocker enable you to do. I gave a speech during the service without spilling a single tear. Dan stood behind me as I delivered it ready to step in when I broke down. But I didn't.

Mark and I met ten years ago in the Hancock pub in Newcastle – a meeting which we both subsequently described as being 'love at first sight'. I can picture him clearly sitting in the midst of a Bacchanalian scene – Guinness flowing, cigarettes being passed around – wearing his trademark turtleneck jumper and flashing me his mega-watt smile. My mother has recently

*reminded me of my words when I saw her the next
morning – 'Mother, I've met the man I'm going to marry.'*

*(...) We married in 2006 and to our great joy little
B was born two years later. Mark talked of B and me as
'his girls', and she and I are both secure in how much he
doted on us. After his emergency heart operation in 2008,
Mark told me that on entering the operating theatre his
last thoughts were that had he not come through it, he
had a lot to be proud of in what he had achieved in his life
through our little threesome.*

*He did come through it, though, and even with the
ensuing complications and gruelling drugs regime, he
refused to be defined or held back by the savage blow he
had been dealt – indeed, his amazing recovery was in
part attributed to his positive attitude and determination.*

*(...) Mark's star was in the ascendant. He had
recently been to Australia with work, had big ambitions
for 2012 and beyond. He had just taken delivery of a
new electric bike in preparation for the spring. He'd
also recently bought himself a new guitar – a pleasure
that he'd been denied following his post-surgical stroke
in 2008 – which he had adapted for play with his own
inimitable resolve – using one of my hair bobbles to
tie his thumb and forefinger together so he could hold
the pick.*

*My only consolation is that Mark died just moments
after tucking his beloved B-B into bed, and the last face*

he saw was that of the person who loved him most in the world – me. From that perspective, I like to think he died a happy man. I want to thank him for the beautiful life we shared, in a home which was always filled with lots of love and laughter. He lives on for ever in me and in B, who reminds me of him in so many ways – not least those big brown eyes and that cheeky smile.

The thought that he will never be just a few paces away again is an unbearable prospect, but as one of the letters I have received said, I feel lucky to have had in ten short years what many people don't have in a lifetime. In the words of one of his all-time favourite musicians, Neil Young – 'Long May You Run'.

I stalked back to my seat, forgetting to thank Dan. I felt bad about that, afterwards.

Mark's best friend John was invited to come and read the speech he had prepared. John was seated a few rows back from me, snottering uncontrollably into his wife's shoulder.

'John? Can John come up...?' Judith looked out into the crowd.

'John sent *you* the speech to read, Judith,' I called out. I'd been cc-ed into the email. 'Remember? He knew he wouldn't feel able when the time came.'

Judith rifled through her notes, false eyelashes fanning like peacock tails. She shook her head and looked plaintively at me and then John.

'I haven't got a copy. John, do you have a copy by any chance?'

John shook his head.

'Do you feel like saying a few words off the cuff?' I shouted to John.

He couldn't formulate a word, never mind a sentence.

'It doesn't matter,' I said.

And it really didn't matter. I wanted this whole farce over with. Judith, Lee, Xanthe, Dennis, they were all people just doing their jobs. No matter how they performed them, it was never going to be good enough. For as hard as they tried, this was the love of my life they were dealing with. And I didn't want them to be dealing with Him at all.

The committal is a solemn moment traditionally heralded by the playing of a piece of poignant music – 'Moonlight Sonata', perhaps, or something by those singing monks. I'd chosen 'Rule the World' by Take That. It was a song Mark had heard in the hospital when He first became ill in 2008 – it played on the radio during the summer. Generally He liked music by bands with names like Them Crooked Vultures and Muse, but for some reason that song by a hairsprayed, perfumed boy band floored Him. After He was released and back home, we would play the song and cry at the memories it conjured up. We thanked God those times were over and we'd come through it intact.

Sitting there in that freezing crematorium, listening to Gary Barlow, I couldn't help but remember a photograph of him in the early days of Take That, where he'd posed naked except for a sock on his genitals. I wished I'd gone for the singing monks.

When the service ended I took one last look at the box that held my soulmate and walked heavily up the aisle. Leaving Him there, on that frigid plinth, I tried not to think about the next and final stop that remained on His journey. I kept my head down as I walked towards the exit, not daring to look at the faces on either side of me lest one of them prompted tears to flow. And I knew once the tears came, they wouldn't stop.

By the time we left the crematorium, our infantile chauffeur had been dismissed and Lee was now behind the wheel of the limo. Immediate family took their seats in the vehicle and we set off for the wake. I watched life go by through the window of the limo. This was an overcast Wednesday in February. Ordinarily we would have been at work. I followed strangers on the pavements with my eyes and longed for the drudgery of everyday existence.

Driving from the City's West End to the pub on the Quayside, I felt waves of weariness and dread converge. I had gone through the motions, done what was expected, but now all I wanted was to close the curtains on the world and let the pain do its worst. I tightened my fists into balls and focused on the sensation of sharp, hot-pink nails digging into my flesh.

Thanks to Facebook, people had got wind of Mark's death and the funeral and flocked in their droves for the free turkey pinwheels and chicken wings. We had catered for sixty, but at least twice that came. The ensuing bun-fight left napkins and cutlery strewn about the Pitcher and Piano mezzanine like one of those teenage parties that ends up as an insurance claim.

I spent most of the wake in a 'meet and greet' role, a sort of lobotomised Beverly Moss from *Abigail's Party*. My strategy was to imagine that Mark was somewhere in the crowd. Occasionally I'd forget myself and absently look about for Him, and then feel panic rise in my guts when I realised He wasn't there. I'd push it back down with a slug of wine and a new conversation, but I knew it was simmering.

I directed guests to the free hot drinks and the paying bar, and regaled them with stories of Mark's death. I comforted those who were crying and took advantage of the goodwill of smokers by taxing them for fags. My glass was never empty of wine, despite my best efforts to drain it.

I met uncles and cousins who had been unknown to me until now. In ten years, Mark had never mentioned them, yet here they were, plates stacked with samosas, reminiscing about when He was a lad. Friends whom I hadn't seen for years turned up, old neighbours, ex-colleagues. When only the last few mourners remained, I picked my way over to the buffet and salvaged a flaccid slice of garlic bread and a few anaemic fries. The only thing I had eaten all day was 80mg of Propranolol, and by then even that was wearing off. It was nearly 7 p.m. and I was ravenous, so a group of us headed to the nearest pizza joint. I stepped outside for a smoke of someone else's cigarette and the first drag whipped up a storm in my brain, as if it had somehow brought together the synapses linking the events of the days and caused them to combust. The breakdown that had been dancing around the periphery of my vision swung into plain view, and I collapsed, right there in Beccy's arms in the street: drunk and totally heartbroken.

Well-Placed Protection

FEBRUARY

Home for Mark and me was an hour away, in North Yorkshire. Now I had the gut-wrenching task of facing an empty house. The journey wasn't made easier by Dad insisting on using his new sat-nav to get us there, despite my knowing the route.

'It's taking us via Whitby,' I said, fists clenched.

'That must be the best way then.'

'No, it's not. Mile for mile it might be shorter, but it's less direct. It takes much longer.'

As far as he was concerned, the voice on the sat-nav spoke the gospel. She was not to be defied. So we wound up and down B-roads and farm tracks, over moorland towards the sea, only to loop back inland towards Malton, arriving into the village a good half-hour later than we should have done. My mouth was tight, fastened shut like a drawstring bag. Rage and heartbreak cut through me and I couldn't bring myself to speak.

We crawled past the butcher's, the chippy (still flaunting their 'Dirty Night In' special deal in the window – fish, double chips, choice of side and can of lager for £6.99), the Star and Garter where Mark sometimes took in a late pint of Guinness. We passed the village hall, of whose committee Mark had been a member, and its adjoining playgroup where our daughter had spent many happy hours before starting school. The furniture of the village, just as we'd left it.

The first thing I noticed was that He wasn't there. He was always there, in that house – it was small, which was why we'd chosen it, so that we were never far from each other. Like Mr and Mrs Tickle, we liked to be able to reach out and touch each other from any given point.

It was cold inside, but the fire was laid. Mark had done it in preparation for our return. A layer of kindling, followed by a bed of coal, topped off with logs and the empty pizza box from our last supper together in the house. I swept my finger across the mantelpiece, hoping to pick up His DNA in the dust.

In the kitchen, the bike He had just bought was propped against the sideboard. He'd spent hours putting it together. My face cream, slathered around the joints as a lubricant, was still tacky. A partial fingerprint was visible.

I was wandering through the house when I spotted the washing basket. It was full of His clothes. Boxer shorts with stains and the odd errant pube. Touring the bathroom, I discovered two of His chest hairs lodged in the plughole in the shower. I picked them out and placed them in my wallet. Bed sheets were skewed from where we'd got up on the morning of 11 February, not ever thinking that we would never be back in them together.

'Shall I get a bag and pack His clothes up for the charity shop?' said Mother.

I threw her an acidic look. 'What are you talking about?'

'No? OK...'

'I can't believe you'd even suggest it.'

She raised her hands in surrender.

'No, seriously, I can't believe you. He's not even been dead two weeks and you want to send His clothes to the charity shop? Fuck you.' I stormed out of the room and slammed the door.

I stopped to touch surfaces; His belongings had taken on a strange new quality. Two guitars in their hard cases, lovingly placed on their sides out of direct sunlight in the spare room. A GCHQ lanyard, from which His identity card hung. The Oxford dictionary I had bought Him for Christmas, still in its cellophane wrapper. A copy of *Agent Zigzag,* bookmarked at page 108 with a Lidl receipt.

So there were three of us – Mother, Dad and me – shuffling about the house, not knowing what to do. We went to the pub for lunch. We came back. We spoke briefly to the neighbour, who couldn't believe that the man who'd been shovelling the snow from her driveway the week before was now dead. We packed a bag of clothes for B and me. We put the bin out. We locked the door and drove back to Mother's.

Via York.

*

We were driving back through the valley between two hills, flanked on both sides by sheep and the ruins of farm buildings, when I received a phone call from the coroner's office. They had the result of Mark's autopsy. Dad pulled into a side road and I scrabbled about for a pen and a scrap of paper.

'One: Left-ventricular hypertrophy,' said the coroner's assistant.

I scribbled down an approximation of what I thought I'd heard. 'What's that?'

'Hmmm... Not sure... Shall I go on?'

'Yes.'

' Two: Ischaemic heart disease.'

'What's that?'

'Furring up of the arteries, I think... Not sure...'

'And?'

'Three: Catastrophic arrhythmia.'

I'd wait and ask our GP.

When the phone call had finished and our journey resumed, I began to notice a slight blurring of my vision in my right eye. No amount of blinking or rubbing would move it. I worried it might be a stroke or an aneurysm or other such cataclysmic affliction, but it didn't get worse. Neither did it shift. We stopped for a sandwich and when I ate, it passed. But when we resumed our journey, I sat in silent fear of what it may have meant, and what on earth my body was going to throw at me next.

*

I had brought back a crate of items from the house which I thought Mark's mates – 'the lads' – might want. The box consisted mainly of CDs I had duplicates of, a stack of war titles (*Stalingrad*, *Gallipoli*, *Black Hawk Down*) and a few items of clothing. On the morning Mark died, the postman had brought Him a package containing brand-new cycling gear – an expensive jacket, winter-proof gloves, two pairs of obscene-looking, padded-crotch cycling shorts. I had exhumed them from the wardrobe where He'd carefully stored them in preparation for His first outing on His new bike. Mark's mate Neil cycled and would no doubt be glad of warm hands and some well-placed protection.

John, Neil and Paul arrived at Mother's to go through the crate. John was last to walk up the path, carrying what looked like a large purple gift bag. I watched from the window, eyes fixed on the bag. I knew what the present was inside. It was Mark. Returning to me and the house in which He'd died in the form of a pile of ash in Dennis's bespoke lacquered box. I'd been unable to go and retrieve His remains from the funeral home myself (I couldn't face another confrontation with the springy-haired receptionist) so had asked John to go on my behalf. And here he was, sauntering down the path with his best friend, my husband, swinging about around his knees.

John handed me the bag. I placed it next to the fireplace in the lounge, not daring to look inside. Paul sat down on the settee in the seat where Mark had sat not two weeks before. Mother took a tea order, and the lads and I exchanged a few jokes. Everyone ventured an occasional sidelong glance at the bag.

And then we set about distributing Mark's belongings.

'Anybody wear a size nine shoe?' I asked, holding up a pair of new-looking brogues.

The lads glanced at each other. It was like the end of a jumble sale, when the scout leader gave stuff away for free.

Neil nodded. 'Yeah...'

'How about this coat? Army surplus, I think I remember Him saying it was Serbo-Croat.'

'He would...'

'I'll try it.'

'That looks good.'

'Is it a bit short in the arm?'

'Let John try it then.'

'It's warm, like.'

'He always went for practicality.'

'I'll take it then. Unless anyone else...?'

'No, you take it mate.'

'He would want you to have it.'

The selection of war books was distributed. No one wanted *The Rise and Fall of the Third Reich,* not even as a doorstop, and there were a few CDs I couldn't foist off, but in all, the crate was emptied. After some persuading, Neil took the cycling attire. Of the various lots, we agreed that this was the hardest to reconcile. For while the jacket, the gloves, the obscene trunks were not long-held, treasured belongings, they represented one of Mark's goals for the future which would never be fulfilled. The electric bike, so meticulously researched and lovingly constructed and the gear that accompanied it had heralded the start of a new era for Mark. He had come so far with His rehabilitation that He felt ready for the next physical challenge. The idea was that He would cycle to work and back, aided by the electric power of the bike.

As it was, Neil would get the benefit of the still-tagged clothing, and the bike would be dismantled, packaged up and returned to the dealer to be resold.

Later, when the lads had left with their sad remembrances, I found myself alone with the lacquered box in the bag. How was it possible, I thought, that just three weeks ago Mark was sitting in the very spot on the settee where I now sat contemplating His remains? And furthermore, what on earth was I going to do with Him now?

I could contemplate it no longer. I picked up the bag and carried it upstairs into Mother's attic, out of sight, until I felt up to making a decision.

MARCH–APRIL

For reasons known only to people who enjoy paperwork, all the bureaucratic bullshit relating to the death of your husband *must* be completed within the first four weeks after His death. During this time, the bereaved spouse exists in a vacuum of disbelief ushered along by family, friends and the likes of Lee the funeral director, all of whom are acting like police officers directing traffic past the scene of a horrific crash. Said spouses are fed, watered (or wined, more specifically), dressed and their hair brushed (their own facility to do so has been temporarily disabled) while responding to requests for birth, death and marriage certificates and other forms of death documentation.

During this short period of time, I managed to do the following:

1. register my husband's death
2. receive the death certificate
3. cancel all of His accounts
4. apply for probate in order to access His final wage packet.

It is inconceivable to me now how I managed to do this. Nonetheless, the checklist grew smaller.

One grey morning less than a month after He'd died, Dad and I shambled into the grubby coroner's office to collect Mark's death certificate. However the certificate wasn't, as I'd hoped, ready for collection. Rather, Dad and I had to sit while an apologetic-looking coroner's assistant took us painstakingly through the events surrounding my husband's death, entering each piece of information on to the computer with a plodding forefinger.

'Is it Mark with a "c" or a "k"?' he asked.

'A "k".'

'And, er, the address at which your husband died – is this correct?' He turned the screen to face me.

'Yes.'

'And, sorry about this, where were you at the time of your husband's death?'

I wanted to say; *'Directly beneath Him.'*

'I was with Him. At that address.'

The coroner's assistant then went through the causes of death, finishing with 'heart valve replacement'. Dad looked at me and mouthed: *Is that right?*

'I don't think that's quite right,' I said, twisting the screen further round towards me. 'His heart valve replacement surely didn't contribute to His death? On the contrary, it kept Him alive.'

The assistant looked at his copy of the coroner's report. 'That's what it says here. If there's any doubt, you'll have to take it up with the coroner. Sorry.'

I deflated back into my seat. At this point, it didn't seem to matter. Mark was dead and this certificate, which I would need several copies of at a cost of ten pounds each, was only required in order for boxes to be ticked, accounts to be closed, for a life to officially end. No one would care about the details.

When it comes to closing accounts on behalf of your dead love, some companies have dedicated 'bereavement lines', where a trained operative with a voice like a sex worker condoles you on your loss, while listing the documents they require in order to close your beloved's account. This seems to be unique to 'big' organisations, like banks and utilities companies.

'Now, Ms Brownlee, I realise this may upset you, but we are going to need sight of Mark's death certificate... Ms Brownlee? Do you need a moment?' (The flow chart reads: *Give customer moment.*)

Other companies, generally mobile phone providers and car insurance dealers, subject you to the tyranny of automated 'options' before you are able to speak to someone under the heading 'All Other Queries'. Apparently, the opportunity to choose the music you wish to 'wait' to should alleviate your distress. When you finally get through, these calls are invariably fielded by students who end every sentence with an exclamation mark.

'So your husband died, Lucie, yeah! Brilliant! OK, I'm gonna need to take some details, yeah! So he was... thirty-seven! That's perfect! I need... the death certificate before I can go any further!'

The exchange normally ends with, 'Have a great day!'

Cancelling appointments has to be one of the most gruelling tasks for the surviving partner to undertake. Appointments, even those that are relatively unimportant, represent plans for a future that no longer exists. Dates for the upcoming year on the calendar are now only good for scratching out.

I phoned the office of a Mr Klaus Fenderbeuller in order to explain why Mark hadn't attended His dental appointment that week. I prefaced my pitch by clarifying who I was and on whose behalf I was phoning. The receptionist 'hmmmmed' in that irascible way that only receptionists know how to do, until the moment I dropped my A-bomb: 'Mark couldn't attend his appointment because He died.'

The sharp inhalation of breath indicated that Mark's excuse was probably going to be acceptable grounds for a no-show.

'Oh. I'm terribly sorry for your loss...'

Some weeks prior to His death, Mark had been done for driving thirty-four miles an hour in a thirty-mile zone. Rather than go for the points, He opted to attend the course, which was taking place in March. I called the company and explained why He would not be there. The cog on the end of the line offered her condolences and assured me that 'the system' had been 'updated' in the light of what had happened.

Three months later a letter dropped on to the doormat, addressed to Mark. (Mail to a dead man continues to arrive, by the way. Have Tesco never paused to consider why He hasn't used His points lately?) The envelope bore the speed awareness company's insignia. I tore it open, and it wasn't just seeing my husband's name at the top of the letter which threw me into a purple rage. The company were writing to inform Mark that because of His failure to attend the speed awareness course on 13 March, they were giving Him notice of their intention to prosecute Him.

Brandishing the letter in a white-knuckled fist, I picked up the phone and dialled the number on the top of the letter.

It was eight o'clock in the morning and clearly the first shift weren't in yet, for a security man answered the call.

'In what way is it appropriate to send threatening letters of this sort to a dead man, a dead man who, incidentally, had been the most law-abiding of citizens and also, by virtue of being an excellent driver, had not been a scourge, but rather an asset to the motoring population?'

The security man told me with a cough that he would try to transfer me through to someone who could help. Turns out that the only cog to be whirring at that time of the morning was one of the biggest ones within the organisation. I let loose into her earhole, concluding my diatribe with a fierce roar of tears. She could only apologise. 'The system' had failed, in this case, most regrettably, and she would personally look into the cause. She couldn't say any more. But it took me the rest of the morning to stop trembling.

The process for applying for probate, meanwhile, was clearly drawn up on the back of a fag packet by a madman with a passion for overcomplicating things. I was advised to pay a solicitor to do it for me, however I saw the forms and their accompanying guidance notes as a personal challenge I needed to surmount. Well, I saw them, and the fee for the goddamn solicitor.

Mark's final wage packet was not significant enough for probate arbitrators to worry about. I filled out the forms and duly received a date for an 'interview' at the offices in York. The interview consisted of a bald man thumbing through the paperwork I'd submitted, asking me to confirm that I was who I said I was, and then holding up a laminated card with an oath written across it.

'Read this out, then sign here.'

To this day I don't understand the requirement for a newly bereaved, shell-shocked individual to have to verbally confirm the fact of their beloved's demise in a cramped office in front of a stranger, however I found myself acquiescing to the bald man's request, tearfully, the words catching in my throat. All for the sake of a few hundred quid.

Four weeks in and I wanted a solution to the relentlessness of grief. I wanted not to wake up in the morning in an indeterminate state of being. I wanted to be able to take in food again, to be able to get to sleep without the aid of a whole bottle of red wine, to sit outside in the unseasonably warm March sun and actually feel it burning my skin. I wanted thoughts other than those of my husband to enter my head. Tears seemed to leak from my eyes whether I was aware of them or not. Sometimes I'd catch myself staring blankly at the sky, or a crack in the path, momentarily dazed by a flashback of Mark's face as He died.

I trawled the Internet for books on grief and underwent an ordering frenzy that resulted in a pile of bereavement literature being delivered to my door. I read voraciously. How had other people got through it? What was the answer to this devastating conundrum?

Some books contained 'road maps' to recovery. Comic-book-style pictorial representations of how to get through the death of your spouse in one piece. According to one book, I was currently in the middle of a boggy, hostile mire, surrounded by dead ends and evil-looking shrubbery. The idea was that I would move through each of the visual depictions (choppy seas, undulating hillsides, a horizon bearing the beginnings of a brittle sun) until eventually I arrived in the rose garden of renewal.

Other books were heavy with case studies and testimonials from people who had gone through it and survived. None of them made any sense to me though, because I still didn't consider myself part of this community of loss. I didn't want to 'recover' because it still hadn't registered in my brain what I was trying to recover *from*. I didn't want to hear about other people's survival stories. I wanted... I wanted... I wanted Mark back.

And here was the nub of the issue. I hadn't anticipated how *conclusive* death would feel. We all know there's no going back, but when it happens to the person you love most in the world, the finality of it is difficult to absorb. Here the books on grief proved correct. The *only* way to cope is to abide the cliché of taking one hour at a time, one minute at a time.

My friend Anna offered to do some further research on my behalf and sent me a list of online resources related to young widowhood. On the list was a forum where bereaved spouses can post about their despair and receive counsel from other widows at various stages on their 'grief journey'.

The forum offered something that no textbooks or counsellors could: the opportunity to offload in real time, and receive a comforting, empathetic response within seconds.

I'd post: *I can't do this. I want to die just so I can be with Him.*

Dina would reply: *Focus on getting through the next hour. Don't look further than that.*

Anon would add: *Yes, come back in a hour and tell us what you did.*

An hour later, I'd be back. *I'm still here. I had a glass of wine and watched my daughter play with her Lego. I didn't have the strength to join in, but watching felt OK. I feel less anxious now though. Thanks all.*

In those early, fraught weeks, I found myself confiding in the forum several times a day, much to the frustration of Mother who saw me existing solely within what she deemed to be a virtual world. But the virtual world had become my artificial respirator. It was a conduit for communication with friends, family and compassionate strangers which bypassed the need for platitudes and eye contact.

My brother Dan, for example, never one to tackle an awkward conversation, sent me the following email soon after Mark died:

My purpose in writing – and indeed in life – is to provide
moments of humour in dark times, and in recent days
I have noted several things that may be of interest.

 [...] At Mark's funeral I was rather surprised to
see Yoda from Star Wars *among the mourners – until*
I realised it was, in fact, [an old family friend] who
appears to have shrunk six inches (or was that because
she was wearing slippers? or is it eighty years of Catholic
guilt gradually crushing her into the ground?).

It was the sort of missive which would have had me doubled over in normal circumstances. But I read it with blank-eyed indifference, and responded with the first stanza of Auden's poem, 'Funeral Blues', in which the poet calls for the excision of the stars, the moon, the sun and the ocean following a loss. In retrospect, it was a self-indulgent reply.

But it demonstrates that even my brother, the person who makes me laugh most in the world, couldn't cajole me through the black fog of the aftermath of sudden death. No one could. And besides, I didn't want to be cajoled through it. In those early days, I had no energy to do anything other than to languish in the pain.

The prospect of a future without Mark stretched out ahead of me and it scared me. I began wondering if I'd missed something. Mark had undergone emergency heart surgery, been hospitalised for a total of three months, during which time He endured procedures and dark nights that I find difficult to contemplate even now. But He was 'fixed'. This is what we thought and this is what we had been told. Indeed, He'd been given the all-clear in November and told that His visits to see the consultant were to be reduced to once every two years. His death, therefore, just wasn't possible.

Any number of preposterous scenarios was preferable to the truth. Had He committed suicide? (I'm ashamed to say that I checked His pill box to see if He had been taking them. He had.)

Had He been assassinated? He had worked as an intelligence analyst for GCHQ since 2004 and I was never given any clues about what He did; perhaps I'd missed the poisoned dart, or the strychnine in the tea? I rehearsed conversations with His boss and His colleagues from the funeral. They had just agreed to give Him a promotion (Mark died not knowing this, despite having worked towards it for the past year). Had He, James Bond-style, uncovered something He shouldn't have?

In fact, GCHQ proved exemplary in their 'aftercare of spouse of deceased employee'. They deployed a liaison officer to come and meet with me personally, to offer condolences, to hand me a cheque from the union and to retrieve Mark's identity card. She was named Lesley and had a manner as soothing as a churned butter sandwich.

We sat in the kitchen of the house Mark and I shared and discussed what further support the organisation would be able to offer. As Mark had been on a secondment up north at the time of His death, they'd already covered two months' rent. They would also foot the bill for the removal firm to pack and store our belongings until a point when I was ready to unload it somewhere new.

She handed me a letter from the director of human resources at GCHQ, who had canvassed Mark's colleagues for opinions on His character and work ethic. While it revealed nothing I didn't already know or suspect about my husband, it was an astonishing tribute to a man who conducted Himself in such an understated way.

...(Mark) was warm, patient and articulate, and always had a positive outlook on life. (He) was an exceptional analyst, always willing to help those around him with less knowledge...The respect in which Mark was held by his peers and those above him was clear for all to see, and he will be sorely missed...

I kept rereading the letter, long after Lesley had gone, my bottom lip trembling with pride and disbelief.

The only other possible scenario pertained to the medical team in Oxford. Had they been negligent in their aftercare of my husband? That little fella, the registrar, with whom Mark and I had high-fived when we left the hospital for the last time. Was he somehow culpable? Or how about another member of the medical team? I phoned Mark's consultant to find out.

'Would it be helpful to come down and have a chat with myself and Dr Graham, Mark's geneticist?' asked Dr Ascensio, the cardiologist who had been responsible for Mark's post-operative care.

I replied that it would be very helpful, thank you, and that I was able to attend a meeting at their earliest convenience. A month later, armed with a list of queries (What exactly did they think had happened? Would Mark have suffered? Why the *fuck* hadn't they picked anything up at the review two months before He died?), Dad and I made the 250-mile trip to Oxford in search of answers.

We spent our first two hours in the city trying to decipher the parking payment system, eventually slipping a vagrant a couple of quid to show us how it worked. (He clearly earned a decent living by taking up a nightly residence next to the pay machines, as everyone else was baffled too.) We then proceeded to the nearest watering hole and, despite vowing to 'only have a couple', we staggered back to the hotel after midnight with the prospect of our Big Meeting the next morning on a hangover.

We arrived at the hospital just before midday, bleary-eyed and ready for a fight. Everything was as it had been a few months previously when Mark and I had been here together for His review. The receptionist with the Jack Duckworth specs. The blue-uniformed medics. The caustic stink. Dad and I wandered through the corridors, past The Friends of The Radcliffe cafe, with its crustless, clingfilm-wrapped tuna sandwiches and bitter coffee, past the lift to the cardiac ward in which I had descended a hundred times, never knowing what news I was about to receive about my husband. I peered through a window down into the courtyard below, and saw the window of Mark's room, shrouded as it always was in a shadowy gloom.

I entered the meeting with the purpose of attributing blame. My beloved was gone for ever and someone had to be responsible. It couldn't all be for nothing. But Dr Asenscio and Dr Graham were in a state of shock too. They had followed Mark's progress since that cataclysmic night in August 2008, and they were confounded by this savage and sudden conclusion.

'We had noted a slight enlargement of the left ventricle on the scans,' Asenscio explained, 'but this was not terribly unusual given the nature of Mark's surgery. It wasn't a cause for alarm.'

I looked at the two genii of cardiovascular illness sitting in front of me, Asenscio with his long crane-fly legs folded one over the other, Graham with his folder of Mark's notes clutched to his chest.

'So why did He die then?' was the only thing I could think to ask.

Ascensio launched into a detailed explanation, the salient points of which seemed to completely bypass my brain. I turned to Dad when he'd finished.

'Did you understand that?'

Dad shuffled in his seat. 'Well, the thing is, what I understand is... er. No.'

Asenscio clearly grasped the level of his audience and went back to basics. He lifted a plastic model of the heart from his shelf and placed it on the table in front of us. 'This is the aorta,' he said, indicating the length of arched piping that slotted into the top of the muscle. 'Mark suffered a dissection which not only extended downwards but also tracked back into the heart itself and up into the coronary artery.' He took each chamber apart to reveal the inner workings of the model. 'The muscle became weakened by scar tissue – which would not necessarily have been visible on a scan. We can't be certain, but what seems reasonable to assume from the coroner's report is that Mark's death was caused by a devastating and unforeseeable arrhythmia, probably as a result of scarring by the emergency surgery He underwent three years earlier.'

The only question left to ask was the one which had troubled me since the moment Mark had fallen on to the pillow next to me. He had been unconscious, but still breathing for a minute or so after the collapse. Did He hear me calling His name? Was He trapped, momentarily, between life and death, able to hear me but unable to respond?

Dr Graham shook his head. 'We hear this a lot – that an individual still appears to be breathing – and it is a cause of much heartache for families. But breathing is an autonomic response and is essentially the last thing to stop. Please be assured that it would have been instant. Mark wouldn't have known anything about it.'

There was nothing more to say. I had to accept that Mark's death was no one's fault. As much as I sought to attribute blame, to find a focus for my fury and devastation, the facts remained: it was a catastrophic arrhythmia, which killed Him outright. But the futility of it all – the struggle we had both endured since He first fell ill and the progress we had made, only to arrive at this empty conclusion – left me bereft anew. Dad and I pulled out of the Radcliffe car park for the final time and I couldn't bring myself to look back. It was the place that had saved my husband and now it had cut Him loose. Dad and I had travelled a total of 500 miles in the vain hope that this journey to Oxford would bring some kind of peace. Yet as we headed northward, the pain in my heart felt as ferocious as the mid-afternoon sun that beat down through the windscreen. And sitting there in Dad's car staring at the road ahead, it seemed impossible to me that it would ever abate.

I had spent little time at our home in North Yorkshire, making the two-hour journey from Mother's only intermittently to pick up more clothes or deal with the mail that continued to stack up behind the door. The place offered nothing in the way of solace – on the contrary, it came to feel like a museum of a previous life, full of artefacts that now only brought pain and gathered dust.

Besides, Mother, Beth and I had become increasingly reliant on each other. Beth's husband Will worked away during the week, and Mother's partner Jim lived up the coast, leaving us three women to deal with the children and the fallout of the bomb blast. We had lived together as a tight threesome when Dad left with Dan all those years ago, and here we were again, turned in to face each other with our backs against the world.

Beth lived one cobbled back lane away from Mother – her bathroom window was visible from Mother's landing – which meant we could be together within thirty seconds of a phone call. We didn't like to be apart for too long, though. One would peel off to do a provisions run, but was always back within the hour. We turned all but the closest friends away, daubing a metaphorical plague cross on the door.

My nieces and nephew too were a vital thread in my safety net. At nine years old, my niece M was the most cheek-blushingly aware of the gravity of the situation, but her pre-teenage rebellion precluded her from verbalising any expressions of grief. After Mark died, she would find me sitting on the step outside Mother's house, looking numbly at the sky. She would kneel down beside me and place her arms around my shoulders and hold me until I stopped shuddering.

'I miss Uncle Mark, M,' I would sob. 'I miss Him so much.'

She wouldn't say anything, but the arms would lock more tightly around my shoulders. Once, only once, did she express her grief in words. I was sitting on the settee in my sister's living room looking at but not watching the TV, and she appeared in the doorway.

'Go on, tell Auntie Lu what you told me last night,' Mother said.

I shifted my gaze to look at her, and she lowered her big blue eyes. 'I said I was really sad about Uncle Mark.'

She said the words, and then she disappeared back upstairs. 'Thank you, M,' I shouted, but she didn't reply.

Then there was my nephew little T, seven years old, whose hobbies included sweet-eating and performing magic tricks. By and large I had never witnessed any response from him with regard to Mark's death. Except perhaps a sidelong look of fear whenever he saw me crying. But maybe, like so many others, he simply didn't know what to say. After all, on the evening of 11 February 2012, T had eaten his dinner with his Uncle Mark, only to be told the next day that He had died. Gone from his life, without cause or explanation. How does anyone, let alone a child, reconcile that? Little T seemed to sense when a low moment had hit. He'd appear before me with a pack of cards and ask me to pick one, making it reappear at the bottom of the deck with well-rehearsed panache.

And even though she didn't live nearby, Dan's seven-year-old daughter G was able to diffuse my grief too. She'd throw her arms around me lavishly and say; 'Hi, Poo-Poo Head!' then shriek when I chased her round the garden as retribution.

It was clear that I needed to move myself and B to the sanctuary of Mother, Beth, the kids and the little village where they all lived. We needed them, and they needed us too. Mother offered up her home as a temporary residence for me and B, and I gratefully accepted. But it was with a shattered heart that I watched the board go up outside the home Mark and I had cultivated and shared, with the prospect of an unknown future without Him looming ahead.

The night before the removal men were to arrive, my old friend Kim and I met up mid-afternoon and walked the fifty yards to the Star and Garter. David, the landlord who also owned the village shop, sat at the counter, sipping Theakston's out of his pewter tankard.

His jowls dropped when he saw me. 'Now then.'

'Can we have a table for dinner?'

'Certainly.'

'You've heard about...'

'Yes, yes. So sorry to hear that.'

'It's... yes... well.'

'Where would you like to sit? Dining room or bar?'

The Star and Garter was famed nationally for its dining room. It wasn't the carpet that covered the floor and continued up on to the seating banks which brought celebrity though. And in my experience it wasn't the food. It was the collection of a hundred porcelain cats that lined the walls. They watched over you as you ate your Hot Beef Dip, as if waiting to pounce for a morsel. David had taken over stewardship of the pub a couple of months previously and had been grappling with the dilemma of whether to ditch the cats or keep them, the pub's USP, intact.

We opted for dining room and were shown to what I assume was the best seat in the house – underneath the pair of gold-leafed Persians – and ordered a bottle of red wine and some cigarettes.

'And, er, matches,' said Kim.

We were part-part-time smokers. Quarter-time smokers, if you will. Only in moments of crisis or celebration would we succumb to the weed, hence neither of us carried a smokers' toolkit. David brought us a packet of Lamberts (the only brand he stocked behind the bar), ready opened, and set it reclining on its hinged lid on the table. We'd ordered a bottle of Chianti and before David could top up the glasses, we were outside under the smokers' gazebo of shame, sparking up our first cigarette of the day.

'I mean, it's just so fucking rude,' I said, ten million noxious chemicals exploding in my brain. 'Sudden death.'

'Aye.' The chemicals were clearly diffusing in Kim's brain too.

'It just wanders in, takes your husband without any warning, then fucks off with Him. It doesn't even have the decency to knock.'

'Fucking rude, like.'

We drew heavily from our cigarettes and stared out at the thin rain. Neither of us spoke for a while, then my mind snagged on a distant memory from when we were girls. 'Remember that time we got caught bunking off English by Mr Fisk?'

Kim laughed. 'Aye. Fisk said,' – and, using our cigarettes as conductor's batons, we both repeated – '"*I take a very dim view of that!*"'

'He was a Nazi, that bloke. Who'd have ever imagined though that twenty-three years later we'd still be best mates, but one of us would be standing here a widow?'

'Come back, Fisk, all is forgiven.'

I stubbed my cigarette out and put my arm around my old friend. 'I'm glad you're here though, mate.'

'I wouldn't be anywhere else.'

Much later, replete with a Star and Garter three-courser and more wine, we were back at the house listening to *Electric 80s* on the CD player. We were preparing to open a couple of boxes of Mark's memorabilia from His three years teaching in Japan. I had never seen the contents of the boxes before. Not that He'd hidden them from me – we just hadn't got round to them, as a couple. Contained within were photos, letters and pictures that revealed a whole other side to my husband.

'Who's this photo of?' asked Kim.

I squinted at the girl cuddling up to my husband. He was young, in His early twenties, with a constellation of angry-looking pustules on his cheek.

'Fuck knows.'

'She looks like...'

'Marge Gyllenhaal.'

'*Marge?*'

'Yes, she's her exact double.'

'*Marge*? Don't you mean *Maggie* Gyllenhaal?'

We rolled about the settee, sending Lambert ash pluming into the air. It was the funniest gaffe we had ever heard.

I pulled a small package from the bottom of a box and opened it. It was a rectangle-shaped oddment, a sort of soap dish on a slant, made out of green-painted brass.

'What do you reckon this is?'

Kim turned it over in her hands. She sniffed it. 'Ash tray?'

'Hmmm.'

We spent an evening trying to decipher His life 'before me'. Of course, we reached no conclusion because there were no answers. The only person who could provide them was gone. Boxes full of unanswered questions would now reside in my loft. I wish I had a few moments just to ask Mark about the contents of those boxes. What? Who? When? Where? But this is the nature of sudden death. It gives you no warning.

We woke the next morning to the sound of rapping at the door. We were both fully dressed with red-wine stained teeth and faces like members of Kiss.

'It can't be,' I said. 'It's only eight o'clock.'

Kim staggered to the bedroom window and peered out. 'Fuck! It's the removal guys.'

'Did we get you up?' asked Nate, chief removal guy and wielder of clipboard.

'Er. Yes.'

'Can you just go through this paperwork and tell me what's staying and what's going?'

I glanced at the clipboard. 'It's all going. Except for the kitchen appliances and the white set of drawers in the bedroom.'

'Sign here, love.'

Kim and I ordered bacon butties from the village shop, prepared and packaged up by David, who had now assumed his 'morning role' as shop proprietor. Ordinarily, he would have made a humorous comment about our hangovers and the amount we had consumed last night. But instead, we stood in silence as the bacon fizzled on the grill.

We ate our butties in the car, drove into Malton and had a rancid coffee at a cafe near Morrisons. We wandered the streets, waiting for the call to say the removal was complete. Finally, we returned to the house to find it stripped bare. An errant hair bobble lay next to a skirting board. A square of Lego, a ballpoint pen, forgotten. The memory of a settee, a chair, a coffee table, imprinted on the carpet. Nate and his crew rumbled off with our furniture – now *my* furniture – and I had no idea when or where I would see it again. I turned to my old friend and shook my head. She came towards me as the tears began to spill.

'I can't do this,' I said.

'One day at a time.' She took me in her arms and I let her stroke my hair as if I were a child. We left the house, and the village, shortly afterwards in our separate cars – Kim heading west, me north. My face felt bloated with tears as I drove away from the place that had been our home and all the dreams it had been part of, back to Mother's with nothing but a few bags of belongings.

APRIL–MAY

Once my status had shifted to 'widowed', a raft of related queries began to emerge. Should I change my daughter's surname to match mine? (I never took Mark's surname, which now meant that my child was, by title, part of a different clan to me.) Were my in-laws still my in-laws, or does widowhood lore state that they now be given another designation? In fact, was I actually still married? The vows said 'till death do us part', but hell, we didn't mean it literally! And certainly not so soon!

As the now sole parent, did I need to bring B back into my fold?

It brought to mind the bitter prescience of an exchange Mark and I had had at customs on our way to France just six months before He died. The customs officer had looked at our three passports and asked if I was the mother.

'Bear in mind that if you ever travel alone with your daughter, that is to say, without your husband, you'll need to bring a birth certificate for B,' he told me.

'Why's that?' I asked.

'Child-trafficking,' he replied, handing us back the passports.

'Given that you have different surnames, we need to be sure she is yours.'

'Wow, really? I didn't know that,' I said.

His mouth crisped into a tight smile. 'Every day's a school day,' he said, waving us on.

In the end, I decided not to change B's name. It felt churlish and insensitive to Mark's memory and to His family. I had lost enough of Him, I figured the least I could do was to keep His identity alive through His daughter.

The queries extended to the tangible relics of marriage too, though. While discussing Mark's coffin arrangements with Dennis, I had suggested that I might like Him to be buried wearing His wedding ring. Ever the sage, Dennis had reminded me that wedding rings, at the end of the day, are but pieces of metal, and anything which wasn't kizzened in the 1,000-degree heat of the furnace would be raked out and discarded. Or possibly sold on eBay.

I elected to keep Mark's ring, and it was returned to me in a small envelope containing the 'personal effects' that had been retrieved from the deceased after He was brought into the morgue. Mark's watch was included in this haul, along with an additional lock of hair that I had requested from Lee. The ring, with its scratches and unpolished exterior, felt heavy in my palm. I didn't want to consign it to a 'memory box' for the rest of my life. I felt a strong need to have it with me. But it was too big to wear on my finger, and I didn't want to adulterate it by having it cut to size. For a while I wore it on a chain around my neck. Then I threaded my own alongside it. But the two seemed to hang there, at odds with each other, somehow no longer representative of our original bond.

I decided to have them made into a new piece of jewellery. They would be welded together to look like bubbles floating skyward, and an emerald would be placed in the oval space where the two overlapped. The gem would represent B – it was her birthstone – and the piece would hang as a pendant from a silver chain around my neck. It signified the unity of our little family, and reflected the mantra that Mark and I would often repeat to each other: 'You complete me.'

I picked the piece up four weeks after commissioning it. It was exactly as I had envisioned it, but suddenly I was racked with doubt. In the process of converting the two rings, the jeweller had polished them up, replated them, ironed out the scuffs. They were perfect, just as the day when we exchanged them. All trace of Mark had gone from His band.

Mark's DNA had now become a finite resource. And I had willingly removed it from the very symbol of our union. I placed the new sculpture on a chain around my neck, along with the locket containing Mark's hair.

'I've done the wrong thing!' I cried to Mother. 'I should have kept the rings as they were!'

'You've done exactly the right thing,' Mother countered. 'You've created something new which has meaning to you all.'

I stared at the mirror at the swags of silverware around my throat. 'Do I look like Mr T?'

'No, of course not. It's lovely.'

'Do you like Mummy's necklace, B?' I asked, kneeling down so that she could see it. 'That little emerald is you.'

B scrutinised the jewel. 'That emerald is me?'

'Yes.'

She looked at me with wide eyes. 'It's a bit small.'

Shortly after we took up residence at Mother's, I enrolled B in the village nursery in order to establish some semblance of routine and 'normality'. After all, the kid had lost her daddy, her home, a handful of little friends, all in the space of two months. Her world had been completely upended too.

But each time I left her there, I'd return to Mother's and ulcerate for three hours until I could go and pick her up. I feared the phone – every time it rang I anticipated it was nursery, calling to inform me of some ruinous disaster involving my daughter. I had to force myself to be calm, circumspect, rational. Mother would hold me in her arms and help me to breathe.

One day I went to collect B, and Mrs Willett the nursery teacher shook her head. 'It's so awful for a little girl of that age to go through losing her daddy.'

For a moment I felt guilty – was it somehow my fault that my daughter had been left fatherless? Had Mrs Willett noticed evidence of my sub-standard, post-sudden-death-of-spouse parenting? Yes, occasionally the vests had gone unwashed in recent weeks, the hair uncombed, the teeth unbrushed. And, OK, there was the occasion when she went out without pants on. But, I wanted to protest, she's fed and loved beyond compare, which some days is as much as I can manage, Mrs Willett!

Mrs Willett told me that B had been crying at nursery. They'd expected it, though – they'd been talking about the Easter story and how Christ died but was risen. She'd watched me do the CPR on her daddy – why wasn't He risen too? But Christ wasn't the only one to blame for the tears.

Earlier in the week, I had taken the rash (drink-fuelled) step of showing her the box containing His ashes. She'd asked to see it, and according to the Gospel of Bereaved Children, you're supposed to be open about everything. And how else does one respond to the question: 'What happened to Daddy's body?'

She'd been lying there next to me in bed (for we have slept together every night since Mark's death, lest she be taken from me as suddenly as He was), her head nestled into my chest. These were moments I relished, when she and I were alone, away from the sympathetic gaze of those around us. Sometimes I would give in to tears, even though I knew Mother didn't wholly approve of it in front of B, and B would wipe them away with a tiny, tender paw.

'Are you sad because you miss Daddy?'

'Yes.'

'Ahh. Don't cry, Mum.'

We would exchange observations and thoughts about life – 'Mummy? Cats say meow.' 'Mummy? I don't want curly hair.'

'Mummy? If I was in your tummy, who is in your legs?' – and it was during the course of one of these discussions that she popped the question.

'Mummy? What happened to Daddy's body?'

Perhaps she heard my heart knocking harder against my ribcage or simply sensed, as she seems so adept at doing, my discomfort, for she turned her face up to look at me, eyes just like His.

What DID happen to Daddy's body? After the funeral I felt the need for an answer to the same question. I had left him there on that plinth in the crematorium, in that cold, precision-measured box, and proceeded to the pub to get pissed. But what was happening to Him while I acted out the ritual of the wake?

I researched cremation on the Internet, just as I'd researched embalmment a few days before. I read about the process with the same detachment. Interesting, but couldn't possibly have been the fate of the body that I knew and adored.

'Daddy's body was burned,' I said.

Pause.

'Was Daddy's bones burned?'

'Yes.'

'Like the logs in our fire?'

'Yes. And Daddy's body is like the ash that you help me sweep from the fire.'

'Ash?'

'Yes.'

Pause.

'Where is Daddy now?'

I contemplated going down the route of Him 'being with the angels' or 'in Heaven.' But He wasn't. He was above us in a box in Grandma's attic. I climbed out of bed, pulled down the loft ladder and exhumed Him from His gift bag. We hunkered down on the floor and placed Him between us.

'Is that Daddy?' she asked, pointing at the box.

'Yes.'

She paused for a moment and then knelt forward and hugged the box. 'Awww,' she chuckled. 'I love Him!' She held Him for a few seconds and then she picked up the box. 'I can hear Him,' she said, moving it gently back and forth.

I could hear Him too. The gritty dregs of a beloved existence.

She put the box down between us again and said, 'Mummy? Can I eat my Easter egg tomorrow?'

It seemed a reasonable response. Overwhelmed, her brain had clearly deferred to its Easter egg synapse.

'Why not?' I replied.

She smiled and looked at me. 'Mummy? Do I make you happy?'

It was a question she'd started to ask with increasing regularity in response to times like these, when I was self-confessedly and visibly *unhappy* without Daddy. My reply was always the same. 'You make me *very* happy, B. Now let's get to sleep.'

I returned Mark to His gift bag and closed the loft. We lay there a long while in silence; she focused on tomorrow's chocolate ovoid, me considering those gritty dregs. They couldn't stay up there indefinitely. But how on earth would I ever decide what to do with them?

'A fucking diamond?' My brother, Dan, turned to his wife. 'Jesus, Helen, when I die, please do not turn me into a fucking diamond.'

'I think it might be nice,' I said. 'He'd become part of an heirloom to be passed down to B and her kids.'

We were sitting around the dinner table at Dad's house, bloated with goose and Karen's home-made simnel cake. I'd prefaced this entire family gathering, the first since Mark's funeral, with a warning that I was not intending to have any fun over Easter, that this would be incredibly hard, and that no one was to expect anything of me except ardent drinking.

The kids, M, T, G and B, were all in the other room consuming their own body weights in chocolate eggs, leaving us adults to have our Annual After-Dinner Argument. This year, though, the argument was more of a debate. After all, no one wanted to further upset the widow.

I had been grappling with the issue of Mark's ashes since I first took delivery of them all those weeks ago. Each time I walked past Mother's house, I couldn't stop my eyes from drifting up to the Velux windows in the roof, thinking of my husband in the box that lay beneath.

Options for the disposal of ashes are mind-boggling. They can be sent to the moon, turned into a coral reef, be sewn inside a teddy bear. And for £2,000, you can have your beloved cultivated into a diamond and set into a ring. Perhaps it's no wonder funeral homes across the world are bursting under the weight of unclaimed remains. People simply can't decide what to do with them.

At almost three months after death, the diamond option seemed to me to be a reasonable one. (Notwithstanding the niggling worry that once the ashes were sent off, the resultant diamond could, in fact, be anybody.) I convinced myself of the idea that looking down at my finger and seeing Mark there, twinkling back at me, would be a fitting tribute and a way to keep Him close. Furthermore, the company on the website said they could now do Him in an array of colours – pink, yellow, blue. The possibilities, and the prices, escalated on a scale of how woozy with grief you were.

'Scatter Him, bury Him, keep Him in the loft, but please, don't make Him into a fucking diamond.' Dan slugged more red wine into his glass. 'It's the last thing He would want, believe me.'

'Well, what would you want Helen to do with you?'

Helen said: 'Oh, this conversation is getting macabre. Let's talk about something else.'

'I'd want her to roll me into a massive spliff and smoke me,' replied Dan. We all laughed.

'On that note, I'm going outside for a ciggy. Anyone want to join me?' Helen said, holding a Benson under my nose.

We stood outside under a brooding North Yorkshire sky and silently puffed on our cigarettes. Two dark waves of cloud – one from the east, one from the west – were beginning to converge overhead. A thin blade of late-evening light tore through, and beyond it, a solitary star shone.

Dad appeared at my shoulder. He pointed skyward and said: 'When I see skies like that, I'm convinced it's Him.'

I turned into Dad's chest and wept, and Dad held my head in his hand and wept too.

'Give me a puff on that tab,' he said, when the tears had subsided. He hadn't smoked for twenty-five years, but this moment merited a drag. 'Fucking horrible that,' he said, handing it back to me. 'Don't know why you ever start.' With that, he stumbled back into the house.

Helen placed her arm around my shoulder. 'I don't know what to say or how to help you. But at least let me dispose of the fag ends.'

As she took the butts to the bin, I looked up at the sky, but the clouds had already closed over.

At the beginning of May, B was going to turn four. Kids' birthday parties have always struck me as a total waste of time, effort and money. People spend the weeks prior organising, planning, ordering bespoke party invitations off the Internet. They dispense the equivalent of two pairs of Office wedges on a chocolate cake with Barbie on it. They spend the day herding other people's children from the bouncy castle to the trestle tables and back again. Then they spend hours chiselling cheese sandwiches off the walls. Only for the child to have forgotten the whole event two days later.

So, newly bereaved and still barely cogent, I decided to organise a birthday party for my daughter. I made myself believe that I needed to do it. The kid had lost her daddy, the least I could do was invest in a bubble machine and gather a crowd to sing 'Happy Birthday'. In reality, it was the first opportunity since Mark's funeral for the adults who loved Him to get together and drink. Streamers and balloons were strewn about, plastic bowls overflowed with Wotsits, and wine boxes perched on the edge of the kitchen bench like birds of prey.

Mark's mates John, Neil and Paul were there, along with John's wife Fran and their daughter Martha. Mark's parents, sister, nephews came too, together with Beth, Will, M and T. Mother hosted, of course, and Dad and Karen put in a late appearance. Ostensibly it was a fourth birthday party, but the message was clear: people had gathered in a show of strength and support for me and for B. For each other. Perhaps even for themselves. And certainly for Mark.

But no one mentioned the latter. Not even me. We sat around Mother's lounge, quaffing wine and passing round the olives, talking about anything but the absence of the birthday girl's daddy.

It was a phenomenon which I came to accept as normality. No one talked about Him, ever. I wasn't sure why that was.

If it was for fear of upsetting me, they needn't have worried – I was already upset. Really, it couldn't get any worse. But people shifted about uneasily if there were tears. They shook their heads and said, 'I'm such an idiot for mentioning it, sorry.'

If I'm honest, I didn't mention Him either. It was easier that way, because hearing His name on my lips made me unutterably sad. I felt the tears teetering like coins in a push-penny machine, and didn't want them to fall, because crying was exhausting. So we talked about work, the weather (unseasonably cold) and possible options for accommodation for B and me.

I read the kids a story and led them on a half-hearted Gruffalo hunt (indoors on account of the gale which raged outside), which culminated neatly at the buffet. The kids ate, the adults drank. And in this way, the birthday milestone came and went, with a stack of presents and no tears. Just a monster hangover, cheese sandwiches as wallpaper and still no husband.

It was difficult to reconcile how much life had changed since that same day exactly four years ago, when B had been born into what was one of our happiest times as a couple.

Mark's job at GCHQ had led us to Gloucestershire, where we were renting the servants' quarters of an old rectory in one of the most breathtakingly beautiful parts of the Cotswolds. I took a teaching job at the University in Cheltenham, and we established a routine which, except for the demands of work, rarely saw us leaving our little village. Mark played bass in the local band (On The Edge) and we became regulars at the village watering hole, but mainly we spent time looking out through the mullioned windows of our flat, over the haylofts, the sand-coloured cottages and the gentle countryside, not quite believing our luck.

The rectory was divided up into five flats, each one inhabited by an improbably wacky character, whose comings and goings we would observe from our vantage overlooking the car park. There was the one-legged Old Major, with his myopic, obese and occasionally vicious canine companion Reggie; there was Juliette, the seductive blond divorcee, with her two small sons, Brett and Rafe; then Cathleen, the Woman On The Top Floor whom we rarely glimpsed; and finally, flying the flag for ethnic diversity in the area, there was Geeta, an incense-burning lone parent living with her tiny daughter, Dhala.

And from their perspective, there was us: a pair of awestruck Geordies trying their best to fit in.

The summers in the Cotswolds were a different colour from up north. They were sand-coloured to match the houses, and you could smell the warmth. We would eat our tea *al fresco* in the wisteria-wreathed grounds of the rectory on balmy evenings, smirking at each other over our goblets of cheap red wine. We had snow-covered winters too, where the roads to the village were impassable and Mark couldn't get into work. Once we got up while the streetlights were still burning and walked around the village, ours the only footprints in the snow.

After ten months of desperately trying to conceive, I finally got pregnant. I called Mark at work to tell Him the news. Every call to GCHQ was subject to meticulous scrutiny, yet He could barely contain His excitement.

'Are you sure, pet?'

'Yes! I've done the test twice and both times it's positive!'

'Well. That's erm, great. I'll try and leave early.'

He was home within two hours, clutching a bunch of service-station stems. 'These were the best I could do,' He said. 'I just wanted to get back.'

The day we returned from the hospital with our precious charge, Mark drove us into the car park to the sight of a welcoming committee on the front steps. Beth was there with Will and the kids, along with Mother of course, but also in the car park were the Old Major and Reggie, Brett and Rafe, Dhala and Geeta and the landlord's wife, who seemed to tolerate all residents from behind a pair of secateurs and a rose bush. They weren't so much awaiting our arrival as loitering about doing other things, but as soon as they saw the car swing in they gathered around, waiting for Mark to lift her out.

It was a yellow-hot day and I had fretted the whole way back about the core body temperature of this new little person we were suddenly in charge of.

'Open the window!' I'd yelled from the back of the car. 'Close the window! Air con on! Air con off!'

I rarely saw Mark flustered – even on our wedding day, the registrar described Him as 'serene' – yet here, bringing His tiny prize out of the car, home for the first time, agitation danced around His lips. He unstrapped the car seat and edged B out of the car, holding her forth in her carriage like a wounded rabbit.

Someone went to reach for her, but He wanted to be the one to carry her over the threshold for the first time. I followed behind trying to shield her newborn flesh from the sun. We walked up the stairs to our flat followed by a stream of pilgrims, and Mark set her down on the table.

'There she is,' He said. 'There's my daughter.' He stepped out of the way and let the cooing commence, opening the fridge and reaching for a Guinness. 'We win, pet,' He said, turning to me and pouring the beer into His glass. 'We win.'

MAY–JUNE

Four months on from Mark's death and the array of physiological insults I was continuing to suffer grew steadily more varied and impossible to predict. I'd had the blurred vision, the retching, the insomnia, the random bouts of crying – by now these were somewhat old hat. The panic attack was next though, hitting me, perhaps predictably, when I was alone and away from the village with no immediate access to support.

I was driving back from Newcastle when it started. A steady creep, from the tips of my fingers, up my arms, through my shoulders and right into the centre of my chest. The traffic was gridlocked and I was caught between a truck and a van, unable to manoeuvre in any direction other than, very slowly, forwards.

We were entering the tunnel before the bridge, the air shimmering with heat. I opened the window and breathed deeply. I inhaled noise and fumes, but I knew I needed to block the path of the attack. I turned the radio up and concentrated on the music. But the panic continued.

I shuffled into the inside lane and waited for the slip road. It would lead me in a loop into Gateshead, completely the wrong direction for where I needed to be, but I was terrified of being on the road when the full force hit.

I found myself in a cul-de-sac in a housing estate, staring at the peach-coloured render on the house opposite, willing my pulse to slow down. I pushed the seat backwards and laid my head against the headrest. The engine was off but my foot pushed at the clutch. I needed to feel tension elsewhere but across my chest.

The cul-de-sac was empty of people and cars; the vacuum created when its inhabitants are out at work or school. The only sounds were the percussive whirrings of heavy machinery from nearby roadworks, and the blood pumping in my ears. I phoned home, where Beth and Mother were looking after B.

'I'm going to wait for the traffic to ease. Then I'll head back,' I told Beth.

'You should never have gone into Newcastle in the first place—' she began.

'Just give me a while to get myself together.'

'Well. Drive safely then.'

She would now be relaying my predicament to my mother, whose brow would have furrowed. Then would follow an hour or so of anxious molar-clenching until I returned.

On this particular day, I had left the village to travel the thirty or so miles into Newcastle to have lunch with Mark's friend Neil. He would take me to Brown's and treat me to anything I wanted off the menu. Being incapable of overt expressions of grief, it was his way of showing he cared. And it suited me.

I had lost weight since Mark's death. It had dropped off without me even trying. The weight loss had been so alarming in its speed and relentlessness I had even been to the doctor about it. I stood on the scales and she conceded that I had lost a stone since my last weigh-in just a few weeks before.

While it made sense – after all, I had only really pecked at food since February – I was now convinced that the world was against me and that it was only a matter of time before the next atrocity struck.

'Cancer!' I thought.

'I'm not worried that it's anything sinister,' she said. 'It's quite usual for people to lose weight after trauma and bereavement. Keep an eye on it, though. If it continues to go down, come back and see me.'

Lunch at Brown's with Neil meant I could legitimately have a glass of wine in the middle of the day without feeling guilty – just one would suffice – in order to facilitate the passing of food down my gullet. Besides, I had made little effort to see any of the lads and felt this might be a good opportunity for us both to catch up. Not that we would talk about Mark – that was a given. But at least we could spend a couple of hours *not* talking about Him, yet be united in a tacit sharing of grief.

I wondered now, as I sat trying to take control of my pulse in a cul-de-sac in Gateshead, whether lunch with Neil had been such a good idea after all. Panic attacks don't need triggers, but I had spent an afternoon forty minutes away from the security of the village in the company of one of Mark's closest friends. Now I had to make my way back.

I looked around the desolate cul-de-sac, considering whether I should knock on a door and ask for help. Tears rolled down my cheeks, which helped. Some of the panic seemed to have been released, and I felt calmer. Three-quarters of an hour elapsed, and I started up the engine. I edged slowly on to the motorway, Simon Mayo blaring out of my car speakers. Forty minutes later, I was home.

'I can't go on,' I wept, allowing Mother to remove my coat, set me down at the table and fill up my wine glass. 'I can't cope in a world without Mark.'

My sister placed a plate of food in front of me, but I retched at the sight of it. B appeared in the doorway and I reached for her. She eyed me cautiously.

'Why are you crying?' she asked.

'Mummy's just a bit sad, darling,' Mother replied, 'but she's all right.' Mother made an attempt to usher her out of the kitchen, but B moved in beside me. I pulled her in and held her tight, nuzzling my nose into her curls.

Mother said: 'She shouldn't have to see you like this.'

But The Gospel of Bereaved Children clearly stated that outpourings of grief should not be disguised. B needed to know that it was normal, and furthermore, OK, to cry.

'She's only four, for Christ's sake,' Mother went on, pouring herself more wine and averting her eyes from the scene. 'It's bad enough when you're older, seeing a parent upset. How must she feel?'

Notwithstanding The Gospel, there was truth in this. On the odd time over the years when Mother had succumbed to open expressions of sadness, it had torn me apart to see her upset. What must this little person in my arms have been thinking, faced with this weary-eyed shell of person who had, overnight, taken the place of her mum?

Something had to be done. I booked myself in as an emergency at the GP's the next day. I got the locum, who never has a waiting list because no one wants to see him. He nodded sympathetically as I spluttered through my sorry tale, and then handed me a leaflet entitled 'Talking Matters'.

'Ring them,' he said. 'And if you feel suicidal, dial 999.'

I bumbled out of his office and duly rang Talking Matters. Turns out in this case that Talking didn't Matter, as they didn't deal with people who'd lost their husbands, suddenly, in the middle of making love. They were strictly stress and anxiety brought on by other means.

'But,' said the kindly lady, 'why don't you try calling Cruse? Bereavement is, you know, their thing.'

So I called Cruse. Counsellors, however, were thin on the ground in my region, and I was looking at a six-week wait for an appointment. I really didn't have that long. After haranguing another doctor at my surgery (I had to wait for an audience with her in order to avoid the locum), I was referred for counselling.

I waited just over a week for the first session, believing that it would provide me with all the answers I needed. After all, these people understood grief. They dealt with women who'd lost their husbands suddenly, during intercourse, all the time. I'd walk in there and they would show me how to pick up the shattered pieces of my life and put them back together again.

The first counsellor I saw greeted me in the reception area with a damp handshake. He wore red Kickers boots under his grey suit trousers, and clutched a ring-binder full of paperwork to his chest. He led me to an airless, fly-filled room with vertical blinds hanging like a bar code at the window.

We sat opposite each other in tan-coloured leatherette armchairs and he positioned his alarm clock on the windowsill. He practised what is known as 'person-centred' counselling. He explained what this entailed as I began completing the first round of paperwork.

'The idea is that you feel safe and secure in this space. You can talk as much or as little as you want. It is my role to listen. To be a sounding board for whatever you feel compelled to say.'

So I relayed the key tragic bullet points of my story to him. 'And that's about it,' I said.

He gave me a searching look and chuckled nervously: 'Isn't that enough?'

We sat in those chairs for an hour, listening to the movement of the clock hands counting out the seconds, looking at each other. The cues had to come from me, he said, when really all I wanted was for him to tell me what to do.

'This isn't working for me,' I said, after fifty long minutes of silence.

'Hmm.'

Two weeks later, I was back in the same armchair, breathing in the same stagnant air, opposite a different counsellor. Her name was Denise and she wore massive heels whose clunks preceded her down the corridor. She was diminutive yet hard as toughened glass. Furthermore, she didn't practise 'person-centred' counselling. Hers was a more direct approach, offering practical ways in which I could help myself. Much more my style.

Every week from then on she'd make me a piss-weak coffee and talk me through her own little diagrams and theories about bereavement and grief, and where I fitted into them.

One such diagram featured a circle with the title 'Grief'. Another circle was drawn closely around the outside. The inner circle represented grief; the outer circle, life. Ergo grief, currently, was all consuming. She sketched it out on a piece of paper and handed it to me.

'However,' Denise said, pushing her expensive, Merlot-coloured glasses up on the bridge of her nose, 'the idea is that eventually you get to this.'

She brought out another picture, where the inner circle hadn't changed size, but the outer circle had expanded to create more space between the two.

'So you see, the grief doesn't get smaller – life just gets bigger.'

I puzzled over the two pictures. 'I don't understand. How does life get bigger?'

'You take on new interests. Things inexorably move on. You may find a new job, new studies. A new partner.'

The latter suggestion was never going to happen. It had taken me twenty-six years to meet the love of my life and soulmate, and a new fella couldn't have been further from my mind. I didn't mention this to Denise, though. I didn't want to burst her circle.

The sessions continued every Tuesday for six weeks. I wailed, she offered me practical advice as to how to get through the week until the next time I saw her. She conceded that I would probably cry for Mark every day for the rest of my life. There was no 'solution' to my grief, but it was possible that one day, I may be able to accept that He had gone. For a non-bereaved, she seemed to understand.

My GP decided on a two-pronged approach to my grief – presumably commensurate with the level of trauma I had suffered, but also to get me the hell away from her office. We went for counselling and pills. I'd investigated the pill debate (for or against) on online bereavement fora: should one should face the savage onslaught of grief full on or cover it with a Prozac plaster? I mentioned this dilemma to the GP but she simply nodded and signed the prescription. I knew that the grief would be lying in wait for me until the plaster was ripped off, but in the interim the little white pill seemed like the only option. I figured I wasn't going to win any awards for braving it.

With my new regime of counselling, red wine and anti-depressants, I prepared for the more savage symptoms of my grief to begin to abate. Or at least become more manageable and less apt to blindside me on the motorway coming back from lunch in Newcastle.

And steeled by the hope born of this new regime, I became restless, feeling the need to make some positive decisions about the joint future of me and my daughter.

I was worn down by the memories contained in Mother's house of the night Mark died. The bed we slept in was the one in which He'd uttered His last words. The staircase was the one He'd gone up alive, yet come down in a body-bag.

His belongings – still in the bottom of the cupboard from the night they were hastily shoved there by Mother – taunted me every time I fetched a dress from a coat hanger. It was time to move out.

It was clear that I was in no position to leave the village. A newly bereaved, newly single mother was not going to cut it alone in the wilds of Newcastle or even inside the genteel walls of Durham. Here I had Beth and Mother on hand, plus my handful of new friends. I viewed a few properties, but finally took on a short-term lease on a house which was originally for sale, but was now also for rent. Kate, the owner, knew my situation and was sympathetic. She undercharged me on the rent and we had a very casual, amicable agreement.

I wondered about my ability to live on my own with a small child though. I felt like one myself. I was frightened of the dark. Felt incapable of dealing with council tax, contents insurance and all the other mysteries of domestic life I had left to Mark to deal with. Yet with all this new responsibility, compounded by the twin aggressors of grief and loss, I saw fit to saddle myself with more aggravation in the shape of an eight-week-old puppy.

It seemed like a good idea at the time, and Mother was on the point of ecstasy at the prospect of me having a 'positive new focus'. So I found myself staring at a phone list of cocker-poo breeders at the start of what I believed would be an unlikely pursuit of the elusive and sought-after breed.

The list started in Aberdeen and extended to Taunton, with just five breeders within a commutable distance from our village. Friends had a cocker-poo, for whom they'd waited eighteen months on various breeder lists. The dogs' temperaments combined with no shedding and 'low odour' make them a popular proposition for families. I wanted black. I wanted a bitch. I wasn't hopeful.

I got my black, albeit male, pup from the second breeder I called. The dog had been reserved up until that day, at which point the prospective owner had decided against it and pulled out. If I didn't want him, he was being advertised in the paper the next day. Even more startlingly, the breeder was just seven miles away.

'Do not wear your heart on your sleeve when we go in there,' I warned my mother as we approached the breeder's house. 'Act cool.'

Thirty seconds later, I was handing over a £200 cash deposit. I would bring the remaining £400 when I collected the dog the next day.

'But what should we call him?' we mused on the way home. The breeder had named him Brucie, but surely we could come up with better than that?

In the event, we couldn't. Just as his acquisition had been serendipitous (the superstitious may call it fate), the breeder's name choice was improbably apt – an amalgamation of B and Lucie, the dog's brand-new, adoring owners.

*

A few days into new dog ownership, I began to think I'd made a terrible mistake. Within the space of seventy-two hours, Brucie had gone from timid ball of fluff to demonic chewer of all our worldly possessions. He destroyed furniture, computer leads, the crotches of my pants. Scarcely a toy remained that hadn't been disembowelled and relieved of all its facial features. His disregard for the home we'd provided for him left me angry and in despair, adding to an already overloaded emotional capability.

Moreover, the bastard wouldn't sleep. He'd drop off for short naps, then wake me up at two in the morning ready to play. He shat all over my rented living room. He wouldn't be left alone for a second, howling like an abandoned child at the bathroom door while I took a bath. In the end, I relented on the latter issue and allowed him in as I bathed. However, in his anguish at being separated from me by a body of water, he would balance on his back legs, rest his forepaws on the side of the tub and lick droplets of water off my shoulders. I missed the attention of an adoring male, but this was not what I'd had in mind.

'I hate Brucie,' I told Mother. 'I haven't got the energy to deal with him. And it's all your fault.'

'My fault? How do you work that out?'

'You forced me to get him. You thought he would take my mind off Mark.'

'I did no such thing—'

'Yeah you did. You want me to forget Mark as soon as possible. To move on. Well, I'm not going to and the sooner you understand that, the better.'

Mother's brow crumpled. It was harsh, but I believed there was an element of truth in my rant. Like any parent, she hated bearing witness to her child's suffering. But unlike a grazed knee or a failed courtship, this time there was nothing she could do to 'fix' it. She wanted desperately for me to be 'better'. But how can anyone, even a mother, minister to a broken heart?

The dog and I sparred for some weeks further. I would give him dirty looks, or the cold shoulder, but his faith in me never seemed to waver. In the end, Brucie and I had a meeting of the minds, assisted by a dog-training manual, *100 Ways to Train the Perfect Dog*, by Sarah Fisher and Marie Miller, which was tactfully bought for me by my dad:

Imagine this: you have arrived in a company where no one speaks your language and no one has told you what to do. You have not been given any training and your job description is vague. You cannot call a friend to ask for help so you try and work things out by yourself [...] Think about how your dog might view his life with you and look at yourself through his eyes.

Like me with bereavement, Brucie had suddenly found himself in a new world where the rules and boundaries were unclear. Once I understood that we were in the same boat, our relationship improved immeasurably. In fact, if Mother's vision had really been of him as the embodiment of a Positive New Focus, it turned out she was right. The task of walking him every day – a mile-long shamble through the countryside surrounding the village – was an enforced opportunity for exercise and reflection. During these walks I could pound the ground with my boot heels and scream into the wind, or else take in great lungfuls of chill north-eastern air to remind myself that I was still alive. I could ponder the clouds in which I often thought I saw Mark – the curvature of His cheek or His hairline arc – or not think at all, just stand on the hill and watch cars snaking southward on the distant motorway.

No matter what I did during these walks, the dog didn't mind; most of the time he barely noticed, but if he did, he'd raise his nostrils from whatever smell they were buried in and come trotting over to check I was all right. He was never far away from my heels, though, and if I lost sight of him I'd call his name and he'd emerge from the bushes and bound towards me, ears billowing, jaws set in what looked like a giant, lopsided grin, and jump up as if we'd been apart for days.

I went from hating the sight of him to becoming as dependent on him as he was on me. I began to refer to him as 'My Man', and before long he had secured his spot on the duvet alongside me and B.

JUNE–JULY

I had made a small group of new friends in the village. Mothers with children the same age as B who rallied around with tissues and wine, plus their husbands who blundered around clumsily in the background, never knowing quite how to deal with this widow in their midst. One of them, Joanne, announced she was hosting a small gathering to celebrate her fortieth birthday. Like Neo dodging bullets in *The Matrix*, I had become adept at dodging invitations to gatherings of adults. The reasons for this were fourfold:

1. Group gatherings meant Couples.
2. Mark's death was a subject around which people skirted, as if it were an open manhole in the middle of the living room floor.
3. My grief was unpredictable, and I didn't want to ruin anyone's night by having a spontaneous meltdown.
4. I felt guilty about the possibility of having fun.

Joanne's fortieth birthday was one bullet I felt I couldn't avoid though. It was to be a small party at their house. Just round the corner from the safety of my little pebble-dashed house, in fact, so I could come away if I needed to. And besides, they were all friends. This would be a good opportunity to put my toe back in the water.

I arrived early and allowed Joanne's husband, Ned, to fill up my glass with wine. People began to arrive. Some faces

I knew, others I didn't. Anxiety stirred. Did these people know my situation, or was I going to have to answer the dreaded question: 'Are you married?' I shuffled about on my stool.

My counsellor had suggested that I come up with a stock answer. It went something like this: 'My husband died last year, but if you don't mind I'd rather not talk about it.' I was to practise it in front of the mirror so that it would roll off the tongue. I repeated the refrain in my head as each new face walked into the party. But mainly I willed them: 'Please don't ask me anything about myself.' I knew from bitter experience though that any line of questioning always led to the cul-de-sac of my widowhood.

'Have you lived in the village long? Oh? Where did you live before?'

'Do you work? And how about your husband?'

'So how did you meet Ned and Joanne? I'm surprised we haven't met before!'

Indeed, since Mark's death, I had cultivated an interviewing technique worthy of *Parkinson*. I feigned fascination in the minutiae of people's lives, their children's lives, the lives of their neighbours and friends. I'd ask a question then pick out a detail of the answer for the interviewee to expand on further. Anything to take the focus off myself and the possibility of having to talk about what had happened. And also to spare myself the sight of the other person's face disintegrating as they heard the response to their seemingly innocuous query.

'This is Dave and this is Christine. They live in the next village.' Joanne was saying, indicating a guy holding a four-pack of lager, and his Sauvignon Blanc-bearing wife. 'This is Lucie.'

'Hi there, Dave, Christine. So you live in the next village? Great. How long have you lived there then?' I said, before either Dave or Christine could open their mouths to speak.

A couple of hours in, and the party had split into two factions: men in the kitchen and women in the lounge. Dave, though, had defected into the lounge and inevitably, as is typical of middle-aged married people who don't get much sex any more, the banter turned smutty.

'Tell you what,' Dave announced, 'When I die, I want it to be between the thighs of an eighteen-year-old virgin!'

Most of the guests knew about Mark. A smaller percentage knew of the circumstances of his death. Poor Dave knew neither, so it didn't occur to him to heed the temperature of the crowd's reaction and quit while he was ahead. He blundered on: 'Ooh, yeah! Imagine that! What a way to go!'

I pushed my Scotch egg around my plate, then stabbed it repeatedly with a breadstick. Would it be inappropriate to launch into an invective about how, while it might sound like fun, Dave, there are downsides to this mode of demise to consider? Namely, the fate of the eighteen-year-old virgin who would be left in the wet patch. If she ever did accept that your death was in no way her fault, what legacy of sexual intercourse would she be left with? How would she ever fully disassociate the act of sex from the image of your lifeless body? And how long would it take for her nervous system to recover, if it ever did, from those initial frenzied moments of blind panic when you collapsed inside her?

By now though, Dave's train of thought had shunted on.

'Talking of death, I met an undertaker the other day.' I noted more and more people in the process of murdering their Scotch eggs. 'Gave me the creeps, he did. Kept looking at me, and I'm sure he was thinking: He's definitely an eight man-er...'

I snuck out of the room and took the opportunity to collar Ned for a top-up on my wine.

'Have you booked your trip to France for that wedding yet?' he asked, topping off my glass with a glug of red.

Mark and I had been invited to the nuptials of a dear old friend of mine, and the celebrations were happening in the Alps later in the month. 'I'm not going, Ned.'

'Since when?'

'Since I have realised that I can't possibly face watching two people at the start of a journey which has just ended so abruptly for me.'

He leaned against the wall and curled the wine bottle into his chest. 'Listen,' he said. 'I've got a book for you. It's about a woman who was dying and she wrote a list of things she wanted her sons and her husband to achieve once she'd gone. I think you should read it.'

'Honestly, I appreciate what you're saying, but I'm not ready to read anything like that yet.'

'I guess what I'm trying to say is that you have to live. You have to go on and do things.'

'It's easy for you—'

'Yes, yes I know what you're going to say, but the fact is, if Joanne died I would not put my life on hold. If anything it would spur me on to do things, for me and for her.'

It is a common assumption held by those who have not been in the eye of a disaster, that they would be certain of the course of action they would take when looking in at it from the sidelines. Indeed, prior to Mark's death I was categorical that if He were ever to be taken from me, I would throw myself off the nearest bridge in order to be with Him. I certainly wouldn't have believed I'd have the courage, or the will, to go on. Somehow, though, I was still here, blundering forwards as best I could, in my own way. And I wasn't prepared to take advice on how I should deal with the death of a spouse from anyone who'd never suffered it, no matter how good the intentions.

I thanked Ned for his thoughts and promptly placed them in my mental Recycle Bin. I sat down and glanced into the kitchen where the men still congregated, propped up around the benches like a commercial for blue jeans. My man should have been in among them too, in His blue jeans.

In fact, He had been, two months before He died, when we came for a Christmas drink. Thinking about His blue jeans, I missed them; the cut of them, narrowing slightly at the knee, worn creases by the pockets. I missed His hands slouching out of those pockets, big man's hands with their wide fingernails and light covering of down.

Draining my wine, I thought about my child, who was staying with Mother for the night. I felt an urgent need to see her, even though she would no doubt be asleep. I wanted to place my hand in the middle of her ribcage and feel the rise and fall of her tiny chest. I checked my phone for messages (a now-instinctive impulse whenever I was away from B) but there were none. My foray into the world of grown-up, couple-led socialising was over for the night. I told Joanne and Ned that I was leaving, and Ned told me he and their fifteen-year-old son Harry would walk me home.

'It's fine, Ned, seriously, I'd rather just run round on my own,' I said, heading out of the door.

'You'll not be running anywhere in heels like that,' he countered. 'Come on, Harry, hurry up.'

They finally caught up with me where the streetlights stopped and the road opened to countryside. The night was black, awash with stars like glass from a shattered disco ball. My heels clicked the pavement and I felt the tears coming. I was too weak to stop them. Ned came up behind me and caught my elbows in his hands, and I let myself go, screaming brokenheartedly at the sky.

'I want Him back, I want Him back!' I yelled, choking on the words. 'I miss Him so much it hurts; it's actual, physical pain.' I clutched my guts and retched on the side of the road.

Ned held me as we walked, Harry hung behind, unsure of what to say or do. Ned shh'd me, told me to be calm, talking me down until we rejoined streetlights on my road. We reached my front door, with its promise of emptiness on the other side, but I wanted the emptiness now, I wanted to walk into its chill and lie down in it until the pain passed.

'I'm sorry, Harry,' I said.

Harry lowered his head and slunk away into a patch of darkness between two streetlights.

'He's OK,' Ned said. 'Are you going to be OK, though?'

'Yes,' I said. 'Goodnight. And thank you.'

I shut the door, opened another bottle of wine and watched the moon through the shutters as it tracked higher into the sky.

Walking into emptiness had its advantages on nights like those. I could drink as much as I wanted with impunity, rail at the four walls without the fear of a furrowed Motherly brow looking on. I could grieve in the manner of my choosing without onlookers standing all tangle-limbed in the corner not knowing what to do or say.

But most of the time, the emptiness felt exactly like what it was – empty. I had lived on my own before, of course, years before Mark and I were married, but now, not only was I trying to come to terms with my own private tragedy, but I had, overnight, become the sole carer of a tiny child.

I had grown used to the economics and machinations of the married household. Labour was divided equally. Mark loved food – and by this I mean he *appreciated* every mouthful and had a passion for each new flavour he came across – so generally, our cupboards would be bursting.

Now I'd spend fifty pounds on fresh produce in Tesco only to find it mouldering in the fridge, untouched, three weeks later. Fruit festered in the bowl, cans of beans began to rust. Even filling the kettle was subject to revision, now that it was only catering for one cup.

Clothes would go unwashed for days. Every time I went to empty the basket and sort the laundry into colour-coded piles, there was never enough of one colour to justify a wash. So I would end up throwing the dirty clothes back into the basket and waiting patiently until it started to overflow. But when I began the triage again, it was always the same problem. The clothes lay on the floor in piles, as if they too had given up hope of ever being clean again, which is why my daughter and I ended up with an entirely pink wardrobe. Frustrated, I committed the cardinal sin of chucking it all in together.

I found myself puzzling over electricity tariffs, car and home insurance renewals, boiler instruction manuals. The cold tap stopped working, inexplicably, one morning, and there was no one but me who could arrange for it to be fixed. Letters would arrive about my daughter's impending school starting date, things that needed to be done, decisions that needed to be taken, and, as the sole carer, those decisions had to be made by me.

Gradually, I discovered the wonder of frozen, diced onion, just-for-one pasta sauces and the ready-meal. I bought individual apples instead of a full bag. I no longer bought pak choi, smelly cheese or exotic fruit – what was the point? My daughter only ate Wotsits, and there's only so much fun you can have with a kiwi fruit on your own.

I managed to surmount a fear of the dark, a hatred of evenings and Sunday mornings (more through necessity than choice), and found that I had successfully managed to insure the contents of the house, our car and also provide a flow of fuel to the house, despite the quantum physics degree that is apparently required to decipher the documentation relating to these issues.

I did appear, to the casual observer and even, sometimes, to myself, to be coping. The pills helped, of course, as did the counselling and the bottle of wine I was consuming each night. But my nervous system had taken a battering along with everything else, and no matter how I chose to self-medicate, the cracks continued to show.

After the blurring in the eyes and the panic attacks came a ringing in the ears. Like thoughts of my husband, sometimes the ringing was loud, sometimes it was quiet, but it was always there, a high-pitched soundtrack to my existence.

Then came periods of dizziness which would accost me at the most inopportune times: driving in the fast lane of the motorway or when I was alone with my daughter with no one to call upon if I collapsed. My hands sometimes began to involuntarily shake and I'd have to sit on them in order to make it stop. One of my upper teeth cracked as a result of being persistently clamped and ground against the lower set. And still the weight dropped off, regardless of how much I thought I'd eaten.

Once again I found myself in the doctor's office insisting on blood tests and full body examinations. It seemed impossible that such a range of physical symptoms could stem from what was essentially a mental illness. I became convinced that I too was going to die and leave my child an orphan. And the further I allowed myself to stray down that path of thinking, the more probable it became.

The Shared Experience

Dr Asenscio, the cardiologist who had been tasked with Mark's aftercare since the events of 2008, made a request that all immediate family be seen for aortic scans. They needed a baseline from which to ascertain the threat to B and her two cousins of this most savage of afflictions.

For B, however, the investigations would need to be more involved. It turns out that when your husband suffers (and subsequently dies from) a spontaneous aortic dissection of the type rarely seen before in the whole of medical science, you and your child are called in for questioning.

Not that we were under suspicion, you understand.

But the aortic dissection was so extensive and caused so much collateral damage in such a young and fit man that the cardiac experts in the NHS found themselves racing back to their textbooks to find a reason why it might have happened.

We were summoned to the Freeman Hospital in Newcastle one balmy afternoon in August. My sister came too. We made a tacit agreement to re-enact that film set in a concentration camp, *Life is Beautiful*, and pretend it was all a game in order to shelter B from the hideous truth of why she was there. We skipped into the hospital, pointed out all the interesting things along the way ('Look at that funny picture of a pair of cancer-ravaged lungs, darling!'), then waited to be called in for the first stage of tests.

It was all so horribly familiar. The cardio-thoracic ward. Coronary care unit. ECG. That sickening hospital stink caught in my throat. The sight of nursing staff walking about in blue scrubs made my guts lurch. What brain-paralysing news were they on their way to impart? At least, I told myself, they couldn't bring any further bombshells about my husband – for Him, there would be no more. But what of my daughter?

My sister and I chuckled away as the Nice Man stuck probes all over B's tiny chest and told her to breathe in and out deeply while he took a reading off the machine to which she was attached. She got a sticker and a rancorous smile off the Nice Man before we were moved on to the next test. We chuckled non-stop for an hour in a Nemo-covered waiting area, until the consultant took us into a darkened room so that my daughter could be probed further – this time an echo scan of her heart.

It was at that point that my chuckle switch hit a malfunction and I had to step out and leave my sister to it. I pressed my ear to the door and listened as they helped my tiny child on to a bed, lifted up her top and examined her aorta to see if there was any evidence that she might be at risk of succumbing to the same fate as her daddy. From the other side of the door, the examination seemed to be taking an inordinately long time. I paced. I returned to the door and listened. Voices were muffled. A nurse approached.

'Is everything all right in there, do you think?' I asked.

'You're welcome to go in, you know,' she said.

'I know. I've been in, but I've come out...'

'I'm sure everything's fine.'

The door opened. I scrutinised faces for evidence of concern. My hands were trembling on my lap as I listened to the doctor tell me that everything was normal. My child was OK. We would be seen again in three years' time, but this was purely routine. So we all left, chuckling.

Yet the investigations didn't end there. A few weeks later, I received a summons on NHS-headed paper, requesting the attendance of my daughter at a genetics clinic in Newcastle.

Anything bearing the insignia of the NHS is enough to send my colon into spasm. It was the case when Mark was alive, and it continues after His death. My immediate assumption was that it was Bad News. Clearly they had identified something in my husband's DNA which indicated that His affliction was genetic. This would mean my daughter would be subjected to a life of tests, pills and blue-garbed medical specialists.

Mother and I took B into Newcastle on the train in a bid to convince her that this was going to be a Fun Outing, not a visit to another airless office, leaden with dread. She sat there for ten minutes looking at the geneticist's beard and then asked when we were going home. The geneticist opened Mark's hefty buff-coloured file and took a pensive breath.

He described the genetic mutation involved in Mark's condition as being 'like an elephant on a motorway'. That is to say it's unusual and anomalous (indeed, hitherto *unseen* in the gene world), but not necessarily a *bad* elephant on a motorway. It could just be a different mode of transport, not yet seen before. In brief, Mark had left us with a mystery.

But what did this mean for B? The geneticist looked at her and smiled. 'Hello, B. I'm Edward. I like your hair.'

She ran a finger through one of her curls. 'Do you wish you had hair like this?' she asked.

'Yes, I do.' Edward handed her a piece of paper and some crayons. 'Would you do me a drawing of your hair?'

She set about the task, no doubt assuming this to be the fun part of the outing, and Edward turned to Mother and me with a serious face. 'Fact is, we don't know what this means for B. Probably nothing. But it would be futile to do any further testing on Mark's DNA at this point in time. It is, after all, a finite resource. We have no way of harvesting any more...'

'Wait – you still have a sample of Mark's DNA?'

'Yes.'

'What does it look like?' I pictured tissue, matter, a tangible, recognisable jigsaw piece left over from His body.

'DNA? Oh, it's a cloudy, sort of cotton-like substance. Doesn't look like much really.'

'Oh. And where is He? It?'

'In a fridge in Salisbury,' he said, casually. 'And we'd be best off leaving it there for now. It needs to be used sparingly and only when it is likely it would yield results. That time is not yet. Genetic science hasn't evolved to the point of discovering the cause of Mark's aortic rupture, but in ten years the outlook may be different.'

I had assumed the only remnants of my husband lay with me – in a lacquered box in the wardrobe, in a curl of hair, a footprint in a pair of shoes. I hadn't considered that He might be spread as far as a fridge in Salisbury. The news unnerved me. I felt upset that part of Him had been removed and stored elsewhere. I resisted an urge to demand the sample of DNA be returned to me, where it belonged.

'My recommendation is that we let B have a childhood before we start intervening with tests and medical procedures. I have no worries for her at the moment, if any at all.' Edward closed the file and turned to B. 'Is that my picture?' B held up her self-portrait. 'That's wonderful. May I keep it?' B nodded and Edward laid it in Mark's file. 'I'll see you all again in ten years,' he said, and showed us to the door.

The 'Glorious Twelfth' of August loomed, and with it, the weight of its significance. Mark and I would have been married six years.

'I'm going away for the day,' I told Mother. 'I need to be alone. To contemplate and reflect.'

She nodded with characteristic equanimity. Inwardly, the duodenal ulcer would be throbbing, but she knew better than to argue with the grieving harridan on her first husband-less wedding anniversary.

'Where will you go?'

'I don't know yet. I just need to get away.' I stalked off to the car and cranked up the engine. I drove to the end of the village and pulled into the lay-by. I tried to decide where to go. Somewhere isolated and windswept, to reflect my despair.

Mark and I had married onstage, at the Georgian Theatre in Richmond, North Yorkshire, on the first day of grouse-shooting season. There was no significance for us in the date – it was the only time the theatre could fit us in – yet people always referred to it reverentially as 'The Glorious Twelfth'.

There was nothing glorious about the weather on that day six years ago, though. The reception was held in a marquee on a plot of land with drainage issues next to Dad's house. It had rained from dawn until the moment the last taxi left at midnight, so by 6 p.m. the path from the tent to the Port-a-Loos was transformed into a fetid mud-slick. Women skittered up and down it in their posh heels, and men just gave up and relieved themselves on the lawn.

Glory came from the fact that I was marrying my soulmate, finally, after four years (and a period of sustained badgering on my part). It came from the look of love on His face as He saw me clambering up the stairs, stage left, trying not to trip on my dress. It came from the friends and family who had gathered in that ancient auditorium to see us wed. It came from the moment we were tucked up in bed on our first night as husband and wife, whispering 'We Win!' to each other over plump duck-down pillows.

Sitting in that lay-by on the first anniversary without Him, I remembered the words of one of our French friends who had been with us on the day: '*Mariage pluvieux, mariage heureux!*' ('Rainy wedding, happy marriage.')

And for six years, it was.

In the event, I couldn't actually think of anywhere I'd rather be on this day than with my family. After ten minutes of deliberation in the lay-by, I turned the car round and returned to the house.

'Oh, hello Mum,' said B, barely looking up from her elaborate Play-Doh project.

'Hello, darling.'

'You're back?' said Mother.

'Yes.'

'Shall I put the kettle on then?'

Mark and I never put much stock in anniversaries, wedding or otherwise. Birthdays were about as excited as we got, usually marked by a card and, if He was very unlucky, a home-made Victoria sponge. What would we have been doing today, had He been here to share it? Most likely we would have exchanged cards, a kiss and a reflection on how much we'd been through these past six years and how grateful we were to still have each other.

I realised I had been worrying about how I thought I *should* behave on this day, rather than focusing on how I really felt. I was numb, bereft, my guts ached. But these symptoms were felt no more keenly today than on any other day. August the twelfth was just one day further away from the last time I saw my husband.

Ten days later, I turned thirty-seven. Cards lined the mantel, but all I could see was a gap where His should have been. It would have been one of those oversized 'For the one I love...' cards, with a scruffy teddy bear holding on to a heart. They became a joke between us, those cards, for their saccharine sentimentality, but secretly I loved the fact that He found a slightly different one every year (teddy holding balloon, teddy holding rose), but always wrote the same message:

To Wife,
All my love, always.
Husband
X

'I feel like putting last year's card from Him up,' I told my friend Anna.

'Why don't you then?' she said.

'Seems a bit daft...'

'I don't see why. Try it, see how it feels. You can always take it down again.'

I lifted Mark's most recent offering from the box of our old love notes and propped it up among the other cards. Last year's teddy was carrying a bunch of flowers, and brought the usual message.

I sat on the settee and looked at the mantel. Teddy looked back at me with a doleful expression. Teddy knew he didn't belong there, with those birthday wishes from the present. He knew it would only make me feel worse to see him, nestling in, testifying to the loss. I took him down and placed him back in the box with the other love notes.

I had deliberately made no plans for the day, but as the morning wore on I realised I needed a distraction.

'I'm taking B out,' I told Mother. 'Just me and her.'

'Oh. OK. Where are you going?'

'To spend lots of money.'

I took my daughter to Durham and we hired a rowing boat on the river. It was a courageous move on my behalf, given the potential for water-based disaster, yet somehow we negotiated the river's sinuous course unscathed, talking all the way. I explained how the oar affected the speed and direction of the boat, and she placed her hand on mine to get a sense of the movement. We peered into the gloamy water looking for sea trout or salmon, finding only leaves and the odd Sainsbury's carrier bag hooked on a log. I indicated the cathedral, where we would shortly go and light a candle for Daddy, and then nearly capsized the tub pointing out a heron which stood, camouflaged, on the bank.

People on the riverside path waved and said 'Aww!' as they saw the two of us pass, she with her flowing Pre-Raphaelite curls, me with my ill-concealed unease. It brought to mind the last time I had been in a rowing boat. Mark and I had been in Evesham, before B was born, and decided to hire a boat on the river.

'I'll row, pet,' Mark had said, taking up the oars and manoeuvring us off upstream.

Twenty minutes later, after a woozy loaf in the sun, I said: 'Can I have a little turn?'

He handed me the oars and sat back, just as a group of alpha males on a stag do came into view on the river path.

'You lazy bastard!' they shouted, laughing and pointing at Mark as I grappled with the boat. 'Do you need a hand, love?'

Mark took it with good humour, but no sooner had we turned the corner than He said, 'Come on, pet, let's turn round and go back now. Pass me the oars.'

He turned the boat around and rowed back past the hecklers with such speed and manly gusto that the bow nearly lifted out of the water. Later, in the pub, Guinness in hand, we rolled about laughing.

'I love it when you get all gallant,' I said.

He posed His arm to His nose like Bruce Forsyth and replied: 'Anything for my lady.'

Back in Durham, B and I walked up to the cathedral with the intention of lighting a candle for Mark. I am not religious, but since Mark's death the majesty of that building had ignited something deep within me and I had found myself wandering in a couple of times during shopping trips, just to sit and be in awe. I liked the fact that it had stood there before Mark was born and would stand there long after I was gone. It had been a bystander through several centuries of human existence, and as such seemed to help me momentarily view death as a part of the ongoing circle of life. Which in turn caused what I call The Lee Effect – it made Mark's brutal demise seem (briefly) 'not quite so bad'.

We entered the cathedral, nodded meekly at the meet 'n' greeters by the door, and made our way towards the glowing votive rack.

'I'd like to buy one for me and one for my daughter,' I told the kindly old man. He brought us both a tealight and we placed them solemnly amid the others, before reaching for the taper to light them.

'Now then,' I told B. 'I want you to light this and think about Daddy.'

I handed her the taper and she stretched her little arm tentatively towards the tealight. At that moment a vacuum cleaner roared into action from behind a pillar, and its wielder (an ancient woman wearing a purple cassock) began pushing it about the stone flags underneath the votive rack. The poignancy of what we were about to do instantly went the way of the crumbled wax.

We hurriedly lit the candles, thought quickly about Daddy, and left in the direction of a jewellery shop, where I did as I had told Mother I would and spent lots of money on bracelets and rings. Things that glittered and looked pretty, but ultimately, when the lustre wore off, would not bring my husband back.

At thirty-seven, I had reached the age that Mark had attained but would never surpass. How much more of life I wanted to see! How many ambitions I had left to polish off! Despite how grief had wearied me, thirty-seven years seemed such a short time to have been on Earth.

Mark had achieved much in His short time. He loved languages and other cultures, mastering French, Spanish and Japanese (and a smattering of comedy German). He never let language be a barrier to communication, though, even if He didn't understand what the foreigner was saying. On our honeymoon in Italy, He simply affected an Italian accent while speaking English, and remarkably, it seemed to work. (Notwithstanding the fact that most Europeans speak English anyway, Italian accent or not.)

He'd lived on three continents – Asia, Australia and Europe – and as a result had acquired a large collection of quirky foreign friends with whom we would occasionally stay on our travels. He taught Himself to play the guitar, a journey that had started as a torturous plucking of random disharmonious chords and had ended just before He died with a heartbreakingly beautiful, note-perfect rendition of the Spanish guitar classic 'Romanza'.

He'd had B, married someone who was devoted to Him, worked in a prestigious and worthwhile job. And with the highs, He fielded the lows. He'd not just *survived* emergency heart surgery – He looked upon it as a second chance, refusing to let it define Him. Once He'd come through it, He pursued His ambitions with fiery determination and a big grin.

And, together, we'd lost a child. It was an embryo, granted, a mere cluster of cells, yet we loved that cluster of cells and had tried for many months to produce it. The moment we found out it was lost, that gut-wrenching moment when the sonographer's screen was black where a heartbeat should have been, He reached for me and held my hand, never wavering until the staggeringly named Evacuation of Retained Products of Conception was complete and we were home, and He could call His sister and burst into tears down the phone.

Perhaps most importantly, though, despite it all, He achieved a level of happiness and contentment that most don't have in a lifetime. He had fought in 2008 because He loved life and had so much more left to give and so much left still to do. I could only lament, as the sun went down on my first birthday without him, what another thirty-seven years might have yielded, and all the things He was going to miss.

By now, we were deep in the throes of the six-week school holiday. Weekends were bad enough for a grieving widow – that gaping forty-eight-hour void in which families *do things together*, even if it's just arguing over the Wii remote.

Now I could do nothing but sit back and watch as these families prepared for their annual break. And everywhere, people seemed to be bemoaning the fact that they were going to have to spend unadulterated time away with their other halves.

'He gets on my tits at the weekend, how am I ever going to survive two weeks?' was the plaintive cry.

This is not to say Mark never got on my tits. He did, especially at holiday time. He would pack everything and everyone into the car before embarking on a trip, then spend ten minutes checking doors and the status of the gas supply inside the house. He wore offensive purple swimming trunks on the beach. He was lax on sharing the childcare, claiming He was too tired whenever it came to sandcastle construction or changing a shitty arse. But this didn't stop me from wanting to shout at all those griping spouses: 'At least you've still got your other half! So stop fucking moaning!'

So I sat on the bench outside my little pebble-dashed house and waited for people to return in the hope that I would feel like less of a freak.

My sister-in-law, Helen, telephoned to tell me that she had organised a last-minute trip to Blackpool, and that B and I were coming, along with Beth, Will and their respective children. Blackpool wasn't my dream summer holiday destination, yet as I couldn't muster the energy or imagination required to come up with anywhere else, I agreed we would go. And as organising holidays is my sister-in-law's favourite pastime, all I had to do was turn up with my daughter and allow myself to be led around like a flatulent dog on a leash.

Helen had sorted accommodation, Pleasure Beach passes, sustenance, and most importantly, she'd identified all the decent drinking establishments so we were never more than a hundred paces from a glass of red wine.

Being Blackpool, most of the hotels have rooms big enough to house an extended family, and ours was no exception. Beth was acutely aware of my spouse-less state and over-compensated where she could.

'Will,' she told her husband. 'You're sleeping on the fold-out. Lucie's in the double with me.'

Will's cheeks flopped, yet he plonked his overnight bag on the wafer-thin fold-out with admirable magnanimity. Once beds had been allocated, we headed down for dinner, where I permitted myself to get roaring drunk without considering the consequences for the following day. Unwittingly, I had condemned myself to a day on the Pleasure Beach in the company of a monster hangover. Spongebob Squarepants never looked so evil.

Wandering around that theme park, the familiar sense of detachment from the rest of the world kicked in. Dads and their offspring seemed to be running around in Instagram-hued ecstasy, plunging down log flumes, doing the thumbs-up on The Big One, intent on baiting the wine-soused widow.

I resented the holidaying families. They had no concept of what it would be to lose it all in an instant. *Stop wasting energy shouting at little Jakey and enjoy your time together*, I wanted to shout. But what was the point?

'Auntie Lu is crying,' announced my niece G.

It was only a matter of time before the meltdown occurred. Helen had located a decent Italian in the town centre and organised taxis to get us all there. Gallons of red wine were ordered, along with plate after plate of food. Sitting in that restaurant, I was starkly aware of the group and my position within it. Spouses were sitting opposite spouses. I was partnered with my daughter. At the theme park we had been scattered about. Here, gathered around the table, the truth was unavoidable: Mark wasn't there.

My mouth quivered uncontrollably and fat tears plopped into my carbonara. My sister sprang into action, ushering me into the Ladies. G and my other niece M followed close behind, not wanting to miss out on the spectacle of an adult on the verge of a breakdown.

'Auntie Lu is just a bit sad,' said Beth.

'Does she miss Uncle Mark?'

'Yes.'

G fetched a length of toilet paper from one of the cubicles and handed it to me.

'Thanks, darling.'

The girls never took their eyes off me as they sidled out of the Ladies, eager to report back on Auntie Lu's emotional disintegration. The tiny amount of carbonara I had managed to ingest was promptly thrown back up into the toilet.

I steadied myself on the side of the sink and looked at the woman's face staring back at me in the mirror. It was pale and wan, streaked with thin fingers of mascara.

'I just want to go back to the hotel.'

I was duly bundled into a taxi not an hour after arriving at the restaurant. More wine was charged to room service, and finally I passed out, fully clothed, on the fold-out bed. Will must have been delighted.

The two days in Blackpool marked our first 'holiday' since Mark's death. As with all aspects of this process, it was not as expected. Despite the perpetual hangover and the jags of grief, I did enjoy it. My daughter enjoyed it. It brought me closer to my siblings and their spouses. Most importantly, it made me realise that I could do it. It was another of those 'milestones', ticked off.

Back on the bench outside my pebble-dashed house, I drank red wine and looked out at the three remaining empty weeks of holiday.

'How about a few days away together?' Beth suggested. 'Just me, you and the kids.'

'Could do. Where were you thinking?'

'How about one of these places where you stay in a chalet and they have activities on for the kids?'

In bereavement, one finds oneself doing things which ordinarily wouldn't enter one's activity lexicon. Blackpool, for example. And holiday parks, with their verruca-ridden swimming pools and chain-restaurant-flanked 'town squares'. For me they are as cheerless as the weather. However, there we were, me, Beth and our three kids, rolling up to the reception lodge of a Holiday Park in our heavily laden car, ready for three days of fun within the confines of a barbed boundary fence.

It had been a long time since I had been away on holiday with a female, let alone my sister, who also happens to be my best friend. I had forgotten the kind of attention that women in this arrangement elicit from men. Like Barbara Windsor and the girls from Chayste Place Finishing School when they pile off the bus in *Carry On Camping*, we became sexual beings, bristling with possibility. And there were plenty of Sid Boggles and Bernie Luggs at this holiday park to choose from.

Will had agreed that he would stay away for the first two days, but would join us on the last day, given that these were the Holidays and while he understood the plight of the grieving widow, he did quite want to spend time with his kids at some point. We offloaded the supplies into our chalet and then joined the line of other vehicles that were snaking back to the car park in order to exchange cars for bicycles – just one of the ways in which the park hoped to promote clean air and serenity. We duly swapped our transportation and peddled off into the forest.

'For fuck's sake, we're back in the red zone,' I shouted, pointing at the sign we had cycled past five minutes before. 'This whole place looks identical.' I placed my feet on either side of the bike, trying to steady B, who wobbled about on the trailer behind me.

'Let's try down this way,' Beth shouted back, disappearing down another tarmacked track through the woodland.

It was some time before we arrived back at the chalet, by which point any intentions of going out for dinner were thoroughly quashed. The navigational skills required for such a venture were simply too complex. Instead, we cooked beans and drank wine until there was nothing left to do but turn in.

The following day, we decided to try out the Subtropical Swimming Paradise, as had, it turned out, the rest of the park's inmates. We fought our way around the Restful Rapids, grappled with other people's limbs in the Spa Pool, and narrowly avoided an altercation with the mother of a particularly pugnacious child who insisted on climbing the wrong way up the water slide. We lasted an hour before the lure of lunch and a lager became too strong, and we found ourselves huddled on the terrace of Café Rouge, bedraggled and trying to keep out of the rain.

That afternoon I had booked a sailing lesson. Despite a fear of open-water swimming, fish and drowning, I had always fancied myself as something of a sea dog. Indeed, Mark had been going to buy me a set of lessons for my birthday. We pitched up on the 'beach' from where I would be setting sail. The tutor, a spotty-faced youth earning extra cash in his school holidays, arrived to greet me.

'I'm really sorry but there's no wind.' He licked his forefinger and held it in the air, just to double check. 'No point in going on to the lake if there's no wind. Could you return tomorrow, perhaps?'

We had archery booked tomorrow, and miniature golf, and in the afternoon, an overpriced facial. Plus I had set my heart on sailing. There was no way I was returning tomorrow.

'Let's just wait then,' the tutor replied. 'I've got no lessons booked in for the rest of the afternoon. The wind might get up. Why don't you go and get into a wetsuit so you're ready when the time comes?'

A couple of other instructors joined us as we waited on the beach.

'She's waiting for your colleague here to come up with some wind,' said Beth, smirking.

'That's normally no problem, is it, Dave?'

'What?' said Dave.

'You coming up with wind.'

'So it's usually windy when Dave's about, is it?' said Beth.

Dave wandered off, his spots throbbing, towards the pontoon to try and summon the tempest.

'You girls staying long then?' one of them asked, yanking a pedalo up on to the sand with a single, fluid movement.

'Just a couple of nights.'

'Got a pass-out from the other half then, eh?' another said.

'Something like that.' I shifted about in my mildewed wetsuit.

I realised, perhaps for the first time since Mark died, that I was single again. I was still married, and the marriage bond still felt alive, but I was in union with a dead man. And I felt sure I would never engage in a carnal act again.

Looking out into the distance, my instructor told me that even a whisper of wind today was unlikely, but that we could still go out on to the lake and practise some moves. I squelched behind him in my sodden wetsuit, and we climbed into the practice vessel that was beached on the grass. After a short lesson in wind speed and direction versus sailing vessel and inept sailor, the instructor saw fit to launch me off on to the lake in my own boat. I tacked and jibed my way from one side of the water to the other, reaching speeds of up to at least quarter of a mile an hour. If an occasional gust of wind blew up, the boat would suddenly take off and I would shriek in fright, much to the amusement of the spectators back on the beach.

The instructor finally had to admit defeat – there was no wind and, despite the occasional frenzy of tack-and-jibe, the truth was that we had spent most of the hour sitting in the middle of the lake, watching the surface of the water for any signs of a ripple. I sensed my sailing career had begun and ended in that hour. I had been happy to pootle about in my little tub, and was even happier to be coming back to shore.

Since Mark's illness and subsequent death, I perceived inherent danger in every situation, and scudding around on a boat, dodging the boom as it swung wildly from side to side, seemed like a fatality waiting to happen. And if the boat didn't see me off, the water would. I asked for assistance climbing out of the boat and back on to the jetty – I didn't want to have got this far only to drown in its murky depths.

Holding out his hand, the instructor laughed. 'I wouldn't worry. This lake is man-made and runs to about a metre deep. Even if you do go in, it'll only come up to your thighs.'

I stalked off to the safety of the changing room and cursed the holiday park anew.

On the final day of the holiday, Will arrived with two bottles of champagne and some chocolates, as if to apologise for the fact that he was a male, a daddy, a husband. We departed on a bike trip, skirting the periphery fence and ending up back in the town square at the last of the restaurants we hadn't tried. After three days of confinement, we had begun to recognise our fellow inmates. We were, after all, all doing the same circuit of activities and restaurants.

Sitting down in the curry house, there were the usual array of faces, and to my widow-weary eyes there didn't seem to be any other group in the same configuration as ours: a couple with their kids, and a singleton with hers. Once again, I found myself thinking of Him, my missing love. He would have been hooting at the sight of me in that soggy wetsuit in the middle of the knee-deep lake, and at the displays of navigational ineptitude around the park (until He got lost too and it suddenly would have become less amusing). He would have scoffed at the kiddies' disco until the groove got Him, Baloothe-Bear style, and He could resist the lure of the dance floor no more. I wondered if there would ever come a time when I didn't miss Him – when it would be OK to be the only one who was without a partner.

I had been warned about 'the six-month point'. This mythical moment in widowhood is when things get *really* bad. It's when the truth finally sinks in and you begin to feel even more suicidal than you did when it happened. So six months came round and I waited for the full force of the shit-storm to hit. And I waited. Yet, despite everything I'd read, I wasn't floored by a tsunami of grief. Instead, I could feel it rumbling on the edge of my vision. Ready to strike at any time.

Friends and family had gone back to their own lives. Their regular cross-country treks to see me had become infrequent, the daily pep-texts had dwindled to once or twice a week. But I couldn't really expect any more of them than they had given. My old friend Kim had four kids and a husband of her own to deal with. Chums from London – Beccy, Nicole, Anna – had the demands of jobs and partners. Mark's friends, John and Neil, had also resumed their commitments. Of all of them, Paul was the only one who maintained a regular vigil. He would visit on a twice-weekly basis, trundling up the motorway in his mother's car to bring me flowers, cupcakes, bottles of Rioja.

To be fair to my other friends, Paul was unemployed and lived nearby, therefore had time on his hands to tend to a lonely widow and her ginger-haired daughter. He loved Mark, and wanted to do his best by Him, and me. He was also newly single, so going through a bereavement, of sorts, of his own. All factors which made him available whenever I needed a bit of cheering up.

B and I looked forward to our days with Paul. They were, after all, one of the few opportunities we had for male interaction which didn't involve someone else's partner or daddy. He would join me for the sort of evenings I missed as a couple; those idle ones featuring Bruce Forsyth and an M & S meal deal. As far as Paul was concerned, these evenings were acts of altruism. He was sparing me another Saturday night of re-enacting scenes from *Sorry!* with Mother. We would sit on the settee, casually draped around each other in the way two people who are grieving, desperately lonely, yet who are observing boundaries do.

Furthermore, since Mark's death, B had had a negligible amount of contact with men. She could go for days without seeing or talking to an adult male, let alone one who loved her and would read *The Gruffalo* three times to her before bed. Paul would blow raspberries on her tummy and let her sit on his head to watch CBeebies. He brought her daft toys and bags of Haribo. She liked having him around.

Paul was entirely focused on us and our well-being, and when we were with him, I felt a weight lift.

For the times when he wasn't around, I sought friendship elsewhere to fill in the gaps. I found it online, through an organisation called WAY Widowed and Young. And like any-one who joins a club, I found I had more in common with these online widows than I did with many of my other friends put together. I was divulging my darkest thoughts to a community on the other end of a keyboard, almost all of whom I'd never met. Moreover, these people understood. These people sent *hugs!*. These people confirmed that I wasn't going nuts and that my reckless behaviours were not unusual. In fact, the majority of these people were doing exactly the same things as me. And like me, they were not telling their friends or family for fear of being labelled a deviant or consigned to the loony bin.

I decided to meet a group of widows from my region. We had arranged to have coffee on the upper floor of Caffè Nero in Newcastle, away from the non-bereaveds who were lunching merrily with their friends downstairs. There were around eight of us, women and men of varying ages, each at a different stage in our grief and each with a different story to tell. Some spent the hour silently contemplating their latte; others seemed ready to burst with the need to share their anguish with people who understood.

We exchanged death stories and grappled with posers such as: *'Should I have gone to view my spouse's body in the funeral home?'* And *'Do I really need to keep those rank, greying boxer shorts with the hole in the crotch, or is it sacrilege to throw them out?'*

'I wish I'd never gone to see Colin,' said Sandy (aged forty-two, into her second year of bereavement after losing Colin to a brain aneurysm). 'Can't get the image of him lying there in a coffin out of my mind.'

Gillian (aged forty-seven, 'an oldie' at five years post-death of her husband from bowel cancer) said, 'Yeah. I kept thinking Gary was going to sit up. Freaked the hell out of me.' We all nodded knowingly.

'I nearly ran out of the room at one point, I was so convinced my Keith was breathing,' said a nervy mouse of a woman whose name, age and bereavement circumstances I never ascertained.

'I wish I'd had the chance to see Ian,' said Cath (thirty-seven, nineteen months bereaved). 'It was a closed coffin, what with him having committed suicide and all.'

There was a synchronised supping of coffee as we considered Cath's predicament. Despite the misgivings, those of us who had been willing and able to see our spouses conceded that it was something that we had felt a strong need to do at the time. Proof, as it were, that our beloveds were truly gone. After all, the last time I had seen Mark, He had been at the mercy of five paramedics on the floor in Mother's bedroom. Who was to say they weren't lying when they said He'd died?

As for the boxer shorts quandary, it turns out I wasn't alone.

'My husband's entire wardrobe is vacuum-packed in the loft,' said Sandy. 'Shoes, crusty old socks, the lot. They're doing nowt but gathering dust but I can't bring myself to throw them away. His family think I'm crazy. Not that I care what *they* think, mind.' She tore at her panini with her teeth.

'I've had one of Ian's shirts made into a memory bear for my daughter,' said Cath. 'It doesn't smell of him any more though, so I keep spraying it with his aftershave.'

'Never mind that,' said Gillian. 'I've got a tin of Baxter's Mulligatawny at the back of my cupboard, five years out of date. Gary loved Mulligatawny. You lot probably think I'm nuts...'

I thought about the food items that were rotting at the back of a cupboard in my new kitchen: a sachet of sweet'n'sour stir-fry sauce (best before 15/6/12), a half-eaten carton of Ready-Brek, a tin of whole peeled tomatoes from Morrisons. I kept them because it was Mark who had bought them. And as such, I couldn't bear to use them, or throw them out.

Gillian's Mulligatawny confession prompted Terry, a thick-set, balding fellow whose neck was the circumference of a dinner plate, to say: 'You think that's nuts? My wife's tooth veneers are in a box next to my bed. They were part of her smile. How could I just chuck them out?'

While it wasn't the most fun I've had in a coffee shop, it served to remind me that I wasn't alone. Widowhood, especially 'young' widowhood, is very isolating. None of your contemporaries are going through it and none of them have the first clue about how to deal with it. Besides, they can't really be bothered to deal with it. Why should they? They're young and don't want to have to contemplate the dirty business of death.

But by virtue of the fact that Terry, Hornby train enthusiast and member of the gun club, lost his wife last year, we instantly had a bond. Gillian, Sandy, the Nervy Mouse and Cath all took on the stature of lifelong friends. And their stories about hoarding clothes, tooth veneers and tins of Mulligatawny seemed absolutely unremarkable.

While very early in the process I railed against Judith and her unsavoury tales of young widowhood, I now found myself wanting to belong to this group of outcasts. For me, the shared experience is more valuable than all the grief textbooks put together.

SEPTEMBER–OCTOBER

Starting school is a lot like those early childhood birthdays. Maximum fuss is made by parents, while most kids have forgotten it by lunchtime. Still, I found myself caught up in the cyclone of B's first-day hysteria. I bought five of every clothing item, assiduously labelling each one with B's name. Her new lunchbox overflowed with a variety of nutritious foodstuffs and an expensive fruit smoothie. I even managed to drag a comb through her matted curls, sending her in with a dandelion clock for a hairdo.

My anxieties were compounded by thoughts of all those daddies who would be Mexican-waving their kids along the route to school, reminding me that this was another milestone in His daughter's life that Mark was missing out on. Nevertheless, Mother and I stepped forth on that first day and delivered a decidedly nonplussed B to the school reception.

There were daddies, but there were also mummies, grannies, granddads. I could fool myself that Mark was just somewhere in the crowd.

What distinguished us from everyone else though was the 'meeting' I had to now go into with B's teacher. It was the one where we would discuss 'strategies' for dealing with the fact that my child was different. What was the response to be if she burst into tears in class? How were they to deal with Father's Day? What questions might they expect to field from her? The school had never dealt with a child who had lost a parent so young, so along with an opportunity for consolation, this was Professional Development Training gold.

Of course, I had no answers. The only advice I could offer was to echo the words of the child bereavement charity Winston's Wish: Don't use ambiguous language. If she cries, comfort her but don't tell her to stop. If she wants to talk about Daddy, engage in the conversation.

I took in a photograph of the three of us, as if to prove to the teacher that Mark did once exist. I wanted her to look at Him and be shocked by how beautiful He was, how young and how seemingly healthy. She held the picture in its frame and nodded. It was as much acknowledgement as I needed. Turns out B never mentioned Him. Not until months later, anyway. Bereavement, I came to learn, is predictable in its unpredictability. There is no way of strategising for how it's going to go.

A week later, some kids from the Big School got off the school bus, and one of them shouted 'Ginger!' at my daughter.

It was a reasonable observation, for she does indeed have ginger hair (give that boy a prize!). But I immediately felt my bile rise and had to resist the temptation to kick the little bastard in the balls. In the unlikely event that they'd dropped yet, that is.

From a safe distance away, I glowered at him from behind my sunglasses. Nevertheless, I felt a nub of angst in the pit of my stomach as I looked over at my little ginger picking buttercups in the grass, unaware she'd been the butt of someone's joke. All kids get ribbed for something – big ears, knock-knees, buck teeth (for me, my slap-head – I was known as Mr Tefal for many happy years). And it wouldn't be the last time it happened in my little girl's life. But at that moment, protective mode took over, and I suddenly wanted Mark so that we could unite against those nasty boys from the Big School who'd teased our daughter.

I could see Him, sitting in Mother's kitchen soon after He'd been discharged from the gruelling three-month stay in hospital. He was watching B as she toddled about around His feet. And He was crying.

'I just want to see her grow up,' He said.

I cupped His face with my hand. 'And you will, love. It's all over now. You're fixed.'

What He meant was, He just wanted to be there for her growing up. If there were bollocks to be kicked, He wanted to be the one who did it. He never cried much, even after His illness. But here He was, His role as chief-bollock-kicker in jeopardy, and it devastated Him. On that September afternoon, I had a stark reminder of my single-parent status, and it scared me. I now occupied two roles, and I worried that I wasn't up to the task. B had become a focus for my angst; and it wasn't just a bout of schoolboy teasing which sent me into a tailspin. Every bump, every bruise was assiduously assessed for its potential long-term effect. I stood beneath climbing frames, monkey bars, zip-wires lest she tumble into certain paraplegia. And we still slept together each and every night so that I could be sure she was still breathing.

Mark's sudden and shocking departure caused me to re-evaluate everything I had previously felt secure about. Anything was possible, no matter how preposterous it may have seemed. Only one thing felt certain: those I held most dear could be taken from me in the blink of an eye. And for now this prospect tainted the way I looked at everything.

September marks one of the highlights in the north-east sporting calendar – the Great North Run. Three people stepped forward and said they were running it this year for Mark – Paul, my cousin Ben and Mark's sister. Everyone hates a charity fun-runner until someone dies and then everyone wants to be a charity fun-runner, or raise money for a charity fun-running friend. It's a way of 'making something good' come out of the pointless and inexplicable waste of a life, a way to redirect the pain from the heart to the feet. And I did want to raise money for them – the gesture was born of love for Mark and the people He'd left behind, and I was deeply touched that they had chosen to honour Him in this way.

I decided the charitable cause for which we would harass people for money would be the British Heart Foundation, specifically for the genetic disorders research fund pot. I set up a fundraising page and started the ball rolling with a donation of £200. It seemed utterly incongruous seeing Mark's face on a 'tribute page', together with an online 'memory book' which people were steadily filling. However, the challenge to see how much we could raise 'in Mark's memory' was on, and we had until September to do it.

The Great North Run is, of course, more than a 'fun run'. It is a serious undertaking requiring training and discipline. Ben and Mark's sister were both seasoned runners and had their fitness programmes already. Paul, on the other hand, had only ever really run between bars along Newcastle quayside. Added to which, he was a smoker and had only recently returned from a round-the-world trip, which had evidently involved a lot of partying. He had always been the loose cannon of the group, the one most likely to end up living on a kibbutz or in the Himalayan Mountains, or else drying out in a clinic in Arizona with Ronnie Wood. It was unlikely he was going to complete the first mile, never mind the full course.

Nonetheless, Paul set about the twin tasks of training and raising money in memory of his friend. He hassled and harangued, canvassed people he hadn't seen for years, old teachers, colleagues, ageing aunts, anyone who would spare him a pound. He initiated a training schedule, factoring in fag breaks and pint pit-stops, and gradually his fitness increased.

'I'm worried about you,' I told him one afternoon, raking my eyes over his shrinking frame. 'You're coming at this from a baseline of abject unfitness. You do know what you're undertaking?'

'Of course, man. I'll be fine.'

'Thing is... you may feel fine, but you don't know what's going on inside. You've been abusing your body for years. I couldn't cope if you collapsed in the middle of the run.' It was my default reaction. It seemed improbable to me that Paul would cross the finish line alive.

Paul took a long drag on his Regal and blew the smoke wantonly into the air. 'Fit as a fiddle, me. Nee worries.'

By the time the day of the race had arrived, Paul had amassed a personal charity fortune in excess of £2,000. I declined to wave on the sidelines, but agreed that we would meet, together with a team of supporters and my cousin Ben, at a pub on the quayside after the event, where I would shout the athletes a few beers. We watched most of the race on the TV, trying to spot our runners among the jostling broccoli florets and Superman costumes. I thought I saw Paul's bald head between a giant wedge of cheese and its cream-cracker running partner, but it was fleeting so I couldn't be sure.

Perhaps it was the lure of the beer, but to everyone's surprise Paul swanned in from the finish line ahead of the other two, a medal swinging brightly from a ribbon around his neck.

'Parched, me, like,' he said, downing his pint in one fluid mouthful. 'Next!'

Ben showed up twenty minutes later, and the collective total raised was confirmed as in excess of £3,500. Mark's sister had gone home, but we ordered prosecco and toasted to everyone's success. We ate steak and drank more wine in a restaurant in which everyone seemed to be wearing a medal.

'I ran for Cancer Research,' one woman shouted across at us.

'Mine was Alzheimer's,' said another.

We all basked in the fragrant glow of charity fundraising, none of us wishing to sully the moment by mentioning why we were all there.

Much later, when the messages of thanks had been posted, when the letter of gratitude had been received from the BHF, when the muscle rub was no longer needed, my spirits plummeted. Mark's fund was at over £4,000. But what did it prove? People cared enough to donate, and to donate generously, but no amount of money would bring him back. Genetic heart conditions were the sort of things other people suffered from, just one of a myriad of threats to human life which resided on the periphery of our consciousness. But this particular genetic heart condition had caught us all out one Sunday evening in August 2008, and had ultimately taken my husband. It had been a blight on our lives for the past four years and I'd had enough of it. Harsh though it sounds, I didn't much feel like raising any more money on its behalf.

By the end of September, The Loneliness had me in its grip. Mark had been gone seven long months, and I was feeling increasingly desperate, for Him, for His company, His humour, for the feeling of His body next to me in bed. I missed seeing His face, the sound of His voice. Even the lawnmower-like roar of His snoring, which had caused so many grumpy nocturnal stomps to the spare room. I now lay awake at night, wishing I could hear it again. But the truth was beginning to dawn on me: I was *never* going to hear it again.

I got the feeling that by seven months people believed things should be 'improving', that I somehow should be 'over the worst'. They made reference to 'the future' and 'moving on' and 'what Mark would want', but these statements were entirely at odds with the reality of where I felt I was in my grief. Indeed, the shock that had anaesthetised me in the first few months was beginning to wear off and a new sense of rawness had kicked in.

Paul continued his twice-weekly pilgrimages to see B and me, providing a welcome dose of maleness into the sisterhood, as well as a mutual sense of comfort in the twists and turns of loss. We had fallen into a sort of easy threesome – me, my daughter and Paul. The triumvirate, back intact. There was laughter in the house again. Male-sized shoes in the hallway. Paul was compassionate, patient, tender. Because of our friendship, and his friendship with Mark, he understood me and handled me with care. I found myself enjoying the company of a man again – a few hours a week in which grief was suspended and some kind of normal life was allowed back in. A new normal, but normality nonetheless. We went to the beach one Sunday and sat on the rocks watching B draw faces in the sand. Paul laced his arm around my back and I nestled my head into his shoulder. *This is what it should have been like*, I told myself. I closed my eyes and inhaled the briny air.

'Imagine if Neil or John came walking up the beach right now,' Paul said. 'What the hell would they think was going on?'

We both sucked on our teeth and wordlessly moved apart.

I realised that I was becoming increasingly (and, I perceived, pathetically) dependent on Paul. I dreaded the moment he would leave us to go home, made him feel guilty if there was an evening he couldn't come down when I felt I needed him. It felt as if our friendship was going from one that had been rooted in equality and respect – and lots of good fun – to one of escalating neediness on my behalf.

Oh well, if you're too busy... I'd text, knowing that he'd relent or change his plans to accommodate me and B.

I hated myself, this person I'd become. I had never been the needy type before, but Paul had slotted in to the space that Mark had abruptly vacated, and it was too easy to let him stay there.

It all began to feel wrong. We both felt it. Furthermore, B began to show signs of disapproval too. Whereas before she had welcomed Paul into the household, climbed over him and swung from his earlobes, increasingly she was rejecting his presence. He would bring her toys and she wouldn't even look at them. Gifts of sweets would be left uneaten.

'Not Paul again,' she would say, if I announced he was coming over.

And the truth was, I didn't want to be with Paul, not really. So eight months after Mark's death, our cosy triumvirate disbanded. It was with a heavy heart that I told Paul it would be for the best if he didn't come around any more. He sensed it was coming – and he understood.

I had been awarded a moderate sum of money – a 'death in service' benefit from those kind people at the pensions company. The consolation prize, as it were. Of course, I was hugely grateful for the support. Many widows are left financially as well as emotionally bereft. In a perverse way, I was fortunate.

But the money presented a dilemma. I hated the fact that my beloved Mark had to die in order for it to come into my bank account. And I hated the fact that when He was alive, we couldn't afford to buy a home of our own, yet because of His death my daughter and I had become financially stable. It's what He would have wanted, I know; it is why He nominated me to receive it in the event of His death. But the money was tainted and utterly without joy. There was, in fact, a large degree of guilt in spending it.

At first, I tried to invest it and not be too outlandish in my spending. I set some of the money aside for my daughter's future. I even consulted Dad's financial advisor, who presented me with reams and reams of FSA-approved ideas of things to do with my money.

'Life insurance is a must,' the advisor said. 'You know better than anyone else how suddenly things can change.'

'But what does it all mean?' I said, looking over the spiral-bound life insurance document he had brought for me. 'Seriously, just tell me what to do. Give me the cheque and I'll sign it.'

The advisor shook his head. 'I'm afraid I can't make the decision for you. It would be unethical. I can only advise on the options.'

I bought Premium Bonds. I bought an ISA. Eventually, I would buy a house. But they were investments in a future in which Mark could play no part – except for having been generous enough to die in the first place, of course. In addition to the investments, I spent money on 'things'. A new pair of £150 boots to lift my spirits here, a new piece of jewellery there; clothing, countless ornaments for the home. My wine bill for the week was into triple figures, and that wasn't counting evenings in the pub. According to my counsellor, profligate spending is a well-documented reaction in grief, together with excessive drinking (guilty as charged), recklessness (also guilty as charged) and a host of other destructive behaviours (*coughs*). I was slowly surrounding myself with things

I wouldn't previously have been able to afford in the belief that they would somehow make me feel better and life more liveable.

However there comes a point where the continual buying of new things is revealed to be an empty pursuit. It was now time to find something other than wine and the credit card to occupy my mind. I resolved to get a job. And within twenty-four hours of making that decision, I got one.

I would be teaching French to small children for one hour on a Saturday morning. Mother reacted to this news as if I'd won the Nobel Prize. For her, it signified a big step forward. It was an opportunity to look outside of grief and death, meet new people who weren't widows and plough my time into something other than thinking about what was lost. I would have to focus on lesson plans and the inventive usage of language props as opposed to the image of Mark's face the moment he died.

I arrived on my first morning and greeted my new class of seven eager young linguists. One thing I hadn't accounted for though was the dads. There were two of them sitting there on the carpet, ready to join in with their offspring. Their presence threw me completely. Saturday morning clubs were, I thought, the sole preserve of mother or granny. Didn't dads watch telly at this time, or play football with other fat-bellied, middle-aged men? Why on earth would they want to sit on the carpet of a community centre singing 'Baa Baa Black Sheep' in French with a load of toddlers? Except, of course, to engage in a bout of widow-baiting, which was clearly their sole intention.

I continued with the class for three weeks before calling time to reassess my position. By now, though, it wasn't just the daddies causing me consternation. The timing of the class was proving to be a drag. I realised that the rest of the world works during the week and likes to get shit-faced on Friday nights. Normally being alone in my drinking midweek, I wanted to be part of this crowd who were drinking socially (and therefore legitimately) at the end of the week. This meant playing Madame Tumble on a monster hangover, which simply couldn't last. Something had to give. In this instance, it was the class.

My boss, a feisty young woman who had bought the franchise, wasn't impressed at losing a tutor so soon.

'Continuity is so important for language learning at this stage,' she told me. 'Plus, I had to pay two hundred pounds to train you and I haven't earned that back yet.'

'You're right. Continuity *is* so important for language learning at this stage,' I heard myself reply. 'I'll stay then. Until the end of the term.'

In fact, my boss succeeded in talking me into taking on a few classes midweek, teaching school kids in school hours, therefore eliminating the daddy issue. But the truth was I didn't want the job. It involved hours of planning, making up of craft examples, a mountain of equipment and props that required storage space. It also demanded a relentlessly chirpy demeanour, which I was finding increasingly hard to muster. I know that if Mark had been around to counsel me He would have told me to resign with immediate effect. However, there I was, doing more hours than I'd ever bargained for, with the promise of more if I could possibly fit them in.

I considered my options. Mark and I had both talked about wanting to continue our studies and undertake a PhD. Mark had completed a masters in the year I met Him, and He had a thirst for education and self-improvement. He had a reputation for imparting His considerable knowledge in meticulous detail – over the years I learned not to ask how the gas burner worked or what that button on the dashboard did for fear of the ensuing lecture. If he started pontificating, I'd close my eyes and pretend to snore.

It seemed fitting, therefore, to invest some of my death dividend in further study. Mark would have approved, I think, and I saw it as polishing off an ambition for both of us. I enrolled on a doctoral programme at Newcastle University, and I knew immediately that the subject of my PhD research would be an American sculptor and patron by the name of Mary Callery.

This American artist had become a source of fascination to me ever since Mother and her partner Jim had stumbled across her on one of their regular cross-continental investigations into some tenuous ancestral link. (Mother, Mark said, loved anything pertaining to graveyards and 'dead relatives'. Since finding out that ancestry could be traced online, she and Jim had embarked on a period of fevered field research into long-forgotten forebears.)

While in northern Spain the previous summer, they had found themselves in a tiny graveyard in Cadaques. They happened upon a small wooden cross underneath an ancient oak. On it was what they assumed to be a British name – Mary Callery. When they came back, it was all Mother could talk about. We had responded to her enthusiasm with the usual mirth, yet Mother insisted that this was one life I might find interesting.

It turned out Picasso had drawn a picture of the back of Mary's head. Man Ray photographed her and sketched her. Alexander Calder made her a brooch featuring her initials. She lived and worked in Paris during the forties and fifties, buying artworks, making introductions, encouraging those she knew to offer commissions. Mother knew I was captivated by tales of literary and artistic Paris of that era. So who was this Mary Callery who all the artists seemed to know? And why were her remains in a graveyard in northern Spain? Despite her connections and influence, there seemed to be very little written about her.

At that point I had neither the time or cause to investigate further. But I found myself returning to Mary, or perhaps she had returned to me, at a time when I was in need of a life outside my bereaved existence in which to lose myself. I had a feeling about Mary, almost as if our lives had collided for a reason. In addition, her name differed from my husband's by a single consonant, Mark – Mary, which I allowed myself to believe was a further sign that this was meant to be.

I discussed my proposal with my supervisors, and it was agreed that a name on a cross was an exciting place to start a period of research. Over the next three years, I would bring Mary Callery back to life, and in doing so would perhaps undergo a kind of reinvention of my own.

My PhD would start in January, meaning I only had my first Mark-less festive season to get through before becoming a student again.

OCTOBER–DECEMBER

'I think I'm going to make Kate an offer for the house,' I told Mother.

A look of delight shot across Mother's face, yet she stayed calm. 'I think that's a good idea.'

Having me permanently anchored in the village was music to Mother's ears. She could keep an eye on me from her vantage just across the road, and buying a house would provide me with another Positive New Focus. Houses require endless attention, from new furnishings to the possibilities of building work, all of which would take my mind off the tragedy which had beset my existence.

'Why don't you call her now?' Mother suggested.

'Slow down, Mother.'

I could feel myself railing against 'moving on' because it seemed synonymous with moving *away* from Him. I resented Time because with each day that passed, Mark receded further into the past. And it seemed impossible to me that He could ever become part of my past. I wanted Him to be part of my present and future, and of those of our daughter. Which of course, in an entirely abstract way He was. But who wants abstract when all you want is the person?

After consulting the usual line-up of advisors (Mother, Dad, Beth, friends), I made Kate an offer for the little pebble-dashed terrace that had become our home. I needed to feel rooted somewhere; a sense of security to counteract the vulnerability of the past year. Furthermore, the house seemed to have cocooned my daughter and me within its hundred-year-old walls. It felt like a safe haven amid the chaos of life after Mark's death. And while it broke my heart to think that Mark and I had only ever dreamed of one day owning our own house, the purchase felt like something He would have approved of. More than another pair of shoes, anyway.

I found myself having to decode terminology pertaining to surveys and land rights, contemplate the relative dangers of radon in the soil nearby, contact local authorities, builders, plumbers, electricians, and pay out a fortune for the privilege of their stamp on a piece of paper telling me everything was in order and the sale could go ahead. The solicitor also appeared to lose every single piece of documentation he was sent, thus requiring everything to be sent out twice. A process which should have taken four weeks ended up extending into the New Year, during which I had to face up to another breakdown-inducing scenario. Christmas.

I announced to friends, family and the Competitive Mother at school that I would not be sending Christmas cards this year. Not even those pointless little ones with an illegible scrawl for a name written on them which are ritually exchanged between five-year-olds. For this year wasn't going to be Happy or Peaceful (and though it was shaping up to be Merry, it wasn't in the way Competitive Mother meant it). More significantly, card-writing involved contemplating the blank space where Mark's name should have been, and somehow, a cute Brucie 'pawprint' just didn't cut it as a worthy replacement. Further to my announcement, one friend nodded sympathetically and said she hadn't sent cards the previous Christmas for exactly the same reasons – it was the year Jimmy had left her for The Other Woman.

Other people's festive cheer is impossible to avoid, however, especially when a small child is involved. I was helpless in the face of lights going up around the village, tinsel-strewn windowsills and the question: 'When are we putting our Christmas tree up, Mummy?'

'Do we really need a tree?'

'Molly's got a tree. Mae's got a tree. Sophie and Jake have got a tree.'

'Right, we'll get a bloody tree then.'

My daughter may have wished we'd never bothered when she returned from school the following day, to find the work of the Yuletide curmudgeon flashing away on the top of the sideboard. It was the smallest tree I could find. In fact, it would probably have been categorised more accurately as a plant. If she was disappointed, she didn't show it though. Her delight filled the room.

'Yay!' she shouted, rummaging through the box of decorations to find the star for the top.

So it sat there, our Christmas Frond, resplendent in its frock of tinsel and baubles, winking at me day and night like a lustful hooker while I tried my best to ignore it.

Later that week, there was a slip of paper in my daughter's schoolbag that read:

B will be playing an ANGEL in this year's Nativity. Please provide a suitable costume by the end of next week.

The familiar sinking feeling ran through me. Another milestone without Mark, another occasion where I would be forced to acknowledge couples sitting together in the audience, of which one half was 'daddy'. Even the story of the Nativity, with its smug loving couple and their celestial offspring, seemed to taunt this widow.

Dress-making has never been my forte, however I decided that B would have something home-made for this theatrical debut. Having lamentable domestic skills myself, I asked

Mark's mother if she could help. She eagerly accepted the challenge. Hamstrung by an aversion to outward shows of emotion, she coped with her grief by 'doing things'. Like making angel costumes for five-year-olds, which she did beautifully.

In the event, I needn't have worried. Hardly any daddies showed up and the narrative was so fragmented by forgotten words, aimless drifting about the stage and the odd bout of tears that it was unrecognisable as anything other than a group of bewildered children shuffling about in pillow cases.

Stepping back into the role he played in my life when we were kids, Dan put a metaphorical arm around me and invited us all to his place for Christmas Day. I accepted, with the caveat that I may not bring with me the most festive of cheer. Or any presents.

Seeing me in the face of such trauma must have been difficult for Dan. As children of divorced parents, we had always been close. Older by eight years, he had seen himself as the one who would help me through life by using humour. We had our own exclusive vocabulary, and he invented stories and characters that he knew would always make me laugh.

The characters he created were based on people we knew, often with a macabre twist. There was Mrs Robertson, an aged spinster who would parachute into humanitarian crises around the world in order to provide comic relief. There was

Mr Geo. Gatenby (deceased) who fashioned the pelts of his own cats into toupees. And there was the mysterious 'Q', whose arrival would be heralded by Dan whistling the theme tune to *Police Squad*.

Dan felt burdened by his role, though, and has talked since of feeling a duty of care towards Beth and me once our dad left the household. But once I met Mark, he must have believed his duties were over. Yet here he found himself again, standing over the pieces of his sister's broken life, trying desperately to use the same old humour trick to get her through it.

'*Given that this Christmas represents a crisis of sorts, I shall ensure that Mrs Robertson is poised with her parachute...*' he emailed in advance of the big day.

I replied: '*Thanks. But ensuring the wine rack is stocked would suffice.*'

Aside from a euphemistic toast to 'absent friends', Mark was hardly mentioned on the first Christmas Day without Him. But it was better that way. If no one acknowledged his death, it somehow allowed that part of my brain to believe it hadn't really happened. The words 'Happy Christmas' were erased from the collective vocabulary, and the only decorative clue to the season was the cock-eyed spruce, now bereft of presents, in the corner.

Had I allowed my mind to wander back to the last Christmas Mark and I ever spent together – the one we had hosted twelve months ago for my family in our tiny North

Yorkshire home – I would have seen kids' stockings hanging from the mantel above the log-burning stove, festive sprinkles strewn over the table, the Dictaphone He'd bought me so I could record story ideas, the joint of beef He'd sourced and prepared; I would have seen Him sitting on the settee in His black fleece dressing gown opening His gift from B (a pebble from the beach, clumsily hand-painted with His initial) and saying, 'B, that's great, pet, awww!'

But I didn't allow my mind to pick over those particular bones. I placed a DIVERSION sign in the path of the memories of that day in the form of three bottles of red wine, several board games and a series of films starring Dick van Dyke.

I couldn't allow the day to pass without a concession to the Mark-shaped void though. I'd brought a packet of sky lanterns for release when the sun went down. The inexorable climb of the glowing pod into the sky and far away was heavy with poignancy. Or so I was told. After the turkey was eaten and plenty of booze had been swilled, we all gathered in the freezing December night, and the kids each lit a sky lantern. We watched as they rose steadily, wafting over the roof tops and up into the sky like fireflies.

'There He goes,' Dan said. 'Happy Christmas, mate.'

'Bye bye, Uncle Mark,' shouted G, chasing the path of the lantern as far as she could, stopping at the end of the lane and waving at the light as it receded into the distance.

There's no doubt it was a touching sight. But my overriding concern was that one of them would get snagged on a power line and we'd be responsible for a mass shutdown of the grid. Knowing my luck, I believed it was a possibility.

'Was that light my daddy?' asked B, slipping her hand momentarily into mine as we shuffled back into the house, once each light had gone out.

'Yes.'

'Awww,' she said. And then: 'I wish He didn't float away.'

Just Keep Going

Dan and Helen had booked a skiing trip for the rest of the festive period, and had to leave the next day. It was a cunning ploy, giving all of us permission to take our leave of one another without seeming ungrateful. On reflection, going away might have been a sensible option for my daughter and me. That way, others would have been spared the awkwardness of being around the grieving widow and could have enjoyed the season in the way in which it was depicted on the Iceland advert. As it was, we'd all braved the first Christmas without Mark, and one more milestone stood in the way of me and the coveted 'one-year' marker. The arrival of 2013.

The first-footer, as all northerners know, is supposed to bring good fortune into the house for the year ahead. Typically, Mark had always been first-footer. A tall, dark stranger (He was an in-law), He had been selected by Dad to fulfil this New

Year tradition. Mark would nip out into the freezing Yorkshire night at one minute to midnight armed with whisky and a lump of coal, and by the time He came in again sixty seconds later we'd have all forgotten that He'd been out there.

'May the whisky bring good cheer,' Mark would say, 'and may the coal bring warmth.'

As He stood there in the early hours of 1 January 2012 clutching His whisky and His coal, none of us could have anticipated that less than six weeks later He would be dead. So much for good fortune and lucky traditions.

As our first New Year without Him approached, I felt like one of those wretched puppies tied to the back of a truck and dragged for miles by a cowardly aggressor. The days and months that had divided us were now about to become a year. This may seem like a question of semantics, but to me, it felt like a seismic shift. Incontrovertible evidence that He was not coming back. I felt guilty that I was leaving Him in 2012. I actually asked for His forgiveness. I can't be certain that He granted it, but I could do nothing in the face of the ruthless march of time.

B, Brucie and I spent New Year with a crowd of others at the house of our new village friends Jeanette and Graeme; those friends who knew nothing of Mark except as a face on the photographs around my house. We fed from a selection of sumptuous *amuse-bouches*, drank prosecco and red wine, sang 'Fairytale of New York' on the karaoke. There was much laughter and absolutely no talk of dead husbands or the abomination of a year we were about to leave behind. Once or twice I felt grief catch in my throat, but each time I swilled it away with a glug of red wine. Grief had no place here, with these new friends. I didn't want to burden them with it at this time of defiant, firework-spangled celebration.

With the kids in bed and Brucie at my heels, I stayed up for the countdown, hoping that the drink and good cheer would stave off any chance of a breakdown. We 'ooohhdd!' as the lights exploded over London, Edinburgh, Cardiff, over houses in our village, and all the other villages extending out to the hills. By 1 a.m., though, each mouthful of booze, like the relentless cheer, seemed to effervesce in my gullet. I ducked out of the festivities without saying goodnight, barely reaching the bottom of the staircase before the tears began to fall. I tip-toed on, clutching my stomach, willing myself not to spray salmon blini all over Jeanette's newly painted landing walls. The dog trotted alongside, occasionally glancing up at me from beneath his eyebrows, waiting for the next move.

I found our bedroom and knelt on the floor next to my sleeping child. Brucie's snout appeared alongside mine and together we watched the infinitesimal twitches of her beautiful, flawless face. I felt my way gently to the other side of the bed and pulled Brucie into the curl of my stomach. Together we lay, she, he and I: a very different threesome to the one who had seen in 2012. I buried my face in Brucie's fur and let the tears convulse silently out of me.

*

Mark's birthday followed on 4 January. He would have been thirty-eight years old. I couldn't help but think back to the same time last year, even permitting myself a glance at a photo I'd taken of Him and B sitting in the kitchen with the cake I made Him. Sadly, having the dexterity of a Dalek in the kitchen, I made too little mixture and the 'sponge' ended up being more of a biscuit – and a half measure at that. Mark arrived home from work to find it sitting flaccidly on the chopping board. Even IT was embarrassed. It was supposed to be low-fat too as we were both on a diet. As if it could get more pleasure-free.

The great, yet unsurprising thing about it, though, was that Mark sampled the cake with the relish of a man who had been presented with a Mary Berry masterpiece.

'Pet, it's lovely,' he said, washing it down with a swig of tea, from where it had jammed in His gullet.

He placed the remaining quarter in a tin and put it at the back of the kitchen cupboard 'for later'. When the removal men came to package up our belongings from the house some surreal months later, one of them unearthed the tin and found that remaining quarter still secreted within it. I watched him sniff it with disdain, then ask me: 'Do you... want to keep this?' (My instinct was to say yes. But I said, 'Just chuck it.')

This year, I bought a tray of cupcakes from Tesco and took them round to Mark's sister's place to share out among her husband and young sons. For myself, I took a bottle of cava, and proceeded to drink it on behalf of everyone, including the birthday boy. We sang 'Happy Birthday' and toasted to our missing guest.

Standing there in that kitchen, I felt an overwhelming desire to just *get it over with*. Not just the song, but also the occasion. It all felt hollow, tuneless. Forced. There we were, hosting a party for a dead man. I'm sure Mark's sister must have felt the same. In fact, part of me felt guilty for inflicting this on her. I had thought it was 'the right thing to do'; what everybody, including myself and B, would have wanted. Looking at the rictus grins around the table that day, I wasn't so sure.

The kids blew out the candles and ate their cupcakes bemusedly, then ran off upstairs when they realised there would be no party bags. Besides, I had started crying by then. They must have thought adults had the worst birthday parties ever.

Two weeks later and I was gearing up for my first term as a postgraduate student. I'd packed my new pencil case and notebook into a satchel like an eager schoolkid, feeling both trepidation and excitement at the prospect of this Positive New Venture. Three days before I was due to start, though, I took a tearful call from Dad. His mother, my gran, had died. She was eighty-nine years old and had succumbed to pneumonia after a period of illness. Gran was a sharp-witted Dundonian, whose fondness for profanity dated from her days in the Wrens. I learned my choicest swear words from Gran, although I could never deliver them with quite the same caustic flourish.

The last time I'd seen her she was sitting in her armchair, squinting at an umpteenth rerun of *Ironside*. She was almost blind and so thin I worried she might break.

'I'm sick o' livin', Lucie,' she told me. 'I just want to be up there, playing ma harp.' She pointed skyward with a knobbled forefinger.

I was sad to hear she'd died, but to a degree it felt like a relief – for Gran, but also for Dad and Karen, whose lives had turned into those of full-time carers in recent months.

'Anyway, she had a wonderful life,' Dad told me through his tears. 'And she was in so much pain at the end. It's a blessing, really.'

But he had lost his mother; great age and physical depletion don't mitigate the reality that a significant presence has gone and will never be seen again. Unlike a year earlier when shock had precluded me from mustering a single tear for my beloved grandma, I cried when I put down the phone. They were tears for Gran, but also for Dad, for Karen, for us all.

Three days after Gran's death, I arrived on the campus in Newcastle and noted two things: firstly, how young and well-groomed students had become since I last checked, and secondly, how people were milling about with *no knowledge* of me, my situation or my husband's sudden death. The events which had defined my life for the past year were of no consequence here: indeed, the air was filled with the excited chatter of a new term, flyers for 'Sports Soc', vertiginous hairstyles, low-slung jeans – this was no place for death or grief. I sniffed this new air. It felt fresh in my lungs.

Students from across the world had gathered in the conference suite of the Daysh Building for the postgraduate induction, and as I took my newly nibbed fountain pen from its box I could barely curb my excitement. We had made it here together – Mark, Mary and I – and we were on the cusp of a new adventure. I took my seat in a row between a thickset Thai man and a husky-voiced woman from Spain. What were their stories? I glanced about the room at all the eager faces and wondered whether I was the only one who had been transported here on the back of a tragedy.

I supped coffee from a Styrofoam cup and listened to the Head of Postgraduate Studies as he delivered a stirring welcome speech. Being a doctor was great, was the message. And moreover, the journey to becoming a doctor was even greater. In fact, there were only great things ahead from here on in. I couldn't help but feel inspired.

During the break, I conferred with my new student peers. I told them about Mary and how I planned to tell her story. In turn they shared details of their mind-boggling research subjects. We exchanged email addresses, useful web-links for postgraduate student socials. Here, in the conference suite of the Daysh Building, I wasn't The Widow. I was The Researcher at the start of the great journey to doctoral success.

And for the first time since His death, I felt that Mark was sharing a moment in my life that wasn't synonymous with sadness and grief. He had studied at Newcastle himself, in the year that we had met. He too had dreamt of doctoral study and His death had provided me with the financial means to fulfil the dream for both of us. Looking out over the city – our city – from this seventh-floor vantage, I could almost convince myself that He was there.

The name on the side of the big white van said:

K.P. Davis.
Plumbing. Heating. Boiler Repair.

I waved from the window but K.P. failed to notice, as he was talking into his mobile phone while reverse parking in front of my car. The house survey had thrown up a damp problem behind the sink, and I had randomly chosen K.P. Davis from a selection of plumbers in the Yellow Pages to come and assess the damage. He'd been due at 11 a.m., yet he was clearly in no rush. It was nearly a quarter to twelve and still he continued his conversation.

I waited for the knock at the door. Eventually it came. K.P. Davis was six foot four, rugged-faced, with tattoos descending like sleeves from his shoulders, down his undulating arm muscles to the apex of each knuckle. His skin was the exact colour of a highly polished mahogany sideboard and each eyebrow was punctured with a thick metal stud. A smile danced around his eyes, and his mouth opened to reveal a set of perfect white teeth. Around his waist, the workman's tool belt.

In fact, K.P. Davis was such a textbook example of all-round manliness that it made me flustered to look at him, yet I couldn't help but stare.

'It's, er, a damp patch,' I said, feebly. 'Behind the sink. I'm buying the house, you see, and there's... a damp patch.'

K.P. flashed his smile then strode over the threshold and into my thin little corridor, filling it with his impossible bulk. Aside from the odd family member, men didn't come into this house. Particularly ones who looked like this. It felt almost surreal. He followed me into the kitchen and released his tool belt in order that he could squat down and take a closer look at the problem. The cupboard under the kitchen sink is where I throw my pans directly from the dishwasher, and there they teeter, large on top of small, lids wedged wherever they will fit. To my embarrassment, this was where K.P's damp trail led him, and he began removing pan after pan from the shelves so that he could access the pipes behind.

'I'm in the process of moving in, so excuse the mess in there,' I lied.

An emotion was stirring within me, as I watched K.P. conducting his excavation, long after I'd resigned myself to never feeling it again. Unmistakeably, there it was: lust. And even the merest thought of it brought me out in invisible hives of shame. How was it possible that I could even contemplate another man after my husband's death, not to mention one I'd met only a few minutes previously? Yet here I was standing over him, trying to focus on anything but the magnificently honed biceps currently entangled in the pipework under my sink. The subject of my libidinous musings looked up at me. 'Can I have a look in the yard?'

Outside, he soon found the issue – a hole in the wall just below the decking ('Shoddy that decking, like. Did you lay it?') and told me with a smile that he would come back tomorrow with his foam gun and fill it, free of charge. He loitered just long enough to enquire (with well-honed nonchalance): 'So, are you married then?'

I felt my cheeks crisp at the question. Although I told myself it was probably just an innocent query related to whom would pay him for his handiwork, I didn't want to drop the W-bomb straight away. I heard myself reply – 'It's just me and my daughter, actually.' Satisfied, K.P. Davis said he would see me tomorrow, climbed back into his van and sped off down the road.

I closed the front door and looked at myself in the mirror in the hallway. For the first time since Mark's death, the pulse of sexual attraction for another man had incontestably begun to beat.

I felt titillated and vaguely horrified in equal measure. What the hell was I thinking? I had sworn to myself and everyone else that there was only ever one man for me, and had that man still been here that fact would have remained. But He was gone. And some beefcake plumber whom I'd known for five minutes had just sent me into a tailspin of shame and self-doubt. With a heady dose of arousal thrown in. It seemed unlikely to be mutual – after all, K.P. Davis could be no more than thirty-five years old and would undoubtedly have his standards pitched above a wine-soused, baggy-eyed widow.

Nevertheless, I found myself waiting with anticipation for his arrival the next day.

Armed with his foam gun, K.P. turned up as promised. It took him ten seconds to fill the hole in the wall, but he accepted my offer of a cup of tea nonetheless. We talked for forty minutes. I told him about Mark and by way of a response he told me about his cousin's friend who'd died suddenly last month aged twenty-five, and how it was no age and how you never know the day, but how it was important to keep your chin up and get on with it in these situations. I nodded in agreement but I wasn't remotely interested in K.P.'s bereavement advice. I was concentrating on maintaining my position in front of the window with the light behind me, so as not to draw attention to my grotesque grief-exacerbated crow's feet.

It had been ten years since I'd engaged in any serious flirtation with a man who wasn't Mark, yet here I was back in the saddle, twisting my hair and flapping my eyelashes like Miss Piggy with Kermit. And if I wasn't very much mistaken, K.P. Davis was responding in kind. He was ribald and charming, and made sure he held himself in such a way that I couldn't miss the six-pack that undulated beneath his T-shirt.

K.P. drained his tea and as neither of us could find further excuse to hold the other in conversation, he left. Within half an hour though, I had received a text. K.P. was sorry if he'd caused any upset by asking questions about my husband's death. He hoped I was OK and it had been nice to meet me. If I needed any further plumbing services, I shouldn't hesitate to contact him.

Disappointingly, the house survey hadn't thrown up any further issues which warranted a workman. And besides, K.P. told me he had a girlfriend. But of course, none of this mattered. After two weeks of increasingly suggestive texts, it became clear that my relationship with K.P. Davis had grown from its client–supplier beginnings into something decidedly more unprofessional. Urged on by desire and the delight-filled goading of my girlfriends, I agreed to K.P. Davis's suggestion that he might stop by my house one evening on his way home from work. My heart thumped in my throat as I went to open the door, not knowing how on earth this courtship was going to unfold.

In the event, I needn't have worried. He strode once more into my thin little hallway, lifted me up against the wall, and without saying a single word, became the first man I would have sex with since Mark's death.

He lifted me into the living room and threw me on to the settee. He pulled his sweatshirt off, revealing the extent of his tattoos. Angel wings spread across his back, and across the pectorals, a set of Mayoral-style chains with a link missing across the heart. His chest was entirely devoid of any hair, thus displaying his honed muscles and their inky legends in stark relief. I had never seen anything like it. It was how I imagine Barbie must have felt on those idle afternoons when my friend and I used to make her have sex with Action Man.

Except I wasn't Barbie. Whereas with my husband I had felt an easiness about my body and all its fuzz and faults, lying there underneath K.P., I suddenly felt like a saggy, wrung-out widow. Questions raged as I succumbed to this strange, unbidden world of sex with another man. Would K.P. be the next victim to die mid-coitus? Was I about to earn some dubious nickname related to my ability to see men off with my thighs? Would it be a turn-off if I asked K.P. to sign a disclaimer, a kind of pre-sex agreement, absolving me of all blame should the worst happen? Furthermore, would it be prudent to ask K.P. to undergo a full health check before we really got down to business?

K.P., however, was unfazed. He continued banging me against the settee, perfectly in time with the percussive barking of the dog who watched from the armchair opposite.

I'd like to say that my thoughts fell to my husband as I lay there beneath K.P. Davis, and that I felt a sense of guilt or betrayal. This is how I had imagined I would feel when this time eventually came. But the warmth and weight of another human's flesh against mine was irresistible. Once my initial fears had subsided, I cleared my mind, threw my head back and allowed myself to enjoy it.

'Fuckin' hell,' K.P. said, sweat-slicked and spent on the couch next to me. 'A thought that dog was gonna bite me cock off.'

I hadn't come, but I sat alongside K.P. radiating the rosy afterglow of fantastic sex. I couldn't believe my luck. Sure, he wasn't the most erudite or considerate of lovers, but for God's sake, look at him! What on earth would he want with me, a thirty-seven-year-old widow with a child and a drink problem, not to mention a dog that barked him all the way to climax? These were the thoughts that prevented me from asking the sorts of questions one is supposed to consider at the beginning of a new sexual relationship, like, 'How about wearing a condom?' or 'Do you have any diseases as far as you are aware?' I didn't want to put him off.

It was only later, when I was sitting, alone again, and semi-naked on the settee, curled around my second bottle of wine, that it occurred to me that I was going to need the morning-after pill. And possibly a trip to the GUM clinic.

I saw K.P. once a week from then on. He would text the evening before to inform me that he would be free for half an hour the following day. He'd call me if there was a problem. But why would there have been a problem? K.P. had it all laid on. He had unleashed a demon within this lonely widow and I began weekly visits to Primark to buy the filthiest underwear I could find. I'd greet him at the door in heels, stockings and not much else, and we'd barely make it up the stairs before he was done and we were in the lounge arranging our next liaison.

I derived little actual pleasure from intercourse with K.P. Davis, but for thirty minutes a week I was able to forget the pain and trauma and the grief, and focus on the tattooed, hairless chest in front of me. Sure, they all returned, along with a liberal dose of self-loathing, as soon as he'd shut the gate and driven off, but it seemed worth it for the moment of respite. And all the initial fears I had relating to sex and death seemed to have disappeared. He was Herculean. Nothing would floor this giant, especially not the simple act of sex. With him, I felt I was immune to the curse of death by intercourse.

Besides, he had a view of life which appealed to me. *Shit happens*, he seemed to say. *You've just got to keep going.* It was an outlook that had no regard for anyone else, and that was fine by me. Aside from my daughter, I couldn't have cared less about the concerns or sensibilities of others. I certainly didn't care what anyone thought about my association with K.P. Davis, but nevertheless, the dissenters were gathering.

11 February 2013. Exactly one year since my world had shrivelled to resemble melted Tupperware. I'd made it. According to The Manual and the wisdom of the non-bereaved,

this was when things should start to get easier. I just had to get over this day, and then ready myself for the renewal.

I spent the day in lectures at university. Start as you mean to go on, I told myself, and signed up for everything on offer. Lectures that particular day included:

Mixed Methods in Linguistic Research

Deconstructing Maps and Other Visual Sources

Noise Cultures and Base/Mass Materialism

It was doubtful whether any of these would have any relevance at all to Mary Callery or the book about her I was about to start researching for my PhD, but I attended each one with all the vim of a new student who is paying in excess of £13,000 for a course of study.

It soon became clear, despite fervent note-taking, that I didn't understand a word of what was being discussed. Even the titles of the lectures were lost on me. Foreign students with their rudimentary grasp of English appeared to have more to say than me. But it didn't matter. Forcing my brain to focus on and grapple with the obscure notions of Noise Cultures and Base/Mass Materialism was the perfect antidote to the bitter significance of the date. In fact, I was so brain-weary and confused by the end of the day that I was able to move from the deconstruction of maps, through a bottle of wine, to between the sheets of my bed with ease, with the promise of the renewal just a sleep away.

But the next day, I felt no different. In fact, entering Year 2, I felt wearier than ever. The prospect of another twelve months without Him stretched ahead like a prison sentence. And then another twelve months after that. No amount of map deconstruction was going to change this fact.

Nevertheless, life cantered on. The house was finally mine, a month after it should have been. I set about making changes. I had a log burner installed, redecorated the walls, pulled down the old blinds and put shutters in their place. I changed the front door, had a loft hatch cut in, planted shrubs and two new trees: a cherry blossom and a pussy willow, symbolic of Mark's place within the household. B and I painted a skirting board remnant and B wrote the word 'Daddy' on it and placed it at the foot of the pussy willow. The following week torrential rain washed the writing and the paint away, leaving a rough-sawn rectangle of wood propped up in the gloom.

Now that B and I owned the house outright, it felt appropriate to bring Mark *home*. The box containing His ashes was still stored in its gift bag in Mother's attic. I hadn't been able to contemplate it up until now. A peek into the bag would reveal the brass plaque on top of the box, with his name and the following words:

Died 11 February 2012, aged thirty-seven years

Seeing my husband's name juxtaposed with such an irrefutable verdict was hard to digest. So for the most part, I avoided it. Now, though, I wanted Him with us where He belonged.

I asked Mother to retrieve the gift bag, but to cover the box with a blanket so I couldn't see the plaque. I hurried across the street with it, took it directly upstairs, and placed it in the bottom of my wardrobe without looking at it. I covered it with scarves and clothes and closed the wardrobe door. Knowing it was there brought a strange sort of comfort. It meant Mark was close by when we went to bed and got up, therefore still maintaining a toe-hold within the family home. Furthermore, it meant I didn't have to think about a 'final resting place' for him just yet. That decision was still to come.

MARCH–APRIL 2013

Over six months had passed since my last round of one-to-one counselling had ended, and although I continued to take the pills, I missed the insights of a trained professional telling me that really, despite what I may have been thinking to the contrary, I was doing OK. I received notification from the GP that I had a place on a six-week group counselling course. It wouldn't necessarily be young widows, but everyone there would be in the grip of a bereavement of some description.

'Thing is,' I told the GP, 'I don't want to be surrounded by *older widows*. They're different from me, their experience is not the same.'

The GP nodded mildly, but I meant it. I had joined the organisation WAY Widowed and Young for precisely that reason. As a young widow, I resented being lumped in with the elderly who'd lost their spouses. They'd had a lifetime with their partners, I reasoned, watched their children grow up together, perhaps had the joy of grandchildren. All things Mark and I had been denied. I hadn't considered how it must feel to be suddenly bereft after all those years of being with your soulmate, of being alone with your memories. But at that stage, I didn't care. Death had hardened me, made me selfish. This group counselling had to be all about me, or I wasn't going.

I arrived in the fusty village hall and took my place next to the other 'bereaveds'. There was Gina, a middle-aged woman with a face like a spent match. She'd lost her daughter two years previously and apparently hadn't eaten since. Helen, of indeterminate age, had lost someone too, but throughout the entire six weeks we never found out exactly who. Then finally there was Susan, rotund and red-faced, whose father had died five years ago and she still couldn't speak about it without breaking down in tears.

Deb, the counsellor, introduced herself and invited us to help ourselves to the cupcakes she had made for the event. She was an older woman who exuded sex from within her grey roll-neck and leather skirt. She spent the first fifteen minutes grappling with the projector, trying to get the image to transmit from her laptop to the screen and then working out how to get the image in focus and up the right way. Technology sorted, Deb sat down and took a swig of tea.

'First off, any questions?'

I raised my hand. 'I'm dubious about the title of the course. "Overcoming Grief". As far as I'm aware, grief cannot be overcome. Is this really what it's about?'

Deb gave me a searching look. 'I understand what you're saying, Lucie. And I agree. Perhaps what we're doing is looking at strategies for dealing with grief, as opposed to overcoming it. Would you mind if we park that for now, and perhaps come back to it in our final review session?'

My issue was duly parked, but my innate cynicism raged on within. It was shaping up to be one of those courses where the delegates took tea every fifteen minutes, and conversations veered wildly off subject. It wasn't until after the first tea break that we got down to the sticky question of why we were all there, how we were all feeling, and did we recognise ourselves in any of the clipart representations of grief that were depicted on the projector screen?

Gina and I were the only two delegates out of four who ventured any kind of discussion. Susan was utterly stymied by her grief and Helen's empty stare seemed to suggest she wasn't ready or able to contribute. Gina, who never took her coat off once in six weeks, seemed fragile as a bird's wing, yet when she got into her stride she betrayed an inner toughness. She had received news of her daughter's sudden death by phone. The daughter had collapsed in the living room of her home and died almost instantly. She was thirty-eight years old, with a small child. The more Gina told us, the further she seemed to shrink into her seat. She sickened for her lost child each and every day, but somehow had found the strength to go on.

As the weeks went on, I found myself looking forward to the group sessions. I liked the sense of solidarity that came from being in a room with other people who were also suffering devastating loss. It didn't matter that these people weren't widows, or if they were young or old. The experiences were all different, but the agony was universal. Unlike individual counselling sessions where the onus is entirely on the person receiving counsel, these group sessions had the effect of momentarily relieving a weight. They gave us permission to remove the masks we all wore in everyday life, thus dropping the pretence that we were getting on with things.

In fact, when the sessions came to an end after six weeks, I told the group I didn't feel ready to let them go. Deb's cupcakes, the projector that she could never quite get level, the coffee, the camaraderie, they were all parts of an elaborate scaffold of weekly support that was about to be dismantled, with nothing to go in its place.

Also, the sessions had helped me to understand the aspects of my grief which I was having the most trouble dealing with: the vivid flashbacks to Mark's face the moment He died, the chaos of the immediate aftermath with the paramedics, images of my daughter crying in the bedroom doorway, even the debilitating physical symptoms I had been experiencing. Deb acknowledged my concerns, which were shared by the other members of the group, and promised further support would be made available.

Two weeks later, I received a call from Deb, informing me that I was on a waiting list for a one-to-one slot with a counsellor who had been in attendance at the group sessions. Her name was Trisha and she would be in touch direct once an appointment became available. They were in short supply, though, and I needed to be aware that I might have to wait a while. In the meantime, why didn't I consider writing down the things I would ordinarily have brought to the group? This could take the form of a diary, or a blog, or even a series of letters to my husband. Deb suggested that it might help in the interim.

I had always written, since I was a little girl, but after Mark's death I had been unable to commit a single coherent sentence to paper. Maybe now was the time to try again? I told Deb I'd give it some thought and awaited Trisha's call.

My evenings had fallen into a woozy cycle of wine and late-night TV, interspersed with pangs of longing for my husband and my previous life. I would wake up, sometimes on the settee, but often in bed alongside my child, not remembering how either of us had got there, or what I had been watching in the hours before I passed out. Mother, I knew, was keeping a fevered eye on the situation, so I didn't worry too much about the consequences.

I found myself furiously texting people on these evenings like a hot-thumbed teen, desperate for contact with the shallow concerns of the outside world. I was only half-aware of B, who was gradually wearing a groove in the laminate with her scooter as she went up and down the hallway. It was over the course of those lonely Rioja-soaked nights that I convinced myself that I had developed feelings for K.P. Davis. I had a vision that perhaps one day we might graduate from ardent fucking on the settee to a meal in a restaurant. (In fact, just a sustained conversation would do.)

My friends in the village had clearly been in conference and decided to try and reason with me.

'It's been fun, but you need to ditch this guy,' Jeanette said. 'Seriously, we're not judging, but we're all worried about you.'

'He's probably moved on to the next woman already,' said Ned. 'I know the type.'

But despite their warnings, I allowed myself to believe that perhaps K.P. cared for me. That when he uttered the words, 'Ahhm so glad a met you' mid-coitus he wasn't just sealing the opportunity for a liaison for another week.

Yet increasingly I sensed he was losing interest. His weekly visits had dwindled to fortnightly, sometimes longer. He would find an excuse not to come around, despite the lewdness of my sexual promises. Late one night, lonely and belligerent with drink, I sent K.P. a text to test his commitment.

I'm sorry but I think this has to end

I awaited the phone's whistle. Within thirty seconds it came. *R U pist again? But if you mean it* :)

It was the sort of response I was after. It seemed to suggest that he would be bereft without me and my increasingly obscene cheap underwear. *OK let's not end it but I am vulnerable and I don't want you taking advantage.*

The response was delayed. Then: *XX But stop textin now, girlfriend here.*

This annoyed me anew. *This is what I mean. I don't want to you to fit me in whenever you can. When r u coming over again?*

Stop textin! Xxx Al call u Tmorrow xx

But K.P. didn't call the following day. Or the following day after that. I held off texting him, trying desperately to remain aloof. But when his silence extended into the following week, I sent him a message.

How r u cowboy?

He kept me waiting over an hour for his response. *Al call u later*

This wasn't good news. I sensed I may have become too much of a liability for K.P. Davis. Sending drunken, needy texts in the evening when his girlfriend was on the settee next to him was not what a casual affair was supposed to be all about.

To my surprise, though, he did call later. Hearing his voice, I felt an immediate lightness in my heart. Perhaps this meant he did care after all? K.P. Davis was a brittle thread of happiness in the safety net, and I didn't want to lose him. But the call signified our swansong. He resented my suggestion that he was taking advantage of me, and had been on the sharp end of questioning from his girlfriend about the identity of the late-night texter. I apologised, promised it wouldn't happen again. He told me he would be in touch. But as days rolled into weeks of no contact, I had to accept that I probably wouldn't see him again.

I pretended to my village friends that it was, as they said, all for the best. They were right, he was a cad, no good, just a bit of fun. But deep down it felt as if another lifeline had gone. I coped with it by employing the tried-and-tested tactic: adding one more steely layer to my emotional carapace, and pouring myself another drink.

People for whom drinking has become a way of getting through life are always on the lookout for the next opportunity to get pissed. The more sociable the drinking the better – anything to make a bottle a night seem normal. I had become one of those people. I could last until around 3 p.m. before the desire for a glass of wine began to worm its way into my consciousness. I couldn't settle until I'd felt that first mouthful of elixir coating my throat. I knew that within an hour or so some of the weight – and it is a physical burden – of the loss of Mark would be alleviated. The sharp edges of my grief would be softened thanks to the healing power of booze.

With this in mind, I welcomed the visit of my friend Nicole one weekend in March. It provided me with an excuse to go out and get smashed. We went for lunch in Newcastle, ploughing through prosecco, a bottle of white wine and liqueurs in the restaurant before staggering on to the next watering hole. Our alcohol trail led us along the length of Newcastle's Quayside and up Pilgrim Street into a lap-dancing club named Red Velveteen. Neither of us had been in one of these establishments before, but a sense of recklessness prevailed. It was 6 p.m. and the club had just opened its doors.

We stumbled inside, down the seedily lit staircase and into the lounge. We ordered a bottle of wine from a disinterested waitress who appeared to be nude but for a few lengths of strategically placed parcel string. Two strippers joined us at our table and talked about how they had got into the trade. A year ago I was signing petitions against these joints; I joined feminist groups, sent letters of complaint to my local councillor. Now it felt as if I just didn't care for these issues any more. If these women wanted to subject themselves to the lustful scrutiny of a crowd of men, let them get on with it.

Finally one of the strippers said: 'Will you be wanting a private dance then?'

'Er...well, how much is it?'

'Twenty pounds each for three minutes. In that booth, there.'

Nicole and I shook our heads. 'We're not staying.'

A group of men arrived and our two strippers shimmied off to where the money was. Nicole and I sat and stared dumbly at a couple of topless dances before heading back upstairs.

Nicole disappeared off to the toilet and I found myself with one of the bouncers as I waited for her to return.

'We get quite a few women in here,' he told me.

'I don't even know why we came in,' I said.

'Bit of fun, isn't it? Nowt wrong in it.'

'I lost my husband, you see... He died suddenly last year... He was only thirty-seven... we have a daughter... I'm just out tonight with my friend...'

The bouncer moved from one foot to the other. 'Sorry to hear that, love.'

Nicole tottered round the corner. 'Here she is,' said the bouncer. 'Bambi on ice.'

We faltered further up Pilgrim Street towards another restaurant. My receipts from that night reveal that we ate lobster ravioli in a cream sauce and consumed another bottle of wine, but memories of this point in the evening come and go. We also took a taxi to a pub out of the city, only to return an hour later and catch a train back to Durham. Nicole wanted to go home, but the devil was in me. I had been left by my husband, spurned by a philandering plumber and I wanted some male attention.

'I want a man,' I said. 'Let's find a bar that's open.'

We found a place near the station playing disco music so loud it made the walls throb. We ordered vodka tonics, which were served to us in plastic cups, and my eyes alighted on a dark-haired lad thumbing his phone beside the dance floor. I grapevined over to him and within a few minutes I had explained about Mark and asked what his relationship status was. He had a girlfriend, but, he said, as demonstrated by my husband, life was short and one should get one's kicks when one could.

An hour later, the dark-haired twenty-eight-year-old, Nicole and I were crammed in the back of a taxi on our way back to my house.

'Mate, are you sure this is a good idea?' Nicole whispered.

'Shhh. Of course it is. You just go to bed and stop worrying.'

When we arrived home, Nicole duly disappeared upstairs, leaving me in the lounge with my prize. My prize, however, was suffering from a bout of cold feet.

'I can't do this,' he said. 'I've got a girlfriend.'

'Yeah, yeah,' I said, popping the cork on a bottle of red wine.

'No, seriously. It's not going to happen. I need to get a cab home.'

It was as if the immutability of the rejection had turned a switch off in my brain, for from that moment I remember little else. I woke up the next morning, fully dressed in my bed, alongside my reluctant catch from the previous night.

'I couldn't get a cab,' he said.

'Did we have sex?' I asked.

'No.'

'You'd better go now.'

'Yes. Sorry. Er. Thanks.'

The last thing I heard was the latch dropping on the front door before I fell back into a shame- and booze-induced sleep.

*

Tell us a few fun things about yourself! We'll use this to send you ideas for your perfect love match!

I stared at the computer screen, unable to think of a single fun thing about myself. This was my first foray into online dating and so far I had managed my name and my geographic location. I scrolled through the photographs of men in my area. They bore no resemblance to the ones who regularly popped up in my email inbox advertising the site I was currently perusing.

I knew what I was looking for. And it wasn't Mark – He was unique and impossible to replicate. I wanted the complete opposite to my soulmate. I wanted K.P. Davis. I entered my height preference as 'Must be over six foot'. Educational achievement wasn't a necessity, but I requested a big build and preferably someone with hair. (These sites are brutal. But I had no interest in being dishonest.) Fun facts about me included a boast about my drinking prowess, and my widow status. I submitted the form and awaited the deluge of love-matches.

One candidate emailed me. And this is where these sites make their money. You join for free, but have to pay to access any correspondence. I paid thirty-five pounds for the privilege of reading a message from Dean from Gateshead. Being six foot two with hair, he ticked two of my 'non-negotiable' boxes. It was enough for me to accept a date with him. We arranged to meet the following week outside a pub in Newcastle.

'Text if you want a get-out call,' said Beth. 'I'll ring you with an emergency.'

'Christ, don't do that,' I countered. 'I've made and received enough emergency calls to last me a lifetime.'

'Well keep in touch then. And take care.' Beth and Mother stood like sentries along the corridor as I clip-clopped off on my date.

I arrived at the pub and as soon as I saw Dean, I knew this wasn't going to work. He was six foot two and thin as a leek. His shoulders were wide, but his heavy winter coat hung off them like a tarpaulin. He had hair, but it was scraped back into a long lacquered wisp. I wished I could have just told him then and there that I was terribly sorry but the nice people at the online dating site had, on this occasion, got it wrong.

The refuge of my car was only a few paces away, yet I found myself spirited into the pub by Dean who was clearly an old hand at online dating. In fact, he told me, he was very popular with the ladies because he was forty-eight years old, solvent, with no ex-wife to muddy things.

'Women on dating sites are often just after someone to settle down with and have kids,' he said. 'I'm a prime candidate.'

'So how come you're still single then?' I sucked my sparkling water through a straw and wondered how long was reasonable to wait before making my excuse to leave.

'I can afford to pick and choose. Not found the right one yet.' He winked at me and my sister's emergency call became instantly more appealing. I found myself becoming increasingly desperate to leave. I went to the Ladies and seriously considered escaping through the tiny window that gave on to the street. But Dean was out for the night. He'd left his car at home specially. He suggested we sup up and continue the trail along the Quayside to the next bar.

I ordered a small red wine and realised that despite his boasts of solvency, this was obviously my round. Perhaps I'd been spoiled by ten years of Mark, but I wasn't used to this lack of gallantry. Furthermore, we were in the bar area of a restaurant that Mark and I had been to, and my mind kept drifting to the last time that we were in here. We had sat over there and shared a starter platter of mixed hors d'oeuvres. In that moment I missed Him more than ever.

I excused myself again and headed to the Ladies, where I sat in a locked cubicle and willed the tears not to spill. Why on earth had I ever thought I was ready for this? Casual fucking was one thing, but being on a real, live date with someone who might actually want more was suddenly quite different. After all, I was still in love with my husband. And poor Dean, with his beautifully starched shirt and his solvency, was looking for a love match and all I wanted was to go home. I needed to remove myself from this situation as quickly as I could.

'Listen, Dean, I'm sorry, I know it's early but I need to get home. My mother is babysitting my daughter and I don't like to leave it too late.'

'Sure. I understand. Can we do this again, perhaps?'

I drained my wine and pulled on my coat. 'I think you know my situation. Being, you know, widowed and all that. I'm finding all this quite tricky to deal with. Can we play it by ear?'

Dean seemed assured that we would be on for round two. He kissed me on the cheek and told me that if he set off now he'd catch the ten o'clock bus, so would I mind if he didn't walk me back to my car. My heels couldn't carry me fast enough out of that bar. I clacked up the road, trying to control my quickening breath. When I got back to the car, I slid into the driver's seat and started up the engine. I sat for a moment, gathering myself, watching Thursday-night revellers in the city's neon glow. How I wished I was one of them again, light of spirit and unburdened by the terrible weight of my soulmate's death. I turned the engine off, put my head on the steering wheel, and wept.

Following K.P.'s rejection and a catastrophic foray into blind dating, I decided to eschew men and focus on my studies and the few hours a week I was still teaching French. While the latter continued to cause me considerable frustration, I persisted with it out of a sense of duty to the boss, who was trying hard to get her fledgling business off the ground. I would arrive at the various schools and playgroups laden down with equipment for the session, sparring with myself inwardly. For despite my passion for French and my tiny, overzealous charges, I still felt I lacked the emotional drive required for the role. But it would be some months before

I summoned the courage to quit. In the meantime, I took solace in the subject of my PhD, Mary Callery.

Her life, I was discovering, had some parallels to my own. She had suffered the sudden and unexpected loss of her daughter Caroline; she had travelled solo to Europe in the thirties, living in France and Spain; she'd volunteered for the ambulance corps in Paris during the war; she had impassioned relationships with a number of men. She was revealing herself to be a woman of mettle and spirit, both traits that I was desperately trying to summon in myself.

I absorbed myself in Mary's life during the day, reverting to a clumsy approximation of motherhood at 3.15 when the school bell rang. Seeing the look of delight on my daughter's face when her eyes fell on me at the end of the school day made my weary heart dance. I'd take her face in my hands and kiss it all over, then we'd wander back home hand-in-hand, discussing the events of the day. One afternoon, though, B's teacher asked me if I could stay behind for 'a quiet word'.

'This week in class we've been looking at people in the community who help us,' she said. 'A policeman came in to talk to us and B got upset. She went very quiet and then burst into tears. Was your husband a policeman? It was perhaps the uniform that did it.'

It was only the second time since the immediate aftermath of Mark's death that I was aware of B acknowledging the events of that evening. The first had come just a couple of weeks previously, when my friend Joanne and her daughter had called in after school. On the sideboard in the lounge are photographs of the family. My nieces and nephews, an oversized baby portrait of B, Mark and I on our wedding day. As Joanne and I chatted, I found myself slowly tuning into the conversation that was occurring between the two little girls across the room.

'Is that your daddy?' B's friend asked, pointing at the portrait of Mark.

'Yes. But my daddy died.'

'How did he die?'

'Like this,' she replied, and proceeded to lie on the floor on her back with her arms outstretched, just as Mark had appeared the last time she saw Him. 'My Mummy was saying, "and 1... and 2... and 3... and 4" and doing this to his chest.' She placed her palms face down on her sternum and began mimicking the last desperate attempts at resuscitation she had witnessed on that night. Joanne put her hand on my forearm.

B's friend considered this dramatisation, then turned her gaze to another photograph on the sideboard. 'Who is that?'

B pulled herself up from the floor. 'That's my G,' she said of her cousin. 'Shall we go upstairs now?'

The scene caused me to consider what on earth was happening in the child's psyche. She never spoke about Mark or his passing to me, so I had made the assumption that she had erased all memories of that night. But her detailed re-enactment was clear evidence that the trauma of seeing the dead body of her daddy was branded onto her brain. How would this manifest in later years, when she had the vocabulary to express it?

I began to wonder whether, like me, she could benefit from some counselling. She wasn't talking to me about it, probably for fear of unleashing a torrent of grief. I already sensed she had taken it upon herself to be the arbiter of my emotions in relation to Daddy – whenever she saw me crying she would run to the bathroom and fetch a length of toilet tissue with which to staunch the flow.

'Grandma,' she would shout. 'Mummy's crying because she misses Daddy. Don't cry, Mummy. It's all right.'

Bereavement counselling for children is done through play, not projectors, clipart and cupcakes, and I was aware of a couple of organisations who offered it. But it wasn't until this conversation with B's teacher that I decided it might be a wise course of action.

'B's daddy wasn't a policeman, no,' I told her. 'But she was there on the night that Mark died and must have remembered the policemen who arrived at the house afterwards.' I chronicled the evening in my mind and worked out that the policemen must have arrived within an hour of Mark being pronounced dead. At this point, His body was still upstairs on the bed, and Mother and I had corralled B in the living room until the undertaker arrived to collect Him. Her brain must have made an association between policemen and the last time she saw her daddy, which came to the fore that day in school on sight of the uniform.

I suggested to Mother that B might need some counselling. Her brow furrowed instantly. Mother has suffered her share of turmoil, but as far as I'm aware she's never used more than a stiff gin and tonic and a blast of Dr Hook to get her through it. Counselling is anathema to her. She simply cannot see the benefit of sitting in a room with a stranger and exchanging negative thoughts for potentially healing ones.

'She's only four,' she said, pouring herself a stiff gin and tonic.

'So? She's clearly processing this stuff and seems unable to talk to me about it. Besides, I'm not sure if I'd know how to deal with it if she did. Perhaps she might profit from sharing her thoughts with a trained professional.'

There was no response, but our mother–daughter telepathy told me all I needed to know about her feelings on the subject. I didn't feel entirely convinced about it myself – it seemed like such a grown-up and serious-sounding intervention for a small child – but I was prepared to give it a go. I'd reached an impasse. I genuinely didn't know what to do for the best for my own daughter, but if she was crying at school, it was something I needed to address. I contacted the GP and began the time-consuming process of referral.

Five months into my new student career, I was enjoying the rigour of academia as well as delving into Mary Callery's past. Yet as any researcher knows, one cannot conduct a lengthy and in-depth study of a subject from the comfort of one's desk. Fieldwork was required, and having made contact with Mary's family on Long Island, it became clear that a trip to the States was unavoidable. They suggested May might be a good time, climate-wise, to make the trip.

This posed a problem, though. I had always been a nervous flyer, but since Mark's death the world had become a place of instability, fraught with unseen dangers. I was edging ever closer to a sort of agoraphobia, which meant I could barely even contemplate leaving the village, never mind the north-east. The village, with its miserable micro-climate and perpetually grey skies, seemed to cocoon me and B, and the people within in it watched over us with a collective eye.

I couldn't entertain the thought of the trip without B – being stranded on another continent away from her would have sent my already angst-frazzled nervous system into apoplexy. So she would need to come too. And if she came, Mother would need to come. And, as it turned out, so would Mother's partner Jim.

'I don't want to go,' I told Mother as we sat in the airport lounge at Newcastle en route to Heathrow. 'I cannot get on that plane.'

'You'll be fine, love. Try to relax and enjoy it.'

I cried as we walked into the departure lounge and on to the flight. B kept looking at me. For her, the tears could only mean one thing.

'Are you missing Daddy?' she asked.

'Yes.' And I was. He was the only person who could have calmed me in a situation like this. He would have pulled out statistics as to why this was the safest form of travel. He would have kissed my forehead, my temple, each eyelid and told me everything was going to be all right.

The sounds of the doors shutting, the tinny voice of the captain, followed by the terrifying groans and screeches emitted from the machinery beneath us caused my bowel to liquefy. I begin a series of slow, deep inhalations with my eyes closed. Mother's partner Jim reached his hand across the gangway and placed it on mine. This is it, I convinced myself. Within a few short seconds, our lives could all be over.

When Mark died, I had a fleeting moment of wishing I was dead too. If it weren't for B, I would have thrown myself in the furnace at the crematorium with Him. At least, that's what I told myself. In reality, much as I wanted to believe I would have joined Him, the instinct to live was too strong. This was one of the revelations I found difficult to reconcile – I discovered that despite my rage and bitterness at the world, I still wanted to be part of it. I had ambitions I still wanted to dust off. I certainly didn't want to end my days here, on this doomed flight to Heathrow.

I ordered a large gin and tonic, drained it immediately and ordered another one before the air hostess had reached the row in front.

'I'm a very nervous flyer,' I told her, apologetically.

The flight cruised until we arrived into Heathrow airspace, at which point a typhoon appeared to have whipped up from nowhere. We were buffeted violently back and forth as we tried to land and I couldn't drag my eyes away from the scene out of the window – the tip of a wing flapping like that of an agitated condor. Once again Jim reached over the gangway and pressed his hand against mine.

'Why doesn't he just land? Why oh why?' I muttered to no one in particular.

Finally, I heard the wheels hit the runway and the air hostess appeared at my elbow. 'Sorry, I should have mentioned it was a bit windy down here. I could see your husband grabbing your hand. You must have been terrified, bless you.'

I pulled my sweating mitt from underneath Jim's. '*He's* not my husband.'

As soon as the mid-flight refreshments were on offer aboard the New York flight, I requested a bottle of wine. And then another. And another. And then the lights were dimmed in the cabin and no more refreshments were forthcoming.

'We have no more wine, ma'am,' the attendant at the back of the plane told me. 'I might have a bottle of champagne somewhere?'

'That'll do,' I said.

She rifled through the drawers and as she did so I craned my neck and peered out of the window. I could just make out ocean waves, like delicate puffs of cotton, far far beneath us.

I staggered back to my seat and noticed Mother's furrowed brow peeking at me over the seat in front.

'What?' I said, popping the cork on the champagne.

'Go easy on the alcohol.'

'Yeah, yeah.'

Shortly after the champagne was emptied, the tears began to fall. Fat little beads, rolling down my cheeks and gathering under my chin like the ties of a bonnet. I looked at the curtain that divided the cabins and willed Mark to come walking through it. I could see Him clearly in my mind's eye. He was coming towards me, smiling, shrugging His shoulders as if to say, 'Come on, pet! I'm here now. Everything's going to be OK.'

I whispered His name over and over again in the LED-lit gloom of that cabin, and could do nothing but let the tears come. The next thing I knew, the cabin lights were on and the map on the screen indicated that we were on the approach to New York. The smell of vomit hit my nostrils. I looked down and realised I had thrown up. A bag of Merlot-coloured sick spilled out over my lap. A disgusted-looking Chinese attendant sidled over and relieved me of it, then offered a damp cloth for my jeans.

'You really have to do something about your fear of flying,' the man next to me said as we taxied to our gate. 'You can't put yourself through that again.'

At that moment, though, I didn't wish to think about the next time I would have to fly. I'd made it to New York and I was ecstatic to be alive.

The Hamptons was the sort of place that those women from *Sex and The City* went to for the weekends to unwind. Manicured townships are dotted along the length of Montauk Highway, each one picket-fenced and fizzing with cherry blossom. Shop signs swing from miniature wooden gibbets and hollow-cheeked women strut between the boutiques, their shopping bags fanning out along their forearms like sets of brightly coloured, shiny feathers. The sand on the east side of the peninsula is white and fine as dust, and the skies constantly change depending on the mood of the ocean.

Mary's family lived a few hundred yards from the beach in a quirky art-studio-cum-cottage that Mary's great-nephew George had designed himself. He and his wife Susan welcomed me in on that first day of my research, setting me up at a desk that had belonged to Mary with a strong coffee and a stack of previously unseen archives, personal letters and photographs.

Mary had been a sculptress of some repute, yet was more noted for her art collection, and was, at one time, the most prolific collector of Picassos in America. She knew, worked and had relationships with Picasso, Matisse, Leger, O'Keefe, and the letters before me intimately documented each one.

'That was taken when Mary was on a date with Pablo,' said George, holding out a black-and-white shot of the fabled artist sitting on a wall holding on to a scruffy-looking mutt. 'She got into photography and took that one of him with one of her dogs.'

On one of the boxes, written in Mary's insouciant scrawl, were the words: *Caroline's letters*. Mary's daughter Caroline had been faceless until this trip, known to me by only two facts: she had had three husbands and she had committed suicide aged forty-one. The letters contained within the box in front of me were ghosts.

It felt like an intrusion, what I was about to do. After all, I had keepsake letters of my own, and photographs; I had a pot of Dax hair pomade, aftershave, a toothbrush, a mobile phone charger, a wristwatch, the four-pack of Guinness that Mark bought half an hour before He died. All of these items were now stored with the sort of reverence one bestows upon priceless antiques. How would it feel to have prying eyes going through those last remnants of my beloved's life?

But Mary had kept the letters (all but those from Caroline's last year, 1966 – these were conspicuously absent). She had wanted them to be read. Archiving a life is a Sisyphean task. What do you keep and what do you throw away? Common sense and decency go out of the window. In the immediate aftermath of Mark's death I didn't want Mother to flush her toilet as the bowl contained Mark's last ever urination. I kept shopping lists He had written, old receipts from His trouser pockets. I unearthed beer bottles from the recycling bin and ran my tongue around the rims, hoping to taste Him one last time. Last desperate acts of preservation, symptomatic of the need to keep the dead person somehow in the land of the living.

I lifted the letters out of the box and placed them on the desk. Each sheet of paper was thin as ageing skin. I fanned through them with my thumb, sizing up the task. As I did so, a tiny envelope dropped out from the pile.

On the front, Mary's writing again:

CCC's hair.

Caroline Callery Coudert. Inside, a leaf of blue paper, folded, and two small square photographs: the first, a sepia shot of Caroline seated with a scarf tied around her head, a clump of curls poking out by way of a fringe. The second was a black-and-white studio shot, a smiling Caroline with her hair scraped into a chignon, black shirt unbuttoned casually at the neck.

I unfolded the blue paper. The curl of cornflake-coloured hair was stapled to the paper, underneath the word 'REMEMBER'.

I ran the tip of my finger around the curl and looked at it for a long time. Caroline: she was tangible, yet so far away. I thought about my own lock of keepsake hair, the one I cut from Mark's head as he lay in his coffin in the funeral home. It now sat, together with a sample of his gingery sideburn fuzz, in a plastic box within a velvet pouch in a display cabinet in my lounge. Occasionally, B asked to see the contents of the box, and I was forced to unlock the cabinet and extract the last recognisable remnant of his body.

We would look at it together, noting the greying strands nestling in the black curl, and the way that the sideburn hair looked like wood shavings. I kept a further lock of His hair in the silver locket He bought me after I gave birth to B and sometimes wayward strands poked out. I may have placed the chest hairs I retrieved from the plughole in that locket too, although I can't be sure.

Outwardly, Mary was 'stoic' following Caroline's death (George's word). But knowing that she had kept this lock of hair, that she had stapled it to a piece of paper and placed it in an envelope with the two photographs, made me believe that she had indeed suffered the agony of bereavement, but in a very private way. The suicide wasn't entirely unexpected – Caroline was very troubled – but even so, just as when an elderly relative dies, the pain of the loss is not diminished. Mary catalogued and kept the ghosts in the box for someone else to read, a set of ciphers with which they could attempt to decode her grief.

Susan and George were keen to give us a flavour of Mary's life in Long Island away from the archives. They invited us all to a cocktail party in Wainscott, where a woman arrived wearing a dress made entirely of neon green pom-poms, matching the outfit of the terrier that sat in her handbag. We ate seafood straight out of the ocean in Sag Harbor, and watched *Gatsby* in a tiny movie theatre right near where the film was set. I had told them about Mark, and they embraced my entire clan with open arms, delighted that I had elected to take up their remarkable great-aunt's story.

It was, for all intents and purposes, the research trip of dreams. Yet I found that, once again, the 'widow's screen' had descended. Invisible to the naked eye, this translucent barrier between widow and rest of world quashed any real enjoyment of my time in this beautiful place. I woke up and cried on the first four mornings because I wanted Him here to continue the adventure with me. Yet here was the truth: He would never have a new adventure again. I bought cigarettes and smoked them alone and deep in thought on the veranda, imagining the covert smirks we would have exchanged about the woman in the poms-poms, or His inevitable lengthy tutorial about how best to eat the crab. I stared down empty stretches of beach, wanting only for my husband to come walking out of the mist. On this far-off continent, I felt more distant from Him than ever.

By the end of our week in The Hamptons, I was ready for the security of my pebble-dashed terraced home. But we had two days in New York before boarding the flight. We were staying on the fortieth floor of a hotel just off Central Park. The vertiginous elevator ride left me unable to sleep for wondering how we would ever get out of the place in the event of a fire. The subway seemed to close in on us as we rode on it, causing us to abandon it for cabs or else pounding the pavements on foot. I passed on a trip around Staten Island, fearing that the ferry would capsize or succumb to some other atrocity – instead I watched B chasing squirrels around Battery Park, while Mother and Jim did the tour alone.

I was again overpowered by a sense of being stranded without Mark, hundreds of miles from home. And I had no choice but to endure the agony of another flight to get back to Him.

I looked into returning to Britain by boat. It would take a week, but hey! It could be fun. These vessels have cinemas, swimming pools, *X-Factor* rejects performing every night. B and I would have a ball! And once we arrived in Southampton, it would only be a mere six hours on the train back up to Newcastle. However, as well as being prohibitively expensive and adding potentially another ten days on to our trip, Mother's face suggested this might not be the best course of action. I too began to have cold feet. Ours would be the ship that would be hit by the freak wave or swallowed in the Bermuda Triangle. I would just have to brave the flight. And that meant getting shit-faced.

'I'm a very nervous flyer,' I belched in the face of the air steward.

'Have you had a few drinks before getting on the flight, ma'am?'

'Er. Yes. But only a couple.'

'OK. Well, don't worry. You're seated in row... 32. I'll let Anton know, and he'll look after you.'

The steward had clearly got straight on the wire to Anton, for I had barely sat down before he was alongside me.

'Could I have a drink, Anton?'

'We'll be bringing them round after take-off. In the meantime, sit back and try to relax.'

Three hours into our crossing, Anton cornered Mother as she came out of the toilet.

'Does your daughter always drink this much?'

'Well, she likes a drink...'

'It's just she's had two gin and tonics, three red wine miniatures, and is still asking for more. I'm afraid I'm going to have to refuse.'

On hearing this news, I took my life in my hands, unfastened my seatbelt and tottered to the back of the plane, where Anton was completing a crossword puzzle.

'Can I have another drink, please Anton?'

'I've told your mother, my darling, no more booze now until we land. Then you can drink as much as you want.'

'I'm frightened though, Anton.'

'Help me do this crossword. What's four down, d'you reckon?'

I loosened my grip on my fear momentarily and looked at the clue.

Sitcom starring Wendy Craig. 11 letters.

'*Butterflies*. "Life is like a butterfly, da da da da da da dadah"!'

'So it is.' Anton began singing too, as one of his pre-pubescent-looking colleagues looked on in revulsion. 'How about this one?'

Anton and I did the crossword, then the Sudoku, then chatted all the way into Heathrow airspace. Arriving back into Britain felt like shedding a skin. I'd been taut for ten long days and now I was home. The final straight – the flight from

Heathrow to Newcastle – was, I'm afraid, insurmountable. We bade a temporary farewell to Mother and Jim, and with my little daughter, the one who had obliviously skipped and laughed all the way through these last ten days while I fended off my own personal hell, I set off for King's Cross and the first train north.

I unpacked our luggage and made a silent vow never to go away again. I was euphoric to be back. I reclaimed my place among my new group of friends, the Village People as they had become known, and looked out at life again from within the bubble of village safety.

With the exception of Joanne and Ned, none of the Village People had known Mark. This was a distinct advantage of the group – with no point of reference, no shared history, Mark was scarcely mentioned. I could put on the 'mask' and head out into social situations with them without the threat of a meltdown or someone reminding me of a happier time. I was making new memories with these people without having to face the pain of what was lost.

I was also gaining a reputation for my recklessness. Having no one to temper my behaviour, or go home to at the end of a night, I would be first to the party and last to leave – if I left at all. I became the friend who was available for a drink at short notice, or when a girlfriend's spouse was away. My sexual exploits had become everyone's business, and I regaled them all with tales of K.P. Davis and fantasies of my next conquest.

But I began to notice discontent in the group. Husbands didn't like the thought of their wives going out drinking with the man-eating widow who had no boundaries. Wives liked hearing the stories of my hapless conquests, yet I sensed an unstated envy at my situation – while none of them wished their partners dead, they all liked inwardly reminiscing about the freedoms that single life affords.

Increasingly, I sensed I was being rounded up, taken in hand, 'saved'. I could not be allowed to wander so wantonly off the tracks. Each couple tried their own method of salvation.

'Our friend Will is coming up from Sheffield at the weekend. He's not long been divorced. Lovely bloke. Fancy getting together while he's here?' My friend Jeanette took a sip of wine and smiled sweetly.

'Are you setting me up?'

'No. Well, maybe. I know you don't want a relationship, but you could have a bit of fun. Will would be up for that.'

'Is he good-looking?'

'In a non-typical type of way.'

'That's a no then. Is he rich?'

'Has his own business. Property development.'

'I'll come for a drink, but I'm not shagging him.'

From behind, Will looked promising. He was tall, dark, with no sign of a bald patch. He was at the bar getting the drinks in, which added to his appeal. He turned round and a 'non-typically' good-looking face beamed at me.

'Hello, I'm Will. Can I get you a drink?'

I decided to give Will a chance. He talked at me for an hour about the trajectory of his career, from paper boy to head of his own company. He had two teenaged sons and was rarely at home because of his all-consuming head-of-own-company importance. Jeanette and her husband Graeme sat opposite us and pretended to be deep in conversation with each other, chancing a look every now and again to see if the look of love was being exchanged between their two friends.

Will didn't ask me a single question about myself, which I took as the result of one of two issues: either he had been briefed by Jeanette and Graeme about my tragic existence and didn't want to exacerbate things by probing too deeply, or else he wasn't interested in me. By the end of the night, Jeanette and Graeme's earnest attempts at restabilising me served only to harden my carapace against the tyranny of the blind date. I resolved not to put myself through one again, no matter who the bloke.

Joanne and Ned's approach was to adopt me as one of their own. They had three kids – one more was not going to make a difference to the balance of the household. They fed me, lodged me on nights when I didn't want to be alone, looked after my child when my own strength to do so had waned. Ned helped me tax my car, change my tyres, mend the fence after it was ravaged by the wind. Joanne brought me flowers and a vase to put them in, or a bottle of wine from their own stash if I needed one and couldn't get to the shop.

One afternoon, Joanne announced they had bought me a ticket to see a clairvoyant who was playing at the local theatre. It was just for fun, and we would all go together the following week. I had heard about this clairvoyant and her well-oiled publicity machine before and it was not the sort of gig I would have chosen to go to. But the ticket was there and my curiosity was piqued. I was pretty sure that Mark wouldn't return to deliver a message via the body of a woman who looked like Barbara Bush, but anything was possible.

I hadn't truly 'felt' Mark anywhere since He'd died, nor had any signs that He was out there. The closest I'd come was that day in the doctoral conference suite on my first day at uni, but even then I didn't feel Him as a physical presence. In fact, there had only been one occasion which caused me to wonder whether He was trying to make contact. One morning in May, B and I came down for breakfast and began the usual rituals. B came into the kitchen and said: 'Mummy. Please will you put the radio on?'

It was something she had never requested, before or since.

'Why?' I asked.

'I just want the radio on.'

Chris Evans was at the tail end of an interview on his morning show.

B stood next to me, listening. 'That sounds like Daddy,' she said. It was true – the low, languorous tone of the interviewee's voice was resonant of Mark's.

'Hmmm,' I said, shaking Shreddies into her bowl.

Then Evans finished the interview, and I heard him say: 'Now then, what year was this one from?'

The opening bars of Neil Young's 'Heart of Gold' throbbed across the kitchen. I hadn't been able to listen to it since the funeral, weighted, as it was, with so much significance to us as a couple. The plaintive strains of the harmonica soared, and I lurched across the floor and turned the radio off.

'Why did you want the radio on, just then?' I asked my child, who by now was shovelling Shreddies into her mouth, oblivious to whether the damn thing was on or off.

She looked at me. 'I just wanted it on.'

I relayed the story to John's wife, Fran.

'We think He gave us a sign the other week,' she said. 'We were sitting in the kitchen talking about Him, when suddenly one of the spotlights flickered and went off and on again. And it keeps happening. Always the same light, always whenever we mention Him. It's become a bit of a joke...'

And while I hated the thought of Him roaming about an afterlife without us, it was comforting to think that He may have been communicating via the medium of Radio 2. Or John and Fran's dodgy electrical fittings. But channelling through a clairvoyant on stage in Hartlepool? It seemed doubtful.

We arrived at the theatre and battled our way through books, DVDs, Barbara Bush-alike key rings to our seats in the section down from the gods. A nub of apprehension began throbbing in my gut. Instinct told me this was bullshit, but what if...?

The house lights dimmed and Barbara strode on to the stage looking younger than her book covers suggested. She had new glasses on, and a relaxed candy-floss coiffe. She waved at the crowd and told us how wonderful we all looked. Within minutes, she had the ghost of Vera on stage with her. Did anyone in the audience know Vera? Vera was standing right there, next to her, looking for Denise. Was Denise out there? A hand went up in the stalls.

'I'm Denise.'

The audience took a collective inhalation of breath. Jesus Christ, maybe this woman was for real. I suddenly felt frightened. I had never wanted to contemplate the thought that Mark could be 'out there' somewhere, watching over me from the ether. The idea of it unsettled me. He would be devastated to know that He'd left me and his beloved B to fend for ourselves without Him. Besides, I'd be mortified if He knew about the plumber. Fancy having to watch that from the afterlife.

'Denise! Stand up for me, love!' the clairvoyant shouted, shading her eyes from the spotlight. The audience clapped as Denise wobbled to her feet. 'I've got Vera here!'

'It's not Vera, it's Val. I think. Auntie Val?'

The clairvoyant paused. 'Yes, it is Val. She wants you to know she's OK. And she loves you very much Denise.'

The camera honed in on Denise's stricken face. She caught sight of herself being projected on to the screen and held her head in her hands. The spirits were active that night on stage in Hartlepool. They'd come from far and wide to make contact with their members of the audience. Jim from the fish shop. Derek who'd been killed on his bike. Lyn who'd gone to Australia and never come back. One of the saddest moments of the evening though was a couple who were seeking contact with their deceased baby son. Barbara thought she'd made a connection, but she couldn't make the details fit. It wasn't him. The couple crumpled back into their seats, heartbroken anew.

Mark didn't come through. I think I was relieved. Those who are bereaved are prepared to believe anything in order to have contact with their beloved again. The land of the dead and the land of the living are devastatingly, irretrievably distinct; it is hard to accept that there is no bridge or tunnel to link the two. While the thought of a conduit is seductive, the thought of Mark being alone on that far-off land makes my heart ache so much that I'd rather believe He was nowhere. He certainly wasn't on stage in Hartlepool, anyway.

As we fought our way out of the theatre, I couldn't help feeling disappointed. My heart longed for Mark, and that night, just before the lights went down in the auditorium, I was given vague hope that I might have contact with Him again; however preposterous it seemed. The fact that He didn't appear seemed to add more weight to the growing body of evidence which indicated that He really wasn't coming back, no matter how much I stood on the seventh floor of the doctoral conference suite and willed it.

A honey-voiced woman called and told me her name was Jill from the children's counselling service. She had been tasked with providing my daughter with some counselling, and could I tell her a little bit of background before the first meeting went ahead? I reeled off my well-rehearsed spiel, detailing how B had witnessed her daddy's death and how she now was talking to everybody but me about it and how that made me feel like the most inadequate mother on the planet.

'It's quite normal,' soothed Jill. 'She may be little, but she's protecting you. Doesn't want to cause you any more pain than you're already enduring.'

I thought about this after the phone call ended. It was true: my daughter's demeanour had changed almost overnight after her daddy's death. She had been a monstrous baby and toddler. She fed awkwardly from the breast, flexing her arms and legs relentlessly while trying to latch on. She had colic and screamed for five hours every night for three months. She would only sleep to the sound of a hair-dryer whirring – in the end Mark downloaded a recording of one from the Internet and we played it on a loop until she dropped off. Once she learned to speak, she would tell people to 'go away' in a low growl. We took her on a speculative visit to a nursery school when she was two and she told the officious head teacher to 'shut up' when she greeted us at the door.

'Does she hear that at home?' the head teacher asked, looking at us down her nostrils like Kenneth Williams.

'We think it may be from *Toy Story*... Woody says it to Buzz at one point...'

'Do you think it's appropriate for a child of this age to be watching *Toy Story*?'

Mark and I stalked around for the rest of the tour, utterly chastened, agreeing via telepathy and a series of choice hand gestures that we would not be sending our child here.

Mark's death and the ensuing fallout signalled a new phase in her personality. At three years old, she seemed to have understood that growling, crying and all the other the trappings of toddlerdom were now redundant. Mummy had no capacity left to deal with them, therefore B would initiate a kind of reversal of roles. She would be the one to soothe the tantrums and the tears, to decide when it was time for bed, to make apologies for her mummy's erratic behaviour.

'Mummy's crying because Daddy died.'

She had become the protector, subtly seeing off people, like Paul, whom she deemed to be threats to the status quo. And here, it seemed, she was shielding me from her own set of complex emotions, even though she couldn't possibly have understood them herself. Jill, I figured, would be a force for good, no matter what Mother or anyone else thought.

'It just seems indecent to me that you should take a child out of a classroom and force them into talking about something they may not even want to talk about,' Mother said, draining a bottle of wine that evening.

Our wine consumption had increased to more than five times the recommended limit since Mark had died, and we regularly found ourselves disagreeing with each other at the bottom of a bottle.

'Well, I'm feeling my way with this and I don't know what else to do. Sadly the sudden death of a husband doesn't come with a rule book.'

'She's dealing with it in her own way,' Mother went on. 'If she wants counselling when she's bigger then fair enough, but not now—'

'Just because you bury your head in the sand about everything—'

'Like what?'

'Your divorce. Relationships with men. Relationships with your family—'

'It's not burying my head in the sand, I just don't feel the need to talk about it in the way that you do.'

'What's that supposed to mean?'

'All the non-stop texting, Facebooking, messaging. Perhaps if you looked out from behind all the technology you'd see there is a little girl here desperate for her Mummy.'

I felt my spirit flatline. I knew she was right. I found comfort in the texts of friends, in the advice from strangers on online forums. I was living in a virtual world, where Mark still existed. Indeed, the seduction of the online world for a widow lies in the fact that it allows you to believe that your soulmate is still alive.

I only needed to log into Facebook to find Him smiling at me in my 'Friends' list. His own Facebook page was still intact – and on it, he 'lives in North Yorkshire' and His status is 'Married'. I was able to hear His voice again through His posts and His daft conversations with friends.

Furthermore, I could communicate with Him on there – post thoughts on His wall, share links to our favourite songs. Other people posted messages on there too, like an unofficial memorial page. To some He was 'mate', to others 'marra', to one person 'Nobfelt' (don't ask). To me, He was 'love'. Mark was so many things to so many people, keeping His page alive and continually revisiting it reminded me how much other people miss Him too and somehow that made me feel less alone.

A couple of months before He died, He went to Australia on that work trip. Looking back through His Facebook page, I noticed that while He was away I'd posted a photograph of Bob Dylan looking forlorn in front of a window in Paris.

'Bob's face is like mine when you're not here,' I'd written.

'Miss you, pet,' He'd replied.

I still had His last two texts on my phone. Sent from a hotel room in Cheltenham a week before He died:

Arrived safely pet. Just about to have a shower. Call you in a bit. X

I had replied: *Don't forget to wash your bollocks X*

To which He replied: *You do it... X*

His email account was still alive too. I logged into it occasionally to clear the accumulated unread messages. To Nissan, Woolovers, Hertz Rentacar, Aston University alumni, He never died. They wrote to Him still. Perhaps I should have deleted His account (I could hear Him telling me to – 'pet, it's a fraud risk') but I couldn't bring myself to do it. Existence in cyberspace is better than no existence at all.

Yet here was my daughter, very much alive in the real world and grappling with her grief – unsure of what to do with this monster that had come crashing, unbidden and unannounced, into her world. And I couldn't handle her.

'Let's just see how the first session goes,' I said to Mother. 'Make a decision from there. OK?'

'OK.'

Jill was a ponderous giant of a woman, with thick glasses and strings of heavy glass beads wrapped around her throat. She was weighed down with props, files, rolls of paper, which she set down with a lusty 'phew!' We met in a stuffy annexe at B's school one Tuesday morning in July. The three of us discussed what the forthcoming sessions would entail. I was required to sign some paperwork, and was then astonished to hear Jill ask B to sign some paperwork too.

'What is she signing up to?' I asked.

'She is agreeing to participate in the sessions,' Jill replied. 'That she wants to talk about her daddy with me – the counsellor.'

'With due respect, you could be Father Christmas. How is she supposed to understand all this and, furthermore, sign up to it?'

Jill looked at me with well-honed tolerance. 'I know what you're saying, but the service requires us to obtain a signature from every client, regardless of their age. It's a formality. I'm afraid we cannot continue without it.'

I watched as B wrote an approximation of her name on the form.

'We offer counsel through play. We will be making a memory box for Daddy, as well as using toys to role-play how we are feeling. B will not be prompted to say anything, but she will be made aware that this is a safe and open environment in which to talk, should she want to. In the meantime, perhaps you would like to borrow this book.' She handed me a copy of *To Live Until We Say Goodbye* by Elisabeth Kubler-Ross. I had come across Kubler-Ross in the very early days of my loss – it was she who coined *The Five Stages of Grief*: Denial, Anger, Bargaining, Depression, Acceptance – and hers was one of the grief manuals I had hoped would be the panacea to my unliveable pain. Of course, there was and is no panacea. And no amount of manuals or reflections on 'the grief process' can minister to the individual experience of loss. I took the book from Jill, though I knew I would never open its pages.

'Fine,' I said. 'So I'll hear from you after the first session then? To discuss anything that came up?'

Jill gave me the tolerant look again. 'I'm afraid I can't

share anything that B might disclose in the session. Client confidentiality.'

'But she's five years old!'

'She has the same right to confidentiality as everyone else.'

I began to think, not for the first time in all of this, that Mother might have been right. I looked at my little cloud-haired child, who was absently poking around in a pot of beads from Jill's prop box. It seemed indecent to be leaving her here.

'OK. Well. I'll leave you to it then. Are you happy, B, to stay here with Jill?'

B nodded without looking up.

'See you later, Mummy!' chirped Jill, and ushered me out the door.

My jaws were clenched tight as I walked out of the school gates and back towards home. What was my child likely to 'disclose' to this woman I had imposed upon her, out of the blue, in the middle of her school day? And what if Jill, in trying to extract said 'disclosure', only succeeded in traumatising my child more than she already was?

That evening, I defied Jill's confidentiality clause and plied B for information. As usual though, it was not forthcoming.

'What did you talk to Jill about?'

'Not sure.'

'Did you talk about Daddy?'

'Hmmm.'

'What did you tell Jill?'

'We made a box. And I got toy.' She ran to her bag and brought out a pink elephant wearing a tutu.

Jill wouldn't have handed over a fluffy pink pachyderm unless it was somehow significant to the grieving process. 'Does the elephant remind you of Daddy?'

B looked at me as if I had just shat in her toy box. 'It's a toy elephant.'

'Right. So what about this box then? Was that for Daddy?'

But unlike Jill, B's tolerance had expired. She flounced off to the sitting room without responding and turned on the TV. Half an hour later I found the elephant in the dog's bed, partially eviscerated and staring at me sadly through its one remaining eye. As an effigy for the grieving process, Jill herself couldn't have done better.

I considered whether to call a halt to B's sessions with Jill. Counselling, confidentiality clauses, Kubler-Ross – these were not words I necessarily wanted to be associated with my little, carefree girl. And did I really want school – that safe haven to which she skipped every morning – to become synonymous with them too?

I consulted the only people qualified to advise me on the subject – my online WAY Widowed and Young comrades. Their experiences suggested that on the whole, counselling through play for bereaved kids was a positive thing. While it didn't solve the underlying problem (what could?), it permitted the child time and space to think about the lost parent. On that basis, I made the decision to see the six weeks through.

B and I had settled into the rhythm of village life, dancing on the tightrope above the safety net of our new, local friends. I had seen less and less of my 'old' friends, those stalwarts who knew me pre- and post-Mark, and I had been lax in keeping in touch. This had partly been a conscious move. While I didn't want to lose them, I found them increasingly difficult to be around. They'd been with Mark and me since we first met in the Hancock pub in Newcastle. They'd waved us off as we departed on our various adventures together. They were on our wedding pictures. Two of them were 'odd-parents' to our child. Each time we got together I felt the M-shaped hole more keenly, that the air between us was heavy with what was not being said.

Some friends dropped off completely, remaining as silent observers to my agony on social media sites, occasionally 'liking' a photograph of B or Brucie. Photos which testified to the fact that I was still going without having to probe further. Others maintained a toe in the mire, but from behind the safety of a birthday card or an email. A hardcore clung on with gritty determination. They knew me well enough to recognise my self-imposed exile for what it was – not a rejection of them, but mechanism for protecting myself against the pain.

These hardy pep-perennials kept a distance, but like a cavalry, they swooped in whenever they felt I was sinking too far in.

'I'm coming up this weekend,' my chum Beccy would text.

'Oh rats, I'm busy!' I'd text back.

'Next weekend then? Or midweek. I've got some holiday to take. I'll come then.'

'Thing is, I'm not terribly good company at the moment.'

'I'm not coming up for your company. I just want to see you and B.'

Cornered, I would find myself the following weekend awaiting the arrival of the 5.50 from King's Cross, frustrated at having to deal with the well-meaning vagaries of a good friend. But then she'd step off the train, arms outstretched and we'd fit with laughter even though nothing had been said.

My friend Anna reinvented herself as my protector, swinging a spiked flail in the face of anyone who challenged my vulnerability. Most of the time her armoury wasn't required. The trauma and the grief I had suffered were usually enough for people to treat me with a velvet glove. But one person who felt the full force was a detractor from an entirely unexpected source: the widow community.

I had finally taken Deb's advice and started writing an online diary about my life since the loss of Mark. Initially I had written anonymously about, among other things, my fling with K.P. Davis, my fears for the future, my admiration for Gary Barlow's insights as a dirge writer. And Deb was right – as I was still on the waiting list for a counsellor, it offered somewhere to go and let off plumes of pent-up grief. It was also a way for friends to check in with how I was doing without the awkwardness of having to ask.

Given the uniquely isolating nature of young widowhood, it occurred to me that I might find some kindred spirits in the ether. So I posted a link to my diary on the widow website Anna had found in the early days of my grief, whose online forum had been such a lifeline to me.

At 9 p.m. on the day I'd posted the link to my diary, I received notification from the site's founder telling me that it had been removed. I was unwittingly in breach of the terms and conditions, which stated that the posting of links to external sites was forbidden. It was a charge that I accepted. But the message that followed was more difficult to comprehend. My diary was ill-written, she told me, and the content 'moronic'. I wasn't even brave enough to reveal my own name. Furthermore, I was banned from using the site with immediate effect.

I read and reread the message in shock and disbelief. Was I somehow sullying Mark's memory by writing about my life since He'd gone? Surely I must be doing something very wrong if someone who had been in my position saw fit to respond in such a way? How could a site which had provided so much comfort now be the source of such bitterness? And what was I going to do now I was no longer allowed access to one of my most important means of support?

I told Anna about the founder's message.

'Hmm. Forward it through to me, let me have a read.'

Within a minute of sending her the email, Anna called me. 'I think I might drop this woman a line this afternoon, if you don't mind?'

Anna spared me the details of her interaction with my detractor, but I know it would have been dignified, controlled and devotedly defensive of my position.

Anna's intervention didn't secure me a place back into the group – I was never allowed to post on the site again – but the incident was a salutary lesson for me. I had assumed that in entering widowhood, that underground 'club that no one wants to join', I would find only kindness and unconditional understanding. But as with the 'outside world', there are hierarchies of tenure to be observed, ways of expressing grief which are palatable to some widows and not to others.

Further to the founder's message, I re-examined the ways in which I was expressing mine. I seriously considered abandoning the blog altogether, but once more, the cavalry of friends and family rallied and convinced me that I must keep writing it. Along with the pills, it had become an integral part of my therapy; it would have been devastating to let it go.

And what's more, it was resonating with other widows. I wrote about how much my alcohol consumption had increased since bereavement:

'*I wonder how many people in our situation would admit to this,*' was one widow's response.

'*I need to find myself a leaky tap!*' came another, after my revelations about the plumber.

In fact, many months later, my online diary went on to win in the Best Personal Blog category at the Blog North Awards. So the conclusion I came to was this: the only people who mattered in this were me, my daughter and Mark. The latter was fiercely proud of me in life. I believe He would have been equally proud of me in death. So what did it matter what anyone else thought?

I missed the text ping-pong. I missed the contact. Yes, OK, I missed the meaningless, roughneck sex. I made contact with K.P. Davis again on a spurious pretext (did he know any tilers who would come and do a job for me?). Inevitably, the lure of extra-curricular sex with a horny widow was too much for him, even despite her tendencies towards instability and late-night accusatory texting. So he saw fit to come over to assess the size of the problem himself.

We both played the game – rubbing our chins and looking at the wall behind the sink, debating how much it would be likely to cost and what sort of tile I should go for. It took fifteen minutes of this before we ended up on our usual spot on the stairs. I had toned down the underwear (this was *entirely* impromptu after all), but K.P. didn't seem to care. In fact, he didn't linger long enough to notice.

'How's it goin' anyway?' he asked, as he pulled his jeans up from where they had gathered around his ankles.

'Oh, fine, fine,' I replied, trying to look smouldering while refastening my bra. 'Have you got time for a cuppa?'

'Nah, I'm on a job,' he said. 'Glass of water'd be nice though.'

I watched as he drained the water in one mouthful. His phone, to which he was surgically attached, rang and he paced about the room as he took the call. His eyes darted about like minnows. He had a look of the hunted about him, which I suppose is what comes of being well-versed in extra-curricular affairs. He wore dusty jeans and white trainers, and his massive six-foot-four frame seemed almost too big for my dainty female-only household.

He ended the call and came towards me. I wrapped my arms around his waist and pushed my face into him. 'Gotta go,' he said. 'Fuckin' tiler hasn't turned up to this job ah've just finished.'

'Sack him then,' I said.

'If it's not him, it'd be some other waste of space. They're all the same, man.' He bent down and kissed the top of my head. 'Ah'll be in touch.'

As he walked off down the path, I didn't know whether I would see K.P. Davis again. But I realised I didn't really care. In the months that had elapsed since my episode of neediness, something had changed within me, and it wasn't until that moment that I became aware of it.

K.P. Davis had been essential in terms of my own 'grief process'. He had stepped into my pebble-dashed home just when I needed him. He provided me with momentary respite from the pain, given me something to look forward to each week and helped assuage some of the fears which had become synonymous with sex.

But in reprising the affair after a hiatus, I was able to see it for what it was. I didn't miss him – I missed the thought of him. And the reality was hollow, shrill and vaguely ridiculous.

Finally I received word that a counselling appointment had become available with Trisha. I was to attend the following week. Trisha's unfeasibly wrinkle-free face belied her fifty-two years (it was genetics, she told me. Her mother's face was the same) and she wore a gold Welsh dragon on a thin chain around her neck, which bounced around furiously whenever she got excited.

Trisha knew my story – she'd been in attendance at Deb's group sessions as a support counsellor – and consequently I knew her well enough to know that our client–counsellor relationship was going to work.

We decided to start by dealing with the recurrent images of a dead Mark that my brain simply wouldn't erase. No matter how hard I tried, my thoughts kept snaggling on the doughy face, the staring eyes, the thumb nerve twitching as His body shut down. And they had the power to paralyse me, these thoughts: walking down the street, washing my hair in the shower, in the fast lane on the motorway.

'You're never going to erase the images,' Trisha told me. 'What we need to work on, though, is removing the power they have to destabilise you. So you need to be able to acknowledge them, but not be incapacitated by them.'

'How do we do that?'

'There is a method used in counselling called Exposure Therapy. It involves the client retelling the story surrounding the traumatising images, but in the present tense. The counsellor will act as a prompt, asking sensory-based questions to help with total immersion in the scenario. The narrative is recorded and then played back to the client.'

I eyed Trisha with suspicion. 'And how does that help?'

'The idea is that by hearing a detailed description of the images, recounted in the present, yet with a level of detachment, the client is able to process them in a different, more constructive way.' Trisha went on, 'That said, some counsellors don't like to use it, because they fear that it risks re-traumatising the client.'

'I really don't want to be re-traumatised, Trisha,' I said. 'Short of a lobotomy, isn't there any other way?'

'There are many other ways, but I am an advocate of this one. For the type of client you are, I think it could be very beneficial. Would you be prepared to at least give it a go?'

I placed complete trust in Trisha, and agreed to try it. Besides, how much worse could it get?

Trisha brought out her Dictaphone and placed it on the desk between us.

'I'm going to begin by asking you some sensory-based questions about the day leading up to Mark's death. If you want to stop at any time, just say the word and I'll stop the tape. I suggest we do about ten minutes, then we'll listen to the tape. Does that feel OK?'

'Yes.'

Trisha began with her first question: 'What's the date today, Lucie?'

I closed my eyes. 'It's 11 February, 2012.'

It's the eleventh of February 2012. It's a freezing cold day, the snow is thick on the ground outside. We are going to Mother's today. My grandmother died five days ago, and we're going to offer Mother some support in advance of the funeral. We all get up together – Mark, B and me – and go downstairs for breakfast.

What is Mark wearing?

He is wearing his black dressing gown; He's barefoot, naked beneath. I talk to my friend Kim on the phone. I tell her I am apprehensive about my grandmother's funeral. I have never been to the funeral of a family member before, I don't know what it's going to be like.

What happens then?

I'm trying to get organised, but B wants to play shops. I ask Mark if He can play it with her while I have a shower. He then goes to take a shower and I sit on the toilet and talk to Him while He's in there. 'I'm a bit worried about this funeral,' I tell him. 'I've never been to one for a family member before.'

How does Mark respond to this?

Don't worry, pet,' He tells me. 'It's rotten, but I'll be there.'
We get dressed and prepare to leave.

Tell me what Mark is wearing.

Jeans, a red plaid shirt and His grey jacket. The postman
knocks at the door with a delivery for Mark – it's new
gear for His bike; a helmet and some thick padded gloves.
Before we leave the house, Mark shows me three pictures
of B He has taken on His phone that morning. They are
close-up shots of her face, all of them smiling. I tell Mark
I want to listen to some Neil Young on the way up to
Mother's. He gets the CD from the shelf upstairs and goes
into the garage to pack the car.

He opens the garage and we drive slowly out of the
village. I am in the back seat, behind Mark, B is seated
alongside her daddy in the front. Neil Young is playing
– 'A Man Needs a Maid' – and Mark says Young would
never have got away with such a song nowadays.

Describe the weather.

The sun is high and the sky is clear. The roads are icy.
Take care, I tell Mark, perhaps go via York instead of
over the moors.

'Heart of Gold' comes on and Mark says, 'Listen
to this one, B, it's part of your education,' and she says,
'Why?' and He says, 'It's a song that makes us think of
people we love.' We drive on and B says she needs a wee,
we stop in a lay-by, but it goes into a dip, this lay-by, and
I tell Mark not to drive too far in for fear that we might
get stuck in the snow. I get B out of the car and the air is
frozen around us, she does her wee and we hurriedly get
back in the car and keep driving.

Whereabouts are you now?

We're driving past the White Horse on the moors and
Mark points it out to B. We keep driving and B asks
for a breadstick. 'Breadstick for Daddy too,' Mark
says, holding His hand out for one. The chimneys of
Middlesbrough come into view and we say, 'Look, B,
Grandma's chimneys, not far now.' We pull up outside my
sister's house and I tell Mark to let me and B out, and to
go and park the car while we run in.

Describe what you can smell as you enter the house.

I smell pizza cooking.

What sort of pizza?

It's got red peppers and cooked meat on it, salami or chorizo. Mark comes in through the back door and says, 'Hiya' to Mother. She steps forward and hugs Him and says, 'Here He is, my boy.'

It's 1.30 p.m., the sky is white, all around us there is ice.

Trisha stopped the tape. I was sobbing through my closed eyes. Details of our last hours together, minute details I had neglected as unimportant, as one does when there's nothing at stake, now suddenly impossible to relive.

'I can't do this, Trisha,' I said, still not opening my eyes.

'No,' I heard her say. 'We'll end there for today.'

My tissue was sodden and black with mascara, and I imagined bluebirds to be circling around my head like poor old tomcat when he is smacked by a frying pan in the cartoons.

'That was harder than I thought,' I said. 'And the worst bit's yet to come.'

'It is very powerful. We'll take it at your own pace. See how you feel next time.'

In the event, we never got to the worst bit. Trisha and I continued our sessions, but we never returned to the Exposure Therapy. Talking through the feelings and actions associated with grief is one thing, but some things are just too hard to relive.

It was only a matter of time before an invitation to an event involving all of Mark's friends came through. It had taken more than a year, yet there it was, on my doormat. The christening of Catherine, first-born child of Andrew and Annabel, a baby that Mark hadn't lived long enough to know was even in the offing. I wondered if Andrew and Annabel were secretly having the same thoughts as me: that it would be somehow distasteful of me to attend. After all, Andrew was Mark's friend. I had been invited, I was sure, out of a sense of duty. But did they really want me hovering over the event like a barrage balloon, just waiting for someone to crash into me with the wrong choice of words?

Mark's friend John called. I had scarcely heard from him since Mark's death. Mark was one of the only people I knew who still had a complete set of friends intact from school days. These fellas meant the world to Him, as they came to mean to me. It had been hard for me to see them since Mark's death though. Not only because they reminded me of Mark, but because I harboured a shameful and utterly unjustifiable sense of resentment towards them – *why wasn't it you who died, and not Him?*

'Hiya, Luce!' John said. 'Listen, Fran and I wondered if you would like to stay at our place after the christening? We could have a bite of lunch here then head off together if you like. Just a thought.'

'Thing is, John...' I began. A series of well-rehearsed excuses ran through my head. I'd been in the business of the avoidance of these people for months. Concentrating on my new life, with my new friends, whose presence didn't cut through me every time I saw them. 'Well, I was thinking I might not go. You know, it might be difficult, for everyone.'

In an uncharacteristic show of lack of reserve, John announced: 'No. You are coming. And you are staying with us. And B is coming too. We haven't seen you for ages and we are looking forward to catching up. Come to ours for twelve. OK?'

'OK.'

But as the day approached, trepidation began to creep in. Mark would be painfully conspicuous by His absence. People would console me on my loss. And the last time we were all together was at a funeral. Mark's. Furthermore, this would be the first time I had seen Paul in months. I ransacked my brain for an excuse to cancel. B was ill. No – didn't want to tempt fate. I was ill – no, idem.

But then I got to thinking. I had become selfish in my bereaved state, judgmental about people I cared about. They wanted me there to share in the day, and as a representative of Mark. This day was not about me, it was about Andrew and Annabel and their new baby, and that must be my focus. That, and the bottles of wine that I knew would be waiting at the after-party. I opened my wardrobe, the one with Mark in the bottom, and scoured the rail for a party dress.

'You look great,' said John, pulling me out a chair at the dining table.

People would say this to me: 'You look great.' Was it the start of a sentence which would conclude 'considering your husband dropped dead eighteen months ago?' if the person saying it could bring themselves to complete it? Or did it mean 'Jesus, YOU look great,' the inference being that my sprightly demeanour meant I was somehow 'getting over' my husband's death? Or was it another one of those platitudes that people feel compelled to wheel out when they can't bring themselves to admit the truth: that you've aged ten years since they last saw you and your purple party dress is hanging off your diminished frame like a set of billowing rags. Whatever John's motivation, I thanked him for the compliment and sat down before a tower of bacon stotties.

In the hour before we left for the church, John, Fran and I sat around the table and talked. Our daughters were born within thirteen days of each other (in a fateful echo of John and Mark's birthdates, which are ten days apart), so over the past five years we had compared everything from shit-viscosity to ferocity of tantrums and all the delights in between. We'd been on holidays together, we witnessed John's proposal to Fran on the steps of the Sacré Cœur. Consequently, the empty place opposite me at the table that lunchtime seemed to be waggling its dick at me more than it usually did. We were a foursome, and the fourth member was missing. It was a relief when John announced the arrival of the taxi, and we set off for the church.

The christening was taking place at the church in which Andrew and Annabel had got married four years before. Mark had been an usher at this wedding; almost exactly a year to the day before the obscene insult that would ultimately steal His life. I found out I was pregnant with B immediately after this wedding too – I had cried to Mark, worrying that my champagne consumption may have somehow jeopardised the health of my unborn cluster of cells. And here I sat, in the same pew as I had four years previously, holding the hand of that cluster of cells, but without the man who made her.

Religious services, like any solemn occasion, always bring out the heckling spectator inside my head, and this one was no different. The priest (vicar? Rector? Who *is* that guy in the dress?) was one of those hip religious types, who tells knowing jokes while dousing the screaming baby with water. Sarcasm and mirth stampeded around in my head, and the only person who would have been able to hear them, via that strange telepathy that only couples who are totally in tune with each other seem to have, was currently in a box in my wardrobe with no means of escape.

I found myself gazing around the church. It was a beautiful fourteenth-century edifice with pitted oak beams overhead and lovingly hewn columns leading the eye to the elaborate filigreed altar, over which a splayed Christ hung on his cross. As the service progressed I felt myself shrinking further into the pew as if a weight were hanging around my heart. The more I watched the priest, the more I became mesmerised, and I suddenly felt compelled to talk to him, to ask for his help in dealing with this great burden I was carrying.

The main part of the service ended and we formed a circle around the font at the back of the church to watch the baptism. Eyes fluttered about, not daring to alight on me or B, and I concentrated on the baby and the priest and the beauty of the font. At the end of the ceremony, when it was time to file out, I heard Andrew say 'See you back at the house' to the priest, and I wondered whether this might be the opportunity, almost heaven-sent, to offload my encumbrance to a man of the cloth.

We raced back to Andrew's place, the location for the after-party, and my chance to tap in to some divine deliverance. I had bought Andrew and Annabel a cherry blossom by way of a christening gift. It was symbolic of Mark and a lasting tribute that they could nurture as a reminder of this day. At least, that was the thinking when I bought it. As I staggered into the house with it, heels sinking into the grass with every footstep, the one remaining blossom flittered off its branch and into the mud. I presented Andrew and Annabel with a twig in a bow.

Mark, it turned out, was not as conspicuous by His absence as I had feared. With so many familiar faces milling about, I could easily convince myself that He was somewhere else in the crowd. As I sunk the first glass of champagne, I simultaneously felt the ragged edges of my tension begin to smooth out. The burden that I had been so keen to offload on the priest was becoming less weighty with each glass I drained. In fact, I had forgotten all about the priest until I saw him staggering off up the driveway and into a taxi two hours after he'd arrived.

No one mentioned Mark. Instead, they marked His absence by taking care of me. They kept a watchful eye over B; ensured I always had a dance partner; made sure I ate, had enough wine, and got home safely. Paul reverted to the friend I had known and loved prior to Mark's death. After an edgy 'Hello,' it became clear that we had both moved beyond the tensions of the previous year. The history and unspoken understanding embedded within the friendships meant that instinctively, they were all *in loco* Mark. Much later, after the dance floor had emptied and the last of the bottles was drained, when I had time in the back of the taxi to lie back and reflect, I realised that for my daughter and me, those fellas always will be.

A Final Resting Place?

JULY–OCTOBER 2013

July, and the end of B's first school year loomed, along with the conclusion of the six-week course of counselling with Jill. I was invited into the final session in order to discuss the situation 'going forward'. Jill handed me a wad of paperwork: copies, in fact, of the documentation that my daughter had been required to sign. I glanced at the top sheet. There were a series of questions directed at 'the client'.

Do you agree to have the counselling that is being offered to you?

Jill had written, on behalf of B: *Yes, I agree to having the counselling that is being offered to me.*

Why do you want counselling?

Jill had written: *Because I want to talk about my daddy.*

B had never expressed an awareness of 'wanting to talk about' her daddy to me. There had been isolated comments, queries, outbursts, but they were set within a context of confectionery consumption, or playing with Barbie. But the conscious desire to set time aside for reflection now seemed very much like the preserve of adulthood. Looking at all that paperwork, I couldn't help feeling that I had foisted this on to her.

I looked at my little girl, perched on the arm of the settee in that hot little room, waiting for Jill and I to agree the next steps before she could be released back into the classroom and the concerns of a five-year-old child. Perhaps she hadn't needed this after all. I had been fumbling, unsure of how to deal with my own grief, never mind that of a little girl who had witnessed her daddy's last breaths. I had believed, or rather hoped, that Jill would be the answer.

Jill pointed at the things on the table – spoils of the six weeks they had spent together 'talking about daddy'. The memory box was there; it had formerly housed shoes, but now it twinkled and shone in its wrapping of gold paper and sparkles.

'Look at how beautifully B has decorated the box! Would you like to show Mummy what's inside?' Jill asked.

B jumped down and opened the lid. Another teddy. A notepad. A set of crayons. A packet of tissues. A photograph of my husband with B on his shoulders. The box should be kept somewhere safe – under the bed, perhaps, or on a special shelf – ready to be brought out should B ever feel she needed it. It could also be used to store items relating to Daddy; a sample of His aftershave or one of his shirts.

'This is Daddy's special box, isn't it, B?' said Jill. B nodded and closed the lid. 'I would like to suggest that we leave it there. I don't feel that at this point B would benefit from any further intervention. She's doing great.' Jill pushed her specs up on the bridge of her nose.

I took the box and the paperwork and thanked Jill for all the intervening she had done up to now. I was relieved that in her professional opinion no more would be required. That evening, I handed B the box and asked her where she would like to store it. She took it from me, emptied it of all its affecting items and sat in it. Was this a metaphor? Was she demonstrating a desire to somehow be in the box with Daddy? Perhaps Jill's intervening had been more damaging than I'd thought.

'What are you doing?' I asked.

'This is my boat,' she announced. 'Can you make me an oar?'

The summer holidays burst into bloom, and for the second time since Mark had died I was surrounded by the cacophony of families preparing to spend quality time together. This time around, I was prepared. With a year to gird myself, I felt somehow less needy, more determined.

According to my online WAY Widowed and Young friends, it was possible to go away alone with your offspring. I hadn't considered this as an option before, mainly because I was worried about all the risks that would need to be assessed for such a trip, the most pressing of which being the possibility of suffering a panic attack in front of my daughter. That, and given my current rate of alcohol consumption, the likelihood of me getting blind drunk and not remembering how to get us both home.

This year, though, perhaps we would do it. She and I, lone warriors in the war against absent husbands and daddies. Cruises are a popular choice for singletons with kids. By all accounts, these vessels are holiday parks on water, right down to the powerlessness to escape your fellow holidaymakers over dinner or in the Jacuzzi. The distinct advantage over the holiday park, though, was that if you chose the right cruise, you would only be accompanied by other single people, and therefore spared the despotism of The Couple in the cabin next door.

Here again, I found myself considering a holiday option which before now would have been an abhorrence. If Mark could have borne witness to my Internet searches relating to cruise liners, he would have had one thing to say: 'Oh no, pet!' Nevertheless, I searched. If the cost wasn't enough to put me off, though, the minimum amount of time spent at sea was. I fancied we could probably manage three nights, a bimble around the Med, perhaps, still within rowing distance of land. But these trips were seven-night expeditions! Sometimes extending to fourteen if you wanted to take in parts of the African mainland and dinner at the captain's table.

The more I searched, the more indecisive I became. I wasn't so sure I was ready to go fully solo after all. In the end, I booked us two tickets to London. We would travel down alone. Take in the sights alone. Circumnavigate the London Eye alone. Watch a performance of *The Lion King* alone. Perhaps even venture into the terrifying underworld of the Tube alone. But we would stay with my friend Beccy in Crystal Palace, just in case.

There was a sense of freedom as we boarded the train at Newcastle. Renewal was in the air. In taking this first journey together as a twosome, I could feel my self-imposed shackles loosening their grip. We waved goodbye to Mother, who was no doubt conflicted by the thought of the trip yet knew better than to express it, and chugged triumphantly off over the railway bridge southward. I'd brought lunch, sweets, books, paper, pens; booty for a successful and fun journey between mother and daughter. Sandwiches were plundered by Durham, sweets were devoured by Darlington, but it didn't matter. We were going on our holidays, and so far, the train was running on time!

The brakes squealed just outside Peterborough. We ground to a halt and a hubbub of disgruntled voices and tutting immediately swelled up. The train guard apologised for this slight delay. We would hopefully be on our way very shortly. I felt a nub of anxiety begin to throb in my gut. Instinctively, I looked about for the emergency window and considered how I might best manoeuvre myself and B out of it, should I have cause.

Half an hour later, the engine whirred and we edged slowly into the station. The train guard came over the tannoy again, apologising once more for the delay. This time, however, there was no hope for getting on our way any time soon. In fact, the train would not be going any further. A body had been found on the track and we were now skirting the periphery of a crime scene. No trains would enter or leave Peterborough station for the rest of the day. Adding my voice to the tutting and the disgruntlement, I hustled B and our luggage off the train and stood on the platform, unsure what to do next.

My mind turned to the poor bastard on the track. Whether they'd been accidentally hit, committed suicide or dumped there, someone who loved them was going to receive a call soon to tell them they had died. Shock would instantly numb the receiver of the news. And then death's circus would begin. But the Circus Masters would be ready to swoop in and orchestrate it all. A Dennis. A Lee. A Xanthe. A Judith. The grief and the trauma would be facilitated until the moment that the tea and Bourbons ran out. Then the bereaved one would have to battle it out alone.

'Come on, darling!' I chivvied, hauling our case up the ramp towards the taxi rank. It would no doubt cost a fortune, but I didn't care. I wanted away from this crime scene, from the blare of the ambulance, the urgency of the police cars.

We joined the queue and ended up sharing a cab with two ageing soaks and a student who was trying to get back to Brighton. B couldn't take her eyes off the soaks and their knobbly red hooters, but they didn't seem to notice or care. They chortled all the way to St John's Wood, whereupon we were ejected from the cab and told that a Tube would be quicker to King's Cross from this point.

B and I – battle-worn urban guerrillas – took our seats on the Tube and finally squealed into King's Cross station three hours later than scheduled. Laden with the weight of baggage, fatigue and the sole responsibility for a small child, I limped out of the station and saw Beccy's raspberry-coloured charabanc waiting for us in the lay-by. She got out of the car and waved. I felt tears flood my eyes; how I wished it were Him waiting with a smile, a kiss and a secure arm. But how good it felt to see my dear friend after our epic journey. And thank God we didn't opt for the cruise.

Despite its crippling effect on my bank balance, London provided a welcoming stomping ground for our first foray into semi-solo travel. The traffic, the noise, the crowds eclipse the loneliness, urging you on when the low ebb descends. You have to be on your toes. And just when you think you might be edging towards a bout of melancholy, it serves up a quirky little watering hole in which to get sozzled.

Grief, however, wasn't going to allow our first holiday as a twosome to pass without making an unexpected and full-blown appearance. We had shuffled our way down a packed row of seats in the Grand Circle of the Lyceum Theatre, and were now wedged in the centre of a line of fellow theatregoers with no opportunity for a beer. It was the fault of the Lion King really – Simba, the lion cub, watches as his father is slain, and stages a vigil over the lifeless body. Given its obvious echoes with my own tragedy, I found it too easy to suspend my disbelief, and began shaking and weeping uncontrollably alongside my oblivious, Haribo-munching daughter. I'd pulled myself round enough to ask, 'Did you enjoy that, darling?' as we shuffled out of the auditorium, and she turned to me and said without hesitating: 'No.'

Eighty quid for a prime-view ticket well spent then.

Thankfully our journey home didn't involve dead bodies or crime scenes, just a flaccid sandwich and an overpriced coffee from the bar. We watched as southern skies turned into those of the north, and as the Tyne Bridge swung into view from the train, I felt a lurch of relief. We'd been away from the homeland and survived. Mother's face was waiting on the platform, sewn up tight, but when she saw us waving through the window, it unravelled.

We loaded our baggage into Mother's car and began the short drive back to the village, and I looked around at the backdrop to my life that I hadn't seen in four long days. It felt as if I was rediscovering the outside world again, taking baby steps, while at the same time my desire to see it was retracting. I seemed to sicken for home whenever I was away, as if the place were as essential to my battered physiology as blood and bone.

When we got back to our little pebble-dashed house and the ecstatic pup who awaited us within, I made a silent vow never to leave again – at least not for long. We'd proved we could do it, my daughter and me. What is more, like everyone else in the village, we'd had a family summer holiday too.

A message landed in my inbox from someone I'd apparently been talking to at Andrew and Annabel's christening. Only some photos on Facebook and his word could attest to this, because red wine had erased any memory of our meeting. His name was Jamie and ten years ago he had lost his girlfriend, suddenly, and he wanted to tell me that despite what I had told him at the christening, I really was doing OK. Furthermore, I was going to survive.

I hadn't the faintest idea what I had told him at the christening, but I imagined it would have included my feelings of desperation, the sense that I was 'taking one step forward and two steps back'. Nevertheless, I thanked him and wrote back, asking how long it had taken him before he began to feel like a normal functioning member of the human race again.

'It happens and you don't realise it. You'll always experience the jags of pain, but the time in between them becomes longer. You'll never be the same person you were, though. But it'll make you stronger. You become more resilient, less bothered by what people think. For what it's worth, I think you're doing really well.'

It was a well-worn platitude in all of this – *you're doing really well* – however I was prepared to accept it from someone who had been similarly bereaved. In fact, Jamie's words caused me to reflect. I looked back at the road I had travelled since that night in February and was surprised to see how far I'd come. In fact, I hadn't just been surviving. I had achieved things. I had organised the funeral of the love of my life, pretty much single-handedly. I had sorted His affairs. I had moved home, started a new life in a new village, taken on a dog, seen my daughter through her first day at school. I had started a new job, embarked on a course of study. And I had just returned from our first holiday as a twosome. I had plundered my inner resources and found that resilience and mettle I had so revered in Mary Callery. I hadn't been prepared to admit how far I'd travelled, for fear that it would translate as 'moving on' or 'moving away' from my beloved. But for the first time in all this, I forgave myself the recklessness and permitted myself to feel proud of how I was coping.

Are you taking me for a drink then?

Jamie and I had been messaging for weeks, yet still hadn't had a conversation. I had sensed a flicker of flirtation between us and decided to capitalise on it. After all, my interactions with men over the last eighteen months had been limited to a series of grunts and the odd suggestive text. A proper conversation with someone who might just provide me with a cuddle to accompany his kiss felt long overdue.

Aren't you worried I might bore you with more crap advice? came the reply.

It may be crap advice, but at least it's crap advice from someone who is well placed to impart crap advice, as opposed to most people who impart crap advice despite not having the faintest clue what they're on about.

OK. Let's go for a drink then. And are you up for dinner too, or will you eat beforehand?

Mother could barely contain herself when I asked her if she would mind babysitting on Saturday night as I was going out for dinner with a friend who was a boy.

'His name is Jamie and he is a fellow widower, of sorts. Don't get excited, Mother,' I told her.

'I'm not,' she lied.

Later that day, Beth called. 'Mother's been asking me what I know about this Jamie.'

'For fuck's sake.'

'She only wants to see you happy—'

'I'm going for a meal, not marrying the guy.'

'I know but—'

I hung up and harrumphed about the house like a hormonal teenager. Typical of Mother, I thought. Desperate for me to 'move on', to 'heal', to 'get better', without the slightest idea of the confused emotions that were involved in agreeing to going out with another man. To punish Mother, I thought, I would not tell her anything further about Jamie or our date. (Which wasn't a date, incidentally. It was two people with a shared experience who were going to sit opposite each other at a table and consume food.)

That said, in the week leading up to the meal I had my nails done, coloured my hair and carefully selected a dress from Beth's wardrobe in readiness. My hairdresser, a heavily tattooed gay man from Gateshead and a demon for gossip, knew something was up.

'Oh yeah? You on a promise or something?' he said, as he snipped the errant ends of my hair off.

'I'm going out for a meal with a friend who is a boy,' I replied, placing my nose further into my magazine.

'Nice, is he?'

'Hmmm.'

The Village People were even worse. Sitting in our usual arrangement in the pub on Friday night, there was much vaudeville-style nudging and innuendo. As was usually the case, Ned didn't attempt to keep a lid on his smutty excitement. 'Don't sleep with him on your first date,' he said.

'Ned!' squealed Joanne.

Everyone laughed.

'I'm not like you, you know, Ned.'

'We're just, you know, pleased you're going out for a nice meal with someone who sounds, well, very nice.' Joanne tempered.

'Absolutely,' said Jeanette. 'You deserve to have some fun.'

'It's not a date date, you know,' I said. 'He's just a friend, who happens to be a boy.'

A row of heads nodded. 'Oh yes, of course. Just enjoy it for what it is.'

'I've got no expectations,' I continued, 'and furthermore, I don't want a relationship with anyone.'

'Look,' said Joanne, 'don't overthink it. He sounds like a nice person who has been through something similar. It doesn't have to mean anything more than that.'

'Exactly,' I said. 'Anyway, enough about me. Ned. I believe it's your round.'

We met in The Champagne Bar, a much-vaunted, newly opened drinks 'venue' in Newcastle. We Geordies love these places. Leatherette-seated luxury at north-east prices, with a real strawberry on the side. And always within tottering distance of a chippy. I arrived first and ordered two flutes of fizz.

I saw Jamie blow in at the far side of the bar. He was dressed in a disappointingly not-on-the-pull type of manner, which made me wonder whether this meant we really were going to be talking about the misery of widowhood all night. The conversation was polite to begin with, but after two more flutes, it got round to the sticky subject of sudden death of a partner and all its associated horrors.

A decade ago, Jamie had come home to find his girlfriend of three years lying dead on the bedroom carpet. The reasons for her death were found to be natural causes, but Jamie remembered little about the immediate aftermath or the funeral. It was, he said, a blur. In fact, his memories seemed to catch up with him only at around eighteen months, when he found himself on a plane to Thailand with a round-the-world ticket in his pocket.

'I fucked around recklessly. Was drunk a lot of the time. Smoked lots of pot. Pretty predictable, I guess.'

I was beginning to realise that actually, these behaviours *were* pretty predictable in grief. Increasingly, my online widowed 'friends' were admitting to similar things. Clearly, I was not alone in some of what I considered to be shameful behaviours: drinking until I couldn't remember how I got to bed; rutting anything that moved like a rampant pit-bull; spending money without regard for the consequences; taking up smoking again (but strictly other people's cigarettes – I wouldn't dream of buying any of my own at that price).

In fact, my counsellor had told me that many of the clients she saw who had been similarly bereaved displayed the same traits. One woman, who had lost a child, was disgusted with herself for getting paralytic and ending up down a back alley with a stranger. My counsellor described it as the third 'F' instinct, along with Fight and Flight. An evolutionary hangover from our reptilian brain, apparently. Or so she'd heard at a conference. But it sounded convincing enough to me.

Jamie and I moved from The Champagne Bar into a restaurant, and the change in air brought about a change in conversation. We didn't mention our respective losses for the rest of the evening. I sat there, opposite a member of the other half of the human race, and actually allowed myself to enjoy his company.

He saw me to the taxi queue and we exchanged a kiss and our phone numbers. We would, we resolved, do this again.

I had spent much of the summer prodding at my keyboard, trying to shape my research from Long Island into something resembling an interesting narrative. I was feeling overwhelmed by the material. Pages and pages of information gathering dust on a shelf in my office, on the hard drive of my computer and still yet to be transcribed from my Dictaphone. Where does one begin to interpret a life?

I decided to start with where I felt most kinship with Mary: bereavement and loss. Since returning from the States I had thought a lot about the lock of hair, and the series of letters and photographs of the dead girl I had been privy to in the archive. In fact, I found I had become increasingly fixated by Caroline. Why would anyone willingly end their life, when others don't get given a choice in the matter?

I had made photocopies of some of Caroline's letters and spent a long time rereading them back at my own desk, in my pebble-dashed house. In one letter to her mother she writes:

I am the first to admit that something is distinctly wrong with me – I shall continue my solitary and lonely existence + probably jump into the Seine or some such thing in the near future [...] Mother forgive me for being the way I am – I guess I'm just a rotten lot. (13 August 1951)

Written fifteen years before Caroline finally jumped from a window, these words must have opened old wounds for Mary had she chosen to look over them again following her daughter's death. Guilt, anger and regret must have converged with equal force. But the letters, and the way they charted Caroline's journey to its tragic conclusion, represented something that I yearned for after Mark's death: an insight into how He *really* felt about His illness, and some written instructions as to what the hell I should do in the event of His death.

How would He have wanted me to grieve? Where would He want His ashes to be placed? What decisions would He have objected to? (Aside from having Gary Barlow sing at the committal.) Yet while we both knew it had been a near-miss in 2008, neither of us dared to venture a discussion about the 'D' word once He had been 'fixed'. It seemed distasteful and a little too close for comfort. Mark died intestate – proof if any were needed that He did not wish to contemplate the worst.

Caroline's letters brought to mind a letter I had found written by Winston Churchill for his wife, entitled 'In The Event of My Death' – a set of instructions, as it were, for when he was no longer around. In it, Churchill urges his wife not to dwell too much on grief, to move forward after his death, to continue to embrace and enjoy life.

With a simple hand stroke, Churchill gave his wife a gift worth more than any inheritance: he granted her 'permission' to live again after he was gone. Caroline's letters to Mary fulfilled a similar function. They became a living will of sorts, absolving anyone else of any culpability for her death. Mary may have drawn comfort from the knowledge that there was nothing she could have done.

I decided to start my book about Mary with Caroline: a short sketch about how it felt to find the curl, the letters and the photos of a dead girl. As the narrative unfurled, I found myself reminded of how powerless I was in the face of Mark's sudden death. It had waltzed in and stolen my husband without even ringing the bell. It left nothing for me to cling on to except a bitter trail of 'what ifs...?' and a set of sickening mental images of His last moments alive. And there was nothing I could do about it, except pound my fury out into the keyboard.

The school holidays had provided me with a reason to adjourn or at least slow down my writing, yet once the term started up again, I had little excuse. Except, of course, for the three hours' work a week I was still doing for the language company.

I worked Tuesday afternoons, and one hour at an after-school club on a Wednesday. But in reality, Tuesday mornings were taken up with preparation, and it took me all day Wednesday to steel myself for the onslaught of twenty seven-year-olds, just released from a long day at school. Of course, at that point, none of them had the slightest desire to speak French, preferring to roll around on the carpet in the classroom and throw paper at each other. It was, for all intents and purposes, crowd control.

'Let's sing the next song, guys!' I'd shout into the wall of screaming. *'Alouette, gentille alouette...'*

'Lucie. Lucie. Lucie. LUCIE.'

Pause song. 'Yes, Tamsin?'

'Your hair is brown underneath and blond on top.'

'Thank you, Tamsin. So... *alouette, gentille...'*

I would leave the classes feeling buffeted and abused, driving home through the twilight hating myself for ever having agreed to continue with it. It felt like a lot of work for little return. Hell, there were cleaners I knew who were earning more than I was. I knew what Mark would have counselled. Ditch it. So in the end, after much ulceration, I did.

My notice period would take me to Christmas. Then I would be free, and able to concentrate, unimpeded, on my research. I limped on, counting down the weeks with a mixture of joy and dread.

NOVEMBER–DECEMBER 2013

News came through that my grandpa – Dad's dad – had died. I had visited him just the week before. At ninety-five years old, he was the last of my grandparents to leave, yet despite my best efforts, I felt nothing in my heart when Dad called to tell me. The inevitability of it all, and what I assumed to be a topped-out grief quota, seemed to cause any emotion to drain away.

Besides, Grandpa had been a Stetson-wearing, cigar-chewing, folkloric character in life. From raggy-arsed beginnings in the back streets of Blyth, he had gone on to found of one of the foremost journalism training centres in the UK, becoming known as the Godfather by the hundreds of students he presided over. Watching him dwindle to a Kit-Kat-obsessed husk sitting in a chair in a care home had been more distressing than hearing he was free.

My sister and I had visited him on his ninety-fifth birthday. He looked through us, to a point in the distance. 'Help me,' he said.

'What do you need help with?' I asked.

'I don't know.'

He cast his eyes about wildly and then said, 'I'm waiting for my granddaughters to arrive.'

'We're here, love. We're here.'

We shared a last Kit-Kat with him. He died less than twelve hours later.

And with a death came a funeral. I had faced three of them in the past twenty-four months – my granny, who had died five days before Mark; my other gran, who died earlier in the year; and, of course, Mark. Four key family members, now extinct. Three of them, though, had died in the order of things. They had all reached the shrivelled heights of their ninetieth year, and beyond. Their deaths were sad, and left an irreparable void. But they were not tragedies. My husband, though, just into his thirty-eighth year, had been denied it all.

Grandpa's funeral took place on one of those clear-skied early December afternoons where you can see your breath on the wind. He was to be buried, intact, in the graveyard which overlooked Dad's house, with its rows of ancient, leaning gravestones like sets of rotten teeth sinking into gums. I still felt numb as we drank coffee in Dad's lounge before the ceremony, so much so that I forgot to take the beta-blocker which would permit me to read a passage at the front of the church.

'He's here,' my stepmother Karen shouted, indicating the contents of the hearse which was crawling up the track towards the church.

We drained our drinks and gathered on the path. The hearse pulled up – that now horribly familiar, highly polished beast – and I looked in its windows at the coffin. It was the same tan-coloured E-Z burn option, as recommended by Dennis. I recognised the gaudy gold handles and the unconvincing striations of the faux wood. I tried to picture the old boy, lying prone in it. I wondered if he was wearing a purple hairdresser's cape, or whether Dad too had insisted on Grandpa's own clothes. I liked to think of him wearing his Stetson, with a cigar hanging from the corner of his mouth. As I mused, my eye drifted to another box on the back seat of the hearse. This one too looked familiar – lacquered, ornate, with a bronze plaque stuck on top. It bore the words:

Margaret Brownlee

   Died 25 January 2013 aged 89 years

Within that box were the remains of another folkloric figure – my gran – who had died earlier in the year. She had a range of adjectives to describe her husband Johnnie, but only when he was out of earshot. Whenever he left the room she would flick him the 'V's, although I suspect their relationship thrived on this pastiche of mutual loathing.

'Is he a hunk or a skunk?' she asked when I first told her about my new boyfriend, Mark. 'I see he's a hunk,' she said on meeting him, unleashing a trademark wheezy laugh. When He died, she told me: 'I think about that laddie every night. I'm heartbroken, Lucie.'

And there she was, a pile of ash in a box on the back seat of the hearse, just below Johnnie's feet. The irony of the positioning was not lost.

I nudged Dan. 'Imagine what she's saying inside that box.'

Dan affected her broad Scottish accent: 'Aye, how dare ye place me on this seat 'neath the feet of that bastard!'

Some situations are so surreal, there's no option than to laugh. The four pall-bearers looked at us as we sniggered at the remains of our grandparents in the back of the car.

We all gave orations at the funeral. Johnnie had been quite a fella and we all had stuff we wanted to say about him. When someone who was larger than life reaches the age of ninety-five and has entered the latter stages of a Kit-Kat coma, people are actually waiting for them to die in order that they can talk about how great they were and permit themselves to reminisce without feeling guilty.

I reflected on my words about Johnnie and those of my siblings and Dad, and realised that all of us had been preparing for these obits for quite some time. Johnnie had become incapable of meaningful conversation, which meant visiting him was painful and a chore. He couldn't remember from one day to the next who had been to see him and who hadn't. But now, just as he was released, so were we.

How different, then, from the funeral of my husband, where I had hastily tapped out a history of our time together through a haze of disbelief. I then read it in the crematorium with as much detachment as if it had been a set of listings from the phone book. Then I listened as others talked retrospectively about the man who eleven days previously had been settling in for a can of Guinness in front of the fire at Mother's, with plans to take the car in for a service the following morning.

The hardest part of my grandpa's funeral was the graveside committal. I had never attended one before, and hadn't been prepared for how brutal it felt. It was lowering the body of a beloved one into the ground intact, effectively to rot. Watching this spectacle, and then seeing Margaret, in her box, being placed on top of him (imagine what he'd be saying about that juxtaposition), I sensed a steady deflation starting in my spirit. Grief finally showed itself and I sobbed at the cruelty of it all.

I thought about my own box of ashes, sitting there in the bottom of my wardrobe. The ones which were increasingly failing to bring me comfort, and were instead becoming a burden. I'd had an email from a family member a few days previously, asking me to give some thought as to what I wanted to do with the ashes, as they felt the need to go somewhere to be with Him and grieve.

It was an entirely reasonable request. But the email destabilised me. It had dropped into my inbox from nowhere, and I read it in a silent, red-wine-infused rage. Where was the logic in having to provide a pile of ash with 'a final resting place' in order that one can grieve effectively, or in order to find the soul of the deceased, I mused? If I chose to scatter the ashes into the sea, what then? Would He be felt in the roll of each wave? Underfoot, between each grain of sand? Would it change the outcome of the situation in any way? Make His passing more bearable? I didn't think so. But the email continued to gnaw away at my psyche, even after I'd reread and rationalised it in the sober light of day.

'Has anyone had this request from a family member with regard to ashes?' I asked the online widows. An avalanche of responses came back. Everyone, it seemed, had faced this issue, one way or another. One widow said she had finally buried her husband's ashes after a year, and had felt a sense of relief. Another balked and said, 'Why the fuck should I care about what they think? They only visited him twice a year when he was alive, why would it be any different now he's dead?'

The consensus was that I should not do anything with them until I was certain. After all, a 'final resting place' was, indeed, final. However, it was important to acknowledge the feelings of those who loved Him – after all, they were grieving too. And, I discovered, the ashes were legally mine, so I could, as my brother suggested, put them in a pipe and smoke them if I so desired. These are things they don't tell you at the funeral home.

As ever, my counsellor Trisha provided me with a sage and balanced view.

'You knew Mark as a grown man, as a husband and a father. You spent ten years of your lives together, intimately, each and every day. Others knew Him in other guises. Which means that you're all grieving for a different person. Therefore, you're never going to agree on what to do with His remains. I see this often in therapy. Very few people, especially family members, understand the need of the widowed spouse to keep hold of the ashes. But that is because very few of them have been in that position. Ultimately, the decision is yours and must not be rushed.'

The canker had taken root in my brain, though. No amount of reassurance from the ether or Trisha was going to stop the spread. The lacquered box which had provided me with comfort when I opened the wardrobe each morning, and closed it again each night, had, on receipt of an innocent and well-intentioned email, become An Issue.

*

'Let's try that restaurant on the Quayside,' Jamie said. 'Unless... well, unless it's inappropriate?'

By inappropriate, he meant liable to send me into spirals of grief due to the memories the place might evoke. Every outing we had had since The Champagne Bar had been subject to this appraisal. Being out with another man was bad enough. Being out with another man in a place I had been with Mark was akin to blasphemy. It had happened only once. Jamie and I had wandered blithely into a restaurant after a few drinks and I had realised too late that not only had Mark and I been there together, but we'd sat at the very same table in the window where we were now perusing the menu. I'd resisted the temptation to vomit spontaneously into my lap, but instead insisted we leave immediately. The waiter, a haughty-looking Albanian with sensibilities that were clearly easily bruised, was not amused.

The restaurant on the Quayside was, however, entirely appropriate. It was new, in fact, thus expunging any possibility of a trace of Mark's DNA being left on the fixtures and fittings. Jamie booked a table and we arranged to meet in town later that week.

I had seen Jamie intermittently since our first date at The Champagne Bar, but we'd been texting each other almost every day. I'd send him queries such as:

'Will the pain of losing Mark ever diminish?'

'Anxiety attacks – did you get them?'

'What did you do with the ashes?'

He'd always come back with a considered and optimistic response.

Jamie was not what I'd call 'my type'. Typically I'd gone for dark-haired men, brown-eyed, stocky... ideally white eyebrowed, with a dazzling smile. Jamie was tall and slim with a close-shaved head and a sidelong smile which he revealed only sparingly. But he was proving to be just what I needed. He was the only man I knew who had been through almost exactly what I had been through myself. He responded to my crying jags with advice like: 'This is normal, you know. And you'll always cry for Him, but the time between cries will become longer.' And I was prepared to believe him – after all, he'd been through it and survived.

We met at a pub next door to the restaurant and ordered some pre-dinner drinks. I pushed my way through the crowds to find a table, spotting one at the far side of the bar. My eyes snagged on the neighbouring table, mainly because one of the men around it had a hairdo sculpted upwards in the manner of Liberace and immediately I saw an opportunity for mirth. Except then, just in time, I spotted a face I knew. It was Dean from my online dating escapade, all those months ago.

'Retreat! Retreat!' I told Jamie, turning and hustling him away.

'What's wrong?'

'I'll tell you in a minute, just move, move!'

We shuffled to the most insalubrious corner of the pub and I inhaled my drink as quickly as I could.

'It's my online date. I can't let him see me!'

'Would he even recognise you if he saw you?'

'I have no idea, but I'm not taking the chance,' I countered. 'Finish your beer and let's get the fuck out of here.'

'Has this become an inappropriate bar then?' Jamie asked, swigging down the last of his pint.

'Yes. But for different reasons.'

We arrived at the safe haven of the restaurant and ordered Bellini aperitifs while we read the menu. It was the sort of place where the waiters casually offered you bread and olives in a way which made you think they were on the house, but then you found them unceremoniously added on the bill at the end of the meal.

'The tyranny of online dating, eh?' said Jamie. 'Problem is, you can never escape them once you've met them. Bump into them everywhere.'

'You saying that from experience, are you?'

'Bitter. Yes.'

We laughed and an elderly man on the next table, who was pulling his coat on in preparation to leave, turned to us.

'Are you two married?' he asked.

'Er. No.' I sipped my Bellini indignantly.

'In love, then?'

Christ, who was this guy? Cupid? I shook my head and looked coyly at Jamie. 'We're just friends,' I said.

The man's wife returned and he held out her coat for her. 'Shame,' he said, lifting the coat on to her shoulders. 'He's got a kind face, your friend. Looks like a nice bloke. Have a good night.'

They shambled out of the restaurant and I said to Jamie: 'Did you pay him to say that?'

Jamie shrugged and we pretended the exchange hadn't happened. But it troubled me. To the outside world, we looked like a couple. Indeed, we were of the age where it would have been safe to assume we were married. The waiters would have assumed it. Other diners, had they taken a moment to consider it, would have assumed it. Dean would have assumed it if we'd lingered long enough at the table next to his. But I wasn't ready for that kind of assumption. I was far from ready, in fact.

We ate our meal and moved on to another bar, by which point the booze had caught up with me and had turned my mood sour. I was brooding on the old man's comment and what I thought it meant in the context of my husband. A friend who was a boy felt acceptable. A reversal of those words did not. And while Jamie had always been nothing but patient, tender and understanding, I began to think that he too, like Paul all those months ago, was somehow invading a role that was not his to claim.

We ended up in a bar on the east side of the city and ordered a drink while we waited for our taxi. I couldn't muster much in the way of conversation. I was drunk and the sombre mood persisted.

Jamie tried to chivvy me out of it. 'See that picture over there?' He indicated a Manga-style drawing of a girl with a huge, bloated stomach which hung on the wall opposite to where we were sitting. 'What do you think that's all about?'

I glowered at the picture. 'It reminds me of being pregnant. Which in turn reminds me of the baby Mark and I lost in September. Which in turn reminds me of the husband I lost five months later.'

Jamie drained his pint. 'I'll go and check if the cab's there.'

I have no recollection of leaving the bar, of getting into the taxi, or of getting back to Jamie's. I woke at six the next morning, fully clothed, with him lying alongside me. I placed a hand on his shoulder but he didn't respond.

'What happened after we left the bar last night?' I asked.

'You don't remember?'

'No.'

'You weren't particularly pleasant to me.'

'How come?'

'You just went into a rage. Threatened to walk off. Told me I wasn't your husband. Which I'm fully aware of, by the way.'

I moved my hand from his shoulder and rolled on to my side. 'I really apologise. I was drunk. It's no excuse.'

He didn't say anything for a while, and then: 'It's all right. It's not like you're like that all the time. If you were, I'd have to kick your arse.'

I pulled his arm around me. 'You do know what you're getting into here, don't you?'

'Of course,' came the reply.

As I lay there in the half-light, it struck me that had I asked myself the same question, I couldn't be certain of the response.

Two weeks on from the email about the ashes, I opened the compartment of my brain which I had closed until further notice and thought about the box in the bottom of the wardrobe. What was its significance? Did it really contain the last vestiges of His soul? Was now the time to dig it out from under the clothes and scarves and consider a more permanent location for it?

Wherever it ended up had to have meaning to me and to B. It was me, after all, who had been with Him, day and night for the past ten years; me who had seen Him through the darkest days of His illness and me who had been with Him at the moment of His death. Selfish though it sounds, as far as I could see the ashes were my concern and no one else's. They were in the bottom of my wardrobe because I wanted Him nearby, and because I didn't know what else to do with them.

The ritual of placing them into the cold, hard ground, covering them with earth and marking them with a headstone would, I felt sure, leave me bereft all over again. Grandpa's body being left to that fate had been difficult enough to witness. How could I do the same with my husband? Even seeing Mark's name on a headstone would be heartbreakingly anomalous, just as it had been on that brass plaque on top of the box. Besides, I wasn't prepared to leave Him in a cemetery in the company of a load of dead people. Who the hell would want to visit Him there anyway?

I was sensing that other people felt the need for somewhere to go and 'pay their respects', though. Even if they went but once a year to lay some freesias at the site of the box's 'final resting place', the act would, it seemed, bring them solace. For the first time since Mark died, I sat down and considered my responsibility to others in respect of His death. Did I have a responsibility to others? And if so, what was it?

Yet I concluded that, ultimately, my only responsibility was to myself, my child and the memory of Mark. How other people viewed the ways I chose to express my grief was really of no consequence. They were not suffering to the same degree that I was, and had not suffered as Mark and I had in the years since His illness. I could keep the ashes in the bottom of my wardrobe until the day I died if I wanted to and no one would have the right to say anything about it.

But perhaps making a decision about a 'final resting place' would bring me comfort and a sense of release. It occurred to me that if I chose to scatter them, I would have to arrange for Dennis's box to be prised open and for the ashes to be transferred into a plastic 'sweetie jar'. I had an idea of what the remains might look like but the thought of coming face to face with them was not a prospect I relished.

That said, being scattered and turned over back into the earth, being part of the 'circle of life', had a certain romanticism about it which would help detract from the true macabre nature of the fertiliser. The only other option was to keep them in the box, which meant that any decision had to be sure and certain, because there was no going back.

Even when narrowed down, the options didn't seem any more palatable. I ricocheted between them like a puck in a pinball machine, only to reach the same conclusion:

'I just don't know what to do.'

Once again, I found myself closing the wardrobe door on the box, resolving that, for now at least, and regardless of the consequences, the ashes would have to stay put.

A text came through from Jamie one idle Sunday in December. He was cooking a lamb joint and did B and I want to come and eat it with him? Given the miserable nature of weekends for those of us who are bereaved, especially chill ones like this one in the run-up to Christmas, B, Brucie and I accepted the offer. After all, we had nothing else on.

We headed to Jamie's, and for the first time since the doomed trinity of B, me and Paul, we found ourselves enacting a rough approximation of a family afternoon. We ate dinner around a table and passed each other the salt. Jamie took charge of the Sky box and set B up with a movie by the fire. B unearthed Jamie's *Illustrated Kama Sutra* from the book shelf before we could stop her, leaving us to field one of those awkward parent–child questions about what was that funny man doing to those three women, and why? We went for a late ramble in the nearby forest and looked for holly to decorate the mantel, and Jamie carried her on his shoulders when she grew tired.

B, I sensed, still regarded Jamie with a sniff of suspicion, though. She wasn't prepared to give herself fully to the interloper. Especially one with the balding head, of which she kept reminding him. Hers were subtle expressions of doubt, imperceptible to anyone else, but we had grown so close, she and I, that I recognised them almost telepathically. An infinitesimal change in her expression or demeanour which meant she wasn't ready to accept this as a family portrait for the future.

When it came time to leave, she asked: 'Is Jamie staying at his house and we're going back to ours?'

'Oh yes, Jamie's staying here,' I replied.
She smiled and said, 'Bye Jamie,' and got into the car waving her holly at him.

Before I pulled away, Jamie asked if I would be up for a night with some of his friends the following weekend. It was his birthday and he was thinking of inviting everyone over for a meal.

'Are they all couples?' I asked.

'Pretty much...'

'Well, as long as they know that we're not, you know, a couple, then I suppose, yes, that would be nice. I'll see you at the weekend then.'

Up to now, I had managed to deflect labels such as 'partner' or even worse 'boyfriend' in relation to my association with Jamie. They seemed inappropriate, and besides, I absolutely wasn't ready to be in a 'new relationship' with anyone. I was still in love with a dead man, and as far as I could tell that wasn't going to change. How could there be room for anyone else? For those who asked, Jamie was my 'friend who was a boy'. Mother had been ruddy-cheeked with delight when she'd gathered that we had been seeing each other, but I stemmed any conversation on the subject. I couldn't deal with the look of hope in her eyes, the sense of relief that I knew was dammed up inside her, just waiting to be released. I was grappling with a set of emotions that I didn't know what to do with. I enjoyed spending time with Jamie, but I couldn't convince myself that it's what Mark would want. But how does one seek approval from a dead man?

The following weekend, I arrived at Jamie's preparing to meet the friends of a friend. As such, I didn't have the apprehension that one normally has in this type of situation. After all, I wasn't seeking to impress these people. I couldn't have cared whether they liked me or not. Mother was looking after B, but I had brought Brucie along with me. He was one more responsibility Mother didn't need, and besides, I wanted an ally. My man, as it were.

However, as the friends trickled in, I started to feel a sense of unease. They were raucous and rambunctious, as is typical of a group of old friends. They talked about people I didn't know, including one update relating to someone who had just dropped dead of an aortic aneurysm.

'The main artery to the heart ruptured,' one friend said.

'How do you mean?' said another.

'Well, the main artery to the heart is the aorta, right? So this aneurysm made it burst—'

I felt Jamie place his hand on my shoulder. 'Right, anyway. Shall we go through for dinner?' He whispered, 'Sorry...' in my ear.

I had an urge to run out of the house, get into my car and drive straight home. These people were not my people, or Mark's people. Being with them felt fraudulent. They had expectations of me, I could feel it.

We sat around the table and someone asked: 'So then, where did you two meet?'

Jamie and I looked at each other. 'It's... complicated,' I said, draining a glass of wine and indicating for more.

'What? What have I asked? Was it online or something?'

'No, no, nothing like that,' I said.

'Can we talk about something else?' asked Jamie, pouring prosecco into flutes and passing them round.

'Oh come on!' piped someone else from the other end of the table. 'Where's the ring? We thought this might be an engagement party!'

I said, 'Oh Jesus!' and took the glass of prosecco. I felt for Brucie, who, as always, was by my feet under the table. He licked my hand.

'Seriously, change the subject,' Jamie said.

I sensed him looking at me, but I didn't dare catch his eye. Hadn't he told them about my situation? If he had, why would they pursue such a blunt line of questioning? They were seeking a mate for their friend, a female to make the group complete. But they got me.

Later in the evening, when wine and good food had worn the sharp edge off my mood, I went outside with a couple of the guys and had a cigarette.

'My husband died last year,' I said, blowing smoke into the freezing night air. 'So you see, me and Jamie... it's complicated.'

One of them put his arm around my shoulder. 'Shit. I didn't know. I just want to give you a hug.'

Much later, when the final couple bundled into their taxi home and there was just us and the detritus of the evening, I said: 'Why didn't you tell them?'

'I did, honest. They must have forgotten.' Jamie placed his hand gently on my knee and laid his head back on the settee.

'I'm not sure I can be who you want me to be,' I said.

But he'd fallen asleep. I tried once to shift him but he wouldn't move.

So I turned off the lights, and Brucie and I went up to bed.

The festive season. It had been whirling steadily around us like a twister, and now it was upon us in full force. The family-centric bent of everything pertaining to this Most Wonderful

Time of The Year had been lost on me up until now. But on approaching my second Christmas without Mark, the family fascists appeared to have ramped up their cause.

Of course, they were around last year. Unavoidable, but somehow less pernicious. I realised that that first Christmas had been mere shadow puppetry. I was there, but in ethereal form. Shock had not yet given way to disbelief. Now the shock had dissipated and I was face to face with the fact that this was Christmas hereafter. He was never going to be part of it again.

Despite having stipulated that I wouldn't be sending cards and neither did I wish to receive any, those folks who simply cannot deviate from their Christmas card list managed to sneak one through. I binned every one on receipt. Mother was appalled.

'That seems a bit mean,' she said.

'And?'

'Well, I can understand maybe chucking the ones from school, but this one from your dad, for example. Why is that one in the bin?'

'I'll see him over Christmas and wish him a happy one in person. Why on earth would I need a card to reiterate the sentiment?'

I wished she'd cease trying to understand. She didn't, and probably never would. This year, as last, I conceded to have a tree, and even went as far as a spangly reindeer decoration for the table. In windows all around the village, LED lights throbbed. In mine, though, nothing. A tacit V sign to the season.

We had been invited to go skiing with my siblings over Christmas, but this would have necessitated not only a plane journey, but also a week's worth of risk assessment on a maniacal scale. I had read that even if you rebounded off the softest of snow, a head injury can be fatal. A tumble from a ski lift was a one-way ticket to paraplegia. Not to mention the inevitable broken limbs, hypothermia and altitude sickness. For my daughter and me, this was not a viable holiday option.

I made a decision that B and I would spend Christmas Day with Kim and her family. Kim had always been a big fan of the festive season, and I knew that she would take everything in hand so that I didn't have to think about anything. Besides, she had four kids, an attentive husband and a huge house, which meant that immediately we arrived B would be absorbed and I wouldn't have to worry about her for a few days.

In the fortnight leading up to the Big Day I attended a total of one drinks party, one Nativity play (this year we had been demoted to Sheep) and one Christmas-themed excursion. I didn't send a single card and did all my shopping in one store on one lacklustre afternoon.

The excursion had been the idea of Jeanette and Graeme. It was a Village People outing to an 'Enchanted Forest' on the outskirts of York, where fun was the law, whether you liked it or not. Ostensibly it was for the kids, with an opportunity at every corner for the adults to part with their cash.

We arrived just before lunch and elected to see Santa first. The children were invited forward one by one by an elf, taken into a 'holding suite' and then directed to one of six rooms each containing a fat man in a red suit with a thick Yorkshire accent and unconvincing facial hair.

'What do you want for Christmas then?' our fat man asked B.

'A Doggie-Doo.' I wondered if this guy was familiar with the charmless Play-Doh-shitting plastic dachshund that my daughter had set her heart on.

'Right...'

He handed over a gift and told B to look at the camera that was rigged up in the corner of the room. There was no obligation, but of course, I bought the photograph.

In the time we had been with Santa, the Forest had got busy. Queues had sprung up for food, drink, ice-skating, Nordic cross-country skiing. Most people seemed to be in the spirit of things, but I found my new-found hatred of the season going into overdrive. This place represented everything I had tried to avoid.

We began the circuit of the Forest, which was flanked on one side by the Nordic cross-country ski trail. This meant that as we sauntered around on foot, admiring the LED-lit flora and fauna, we were treated to the gratifying sight of people blundering about alongside us on a length of green matting, grappling with ski-poles, falling over skis. And all for no discernible reason. For me, it was the highlight of the day.

Finally, we took to the ice rink. It was a potentially magical experience – a glistening pond of ice set against the glorious, Technicolor Forest – yet inevitably I was fraught and unable to enjoy a single second. I dragged B around the ice, never daring to leave the safety of the handrail.

Ned skidded up behind me. 'Do you want me to take B for a bit?'

I nodded and placed her tiny hand in his. 'Be careful with her, though. No messing about.'

I watched as he took her around the rink with the casual ease of a man who had fathered three children and got them all safely through this stage. My thoughts returned, as they always did, to Mark and how much He had been denied. I wondered if my friends felt it too as they watched somebody else's daddy taking up the slack with my daughter.

It was dark when we arrived back in the village. B and I were deposited home and I contemplated the few black hours between dinner and bed. These were the times I missed Him most. I poured myself a large glass of wine and agreed to some film or other even though it was probably too late. We sat on the settee, B, Brucie and me, curled into one another like a single homogenous being.

I looked across at the other settee, the two-seater, Mark's favourite. It was, of course, empty now, but I tried to picture Him sitting there, teasing the ring pull from the top of a can of ale and glugging the contents into a glass, then setting it down on the side table. He would reach across the arm to me and entwine His fingers with mine, and we would sit like this for most of the evening, before going up to bed and re-entwining our fingers under the duvet as we drifted off to sleep.

The season felt different, this time around. Darker, thicker, more apt to make me cry. The wine would have been drained, of that I am sure. Somehow, we got to bed.

It was 23 December and while storms had buffeted the south, up north we had barely had a whisper. High winds were forecast, though, but as forecasts generally only apply south of Birmingham, I figured that it would be safe to embark on the two-hour journey to Kim's on the other side of the Pennines.

'High winds are forecast,' said Mother. 'Are you sure you want to go today?'

'Jesus Christ, stop worrying. Of course I want to go today. There'll be no point otherwise.' No point, and also Kim was hosting a cocktail party that night, which I was keen to attend. A breeze barely strong enough to dislodge a conker wasn't coming between me and my mojito.

I loaded up the car with luggage, presents, child and dog, and headed off into the wind. And it was wind. High wind. As we hit the A66, it appeared we'd entered a tunnel of the stuff. My white knuckles could barely control the steering wheel. Furthermore, there was snow on these tops, it had gathered like a frill in the lay-bys, and it blew across the road in a series of terrifying mini-tornadoes. Then the downpour started. Shards of icy rain pelted the windscreen faster than my wipers could sweep them away.

'Isn't this fun, B?' I said, trying to eradicate the fear from my voice. Under the circumstances I permitted the iPad and the scourge of the Minions – anything to distract her from the prospect of certain death on this godforsaken road. Why the hell hadn't we waited until tomorrow?

I tried to calm myself by imagining Mark's voice. 'They would have closed the road, pet, if it was dangerous. Just keep your eyes to the front and take it slow.'

I took deep breaths and followed His instruction. High-sided lorries thundered past me on the inside lane, sending geysers of water into the air. I drove the whole distance at fifty miles an hour, arriving, ashen-faced and trembling, on to Kim's drive two hours later than scheduled.

'Mojito?' was Kim's first word.

'Aye,' I replied, leaving Steven, her husband, to unload the car.

'They've closed the A66 you know. You did well to get over when you did.'

I didn't want to think about the A66, though. Mojito in hand, I sank back into the chair, with every intention of staying there until Boxing Day.

Christmas Eve in the Harrison household involved phases of frantic activity, followed by periods of boozy calm. The three of us – Steven, Kim and I – drank throughout the day, stopping only to walk the dogs, tend to a twisty child or wrap the few remaining presents in time for the morning. I'd brought Martini, which we devoured with ice cubes and gusto. We moved around each other with the ease of old friends. But I felt the drag of intense sadness in my guts. It had been building and building, worsening with each festive film, each Christmas song. Indeed, this year felt worse than last. I felt less capable – or perhaps willing – to pretend that everything was all right.

Steven's family arrived and brought lunch – a selection of grotesque meat cuts from the local butcher and a flabby, anaemic-looking tripe – and we toasted to each other's good health. Steven's mother offered me a taste of the tripe, which was, apparently, best served cold with malt vinegar and a pinch of pepper. I opted for a tiny morsel and instantly regretted it. The rancid taste lingered on my tonsils for the best part of half an hour, despite my efforts to remove it with a variety of alcoholic astringents.

That the Harrisons were prepared to take me and my daughter in on this most intimate of family occasions was verging on the biblical. Kim and I had, of course, been friends for more than half of our lives, but they were, in my opinion, taking a risk with this decision. I stood to ruin Christmas for them. Who wanted tears on Christmas Day when really it was all about pudding and Slade?

The children were, in the end, the saving grace. By their very nature they have fleeting interest in anyone else but themselves. They force the grieving widow out of her navel-gazing and into the moment, which is the best place to be. Kim's youngest child decided to attach herself to me, stymying any desire I might have had to enter a realm of self-pity. So I managed to remain buoyant and tear-free. Until Christmas Day.

B woke at 6.30 a.m., which was unheard of. This was the kid who required a chisel and a winch to remove her from bed for school in the morning.

'I doubt Santa's been yet,' I said, rubbing her back, trying to persuade her back to sleep.

'He must have been. It's up time.'

'Not quite.'

She prised my eyes open with a thumb and forefinger. 'Yes it is.'

I heard voices downstairs and assumed that Kim's kids were up and waiting for us, despite the insanity of the hour.

'Come on then. Jesus Christ, it's barely even daylight.' As I pulled on my socks and dressing gown I recalled how Mark used to greet me each day with the words: *Morning, Sunshine!* in reference to my foul fore-noon mood.

We arrived in the kitchen and found Steven up with the youngest child. Kim was still in bed, as were the other three kids.

'Has he been?' B asked Steven.

'We think so, but we need to wait for the others to come down, B. Then we can all go in and look together.'

I looked at my child as she sat alongside her little friend and drank the milk that Steven offered her. It struck me that this was the first Christmas that she had really embraced the excitement, the concept of the gifts and the sense of togetherness that encapsulated Christmas. Nothing ever got her – or me – out of bed at 6.30 a.m. except for the promise of Santa and the anticipation of Christmas Day. I felt pleased for her that we were here, in a little nest of family life, where there were symbols of the season on every corner – decorated trees, branches, cards, stars, fake snow. The things I had wilfully expelled from our home.

The three remaining children woke and came running downstairs, and we prepared them all for the big reveal. Steven went ahead into the room in order to film their faces as they first glimpsed the majestic spruce bursting with presents.

'He's been!' came the first gleeful shriek.

'There's a footprint!' came another.

'He's eaten the mince pie!'

'And drunk the brandy!'

'Here's a present for me!'

B scurried in with the rest of them and then turned to me when she saw the mountain of presents. 'Where's my Doggie Doo?' she asked.

'Here, my darling,' I said, plucking the box from where I'd laid it the previous night. 'Let's open it together.'

The tears threatened then, at that moment, amid the presents and the elation, for this was not just Christmas, this was the Christmas of my dreams, an apricot-hued, soft-focus Christmas featuring Mum, Dad, kids, canines, and my man was missing it, He was missing the face of our child as she opened some crappy mass-produced toy and grinned from ear to ear.

I didn't want to look at the pile of presents that Steven had reserved for his wife, the perfume, the fancy shades, the expensive eye cream or the bottle of special reserve gin that he just knew she'd love. I concentrated instead on the delight of my child as she unearthed the gifts that Kim and I had bought her and opened them, one by one.

'Champagne?' Kim said once the final gift had been unpacked and discarded in favour of the paper.

I looked at the clock. 8.45 a.m. 'Aye.'

She disappeared into the pantry to retrieve the champagne and I stood at the kitchen window and wept. Fat tears formed rivulets down my cheeks, and they wouldn't be staunched. Kim returned and looked at me.

'I know, pet,' she said, and popped the cork on the bottle. She filled three flutes and handed me one. 'Now then. Why don't you go and get yourself ready. We're having smoked salmon at 10 a.m. Be down and beautiful for that.'

In a hiatus between the salmon and the Christmas dinner, one of those quiet moments when everyone is absorbed in their own thoughts and activities, my gaze drifted to Steven, who stood, propped up against the oven, watching the TV. He had unquestioningly accepted my daughter and me into his home during this most intimate of festivals. He was a man of few words, yet for whom actions go a long way. Also, he was wearing one of the comedy moustaches I'd bought him, which somehow added to his allure.

I got up from my chair and threw my arms around his neck. I buried my nose in his shoulder and cried. Kim busied herself around us as we held each other, then I pulled away and ran to the toilet to compose myself. When I returned, my daughter was waiting for me with the Doggie Doo.

'Can you help me with this?' she asked.

Within minutes of my breakdown, I found myself stuffing a lump of Play-Doh down the throat of a plastic dachshund and watching it emerge in the form of a turd out the other end.

B and I lived in a pebble-dashed bubble of tranquillity, like a latter-day Bert and Ernie. Here, though, we were in the midst of a cyclone. No sooner had the turkey been placed on the table than it was reduced to an obscene-looking splayed skeleton. Roast spuds were digested at one end of the table before they had chance to reach the other. It was impossible to take two successive mouthfuls of food without fielding a request for juice, water, bread, another spud, more turkey. Dogs woofed in unison whenever a chair moved, and waited, unblinking, for the moment that one of the kids dropped a morsel of food on the floor.

Once the meal was finished, the clear-up job began. Industrial-sized baking trays had to be washed, hundreds of plates, utensils, items of cutlery needed to be cleaned and put away, and then dessert would follow and the whole rigmarole would begin again. That evening, some of Kim's friends dropped in for a drink, unleashing three further children into the mix. B and I sat together on the settee in the lounge and stared dumbly at the TV, in a food-and-screaming-induced catatonia.

Later that night when I took B to bed, and we lay opposite each other for one of our pre-sleep chats, she said: 'Can we go home tomorrow and see Grandma?'

'Yes, darling. I think that's a good idea.'

'And Mum?'

'Yes?'

'When it's Christmas again, can we have lights in our window and a big tree, like at Kim's?'

I kissed her forehead and traced a finger around the outside of her face. 'Maybe.'

Jamie announced that he wanted to take me away for a night between Christmas and New Year. Or two nights, if I could manage it. We hadn't seen each other over Christmas and weren't going to see each other at New Year. After all, these are the days that couples typically spend together, and we were by no means a couple. We were two people who enjoyed each other's company, as well as sharing an understanding of a situation which is not understood by many.

I conceded to one night. I would fret for B if I was away for longer, fearing the worst might happen and that I wouldn't be able to get back to her.

'We're going to Edinburgh,' Jamie told me. 'Pack a nice dress.'

He picked me up on the Saturday morning and we took the route north through the Northumberland hills. The sun was low behind us, casting a lemony light across the knitting-needle grassland, poking through the rheumatic branches of the ancient oaks. It was a part of the world Mark loved, where we'd always dreamed of living. I fell into silent contemplation, feeling guilty about admiring its beauty with another man.

We arrived at the hotel at noon. It was a smart, wood-panelled residence in the curve of a Georgian crescent. Jamie had booked us a suite whose three massive windows looked out over parkland and the Firth of Forth beyond. We had a brunch reservation at 12.30 p.m., which we would take up while the room was being prepared.

Brunch was in one of those places which can't decide whether it's a cafe or a bar or a restaurant, so it calls itself a 'kitchen'. The sort of place where denotations of currency on the menu are considered to be extraneous, so instead prices are written as simply '10' or '10.5'. I ordered the eggs Benedict (7.5) and a Bloody Mary (7).

'Let me at least pay for lunch,' I said, stirring my drink with a celery stick.

'Absolutely not. It's my trip, I'm paying.'

A woman at the next table was fighting with a small child in a high chair, trying to get him to bend his pudgy little legs in order that he could be seated. He held himself straight as a rod and emitted a loud scream from the depths of his tiny, tyrannous lungs. I couldn't help reflecting on B at that age. A bundle of fury and rage who growled at anyone who came near. I remembered calling Mark once on a rare afternoon when He'd taken her out to a local cafe on His own.

'All OK?' I'd asked.

'Just sitting here, having a cheese sandwich and a coffee with my lady,' He replied, at which point His lady had interjected with a bloodcurdling screech followed by a strident chorus of tears. 'Er. I'd better go.'

I watched the woman as she tried to waft her errant fringe out of her face at the same time as attempting to silence her child.

'Thank God I'm past all that,' I said, taking a slug of the Bloody Mary. 'This is so nice.'

The main challenge of the afternoon was choosing which sort of liquor I wanted in my chocolate. Sitting at one end of the spa bath back at the hotel, I scrutinised the box. I plumped for the gin crunch and washed it down with a mouthful of Rioja.

'What time are we going out?' I asked.

'You need to be ready by seven thirty.'

'Where are we going?'

'You don't need to know that.' Jamie smiled from the other end of the bath. 'Pass me the chocolates.'

'It's a shame that these water jets aren't a centimetre to the left,' I said, sinking deeper into the bubbles. 'That way, they'd be exactly on my bad back.'

'I knew you'd find something to complain about,' Jamie said. 'Do you mind if I eat the amaretto one?'

I laughed. 'Go ahead. I don't like amaretto anyway.'

The conversation made me think about Mark. There was a joke between us: No matter how good something was, I'd always say; *It's nice, but it's a shame that...*' As if I had an intrinsic predilection for disappointment. Here I was guzzling chocolates in a spa bath in Edinburgh, rehearsing exactly the same words.

The taxi arrived at 7.45 and spirited us from our hotel to a wine bar near the station. Dinner was at eight at a restaurant named La Garrigue.

'I know you like anything French, so I thought it was probably a good bet,' Jamie said as we walked, arm in arm, along the street. 'We can't have you complaining now, can we?'

I couldn't help but think that this bloke had got the measure of me. That somehow, even though he wasn't my dark-haired, white-browed ideal, I'd met my match.

The meal began with white Dubonnet and cold lobster, was followed by cassoulet and an unexpected jag of tears, and ended with cheese and an Armagnac.

'I'm sorry,' I said, returning from the restroom where I'd spent five minutes trying to remove the riverbeds of mascara from my cheeks. 'I have no idea where that came from.'

'It's no problem. It will happen. Don't forget, it's to be expected.' Jamie smiled at me and picked up the cheese knife. 'Now then. Which do you fancy? Camembert or some of this rancid-smelling shit here?'

I took Jamie's hand and entwined my fingers with his. He leaned in and kissed me, leaving a taste of warm brandy on my lips.

We finished our meal and wandered out into the December night. The castle loomed through the darkness like a charcoal drawing over Princes Street Gardens, where the trees glittered like sparklers. Scarf-swathed skaters glided about on the flood-lit ice rink and the alpine chalets of the Christmas market glowed, just like the one Mother always used to put on the mantel at Christmastime when we were small. Jamie pulled me in next to him and we held each other tight against the cold while we waited for the taxi.

That night, I gave in to being half a couple with someone other than my husband. I allowed myself to hold another man's hand in the street. Permitted others to assume that we were together. I allowed him to take over, to take on the burden of organisation, to be my foil. And like those alpine chalets, something glowed within me; but this time, it wasn't the fierce burning of a broken heart. After so long I couldn't be sure, but I thought I recognised it – a kernel of contentment. My brain still resisted in part, but I felt a deep sense of peace for the first time in almost two years.

Epilogue

The impending New Year was the second of four challenges I had to surmount before I could consider the months ahead. Christmas had been the first and I was now able to tick that off. Mark's birthday, on 4 January, would be the third. I had an idea of how I wanted to mark this, and it would involve just me and Mark's three closest buddies, John, Paul and Neil. It had been quite some time since we had spent time all together, and I felt strong enough this time around that I wanted to do something to 'remember' my husband.

The fourth would be 11 February, the anniversary of Mark's death. The date swung out there in the void on a creaking gibbet, daring me to approach.

B and I were spending New Year at Dan's with the rest of the family. My siblings had been skiing and I hadn't seen Beth for almost two weeks. It was the longest a single member of our feminine triad had been away, and I was starting to pine for her. But I pined for the others too – Dan, who could make me laugh with a look; Dad, from whom I'd inherited my snaggly bottom teeth and tendency towards cynicism; Helen who supplied me with cigarettes and a level-headed viewpoint; and the kids, oh the kids, each one of them like a lifebuoy on a squally sea.

And again, as I prepared to dive off the cliff into another year without Him, this time felt different to the last; the pain was more livid, the truth in starker relief. I could scarcely control my bottom lip as I was reunited with my family on the eve of a new year. After this point, I would no longer say 'My husband died last year', but rather, 'My husband died two years ago', which was only a difference of words, yet signified so much.

We started early on the champagne. Dad disapproved volubly from behind his paper, but soon gave in and joined the rest of us. Once the final bottle was upended, we opened the wine. We ate from a home-cooked ham and a board laden with cheese, but I was agitated, watching the minutes tick by on the clock. Perhaps sensing my steadily deflating frame of mind, Dan disappeared and presently I heard the strains of 'Silver Lady' by David Soul welling up from neighbouring room. It was a song my brother and I shared, the soundtrack to an in-joke from when we were kids.

He threw me a rope and I took it, bounding into the room just as he was coming out to find me. We bumped into each and laughed, and pointed at the stereo in glee. Beth appeared then, and the three of us held each other and belted out the chorus in unison.

We exorcised our dance demons to a catalogue of other Soul classics, joined eventually by the kids who couldn't resist the lure of the great, be-cardiganed man.

But Soul was merely a temporary fix. As midnight approached, I heard Dad say, 'Right, now we need a first foot... Will, it'll have to be you, you're the only one with dark hair...'

The cyclone that had been stirring in my brain whipped up to full force, and I ran and hid in a far room, hoping that no one would notice I was missing.

Helen found me first.

'I'm tired of pretending everything is OK, Helen. It's not. Nothing about this is OK.'

'There's nothing I can say, is there?'

I shook my head. Dad arrived with Beth and M.

'This is the special one,' I said, holding M's head close to my chest. 'She was born the month I met Mark.'

'Come on now, come on,' somebody said.

Dan came in. 'Right, Will's outside freezing his 'nads off. Pull yourself together, it's nearly midnight.'

'I can't. I don't want to.'

He grabbed my hand. 'Yes, you can.'

'I can't. Mark was always first foot, it should be Him.'

'Well, He's not here and Will's doing it. So come on.'

But I couldn't. I missed the countdown, the fireworks, the birth of the New Year. I overheard it all, alone, from behind a settee in Dan's house.

Aside from a hangover and the inevitability of my situation not having changed, what did the next morning bring? I drew back the curtains on the 688th day since I'd last seen my husband alive, and felt weary. Weary of being defined by my loss, of using grief as an excuse for my erratic and reckless behaviours. What tools had Mark given me with which to battle on into another year, and how could I use them to banish the weariness?

Firstly, He'd given me B. In the early days of my grief, I'd wondered whether this bequest was a blessing or a curse. She was a constant reminder of Him and what was lost. Not only did she look like Him – who could mistake that smile, those eyes? – but her existence defined me as a single mother. But now, she was the biggest and single most important buoyancy aid I had. We had become inseparable since His death, she now completed me, just as Mark had.

But He'd also given me ten years of unconditional love and happiness, as well as the legacy of His own personality and extraordinary courage. And like a kind of alchemy, these elements had transformed after His death into a source of inner strength to get me through. For the first time since His death, I felt myself acknowledging the faint beginnings of hope. Maybe things *would* eventually get better.

EPILOGUE

*

I woke up on the morning of Mark's birthday with my head on Jamie's chest. The sound of a heart beating beneath a ribcage unnerved me. It had become synonymous with the eerie click-whoosh of Mark's mechanical heart valve which could be heard across a silent room.

'I hate hearing that,' I'd tell Mark, placing my fingers in my ears.

'Why, pet?' He'd reply. 'It's life-affirming.'

Instinctively, I moved my head from Jamie's chest on to the pillow. I looked at the photographs of my beloved, which hung around the room. A black-and-white shot of Him on the pier at Port Melbourne. Him sitting in Mother's garden, squinting even though there was no sun. Our initials, etched into sand. *L 4 M*. It was He who had drawn them, a piece of driftwood for a pen.

I wanted Jamie to leave, but I was afraid that I might shatter if he went – literally, break apart into a million shards on the floor. We got up, ate, looked at the clock. I knew what the day held. I would leave the house at 2.15 and head up the coast to John's house, where Paul and Neil would have gathered. I had planned a ritual. An honouring of my husband on the day He would have turned thirty-nine.

Jamie, aware it was Mark's birthday and perhaps sensing my need for solitude, left at midday. I didn't break apart, not at first, but I spent some time sitting on the edge of the bed, staring at the wardrobe where Mark's ashes were.

The dog came upstairs, searching for me as he always did. He immediately sensed my mood, and flattened himself on the carpet a short distance away from where I was perched, watching me through the thicket of his eyebrows. I felt the inexorable tide of tears approaching, and I crawled to the floor, clutching my stomach as if I might throw up.

'Love,' I whispered. 'Oh, love.'

The dog rose and walked over to me. He placed a paw on each of my shoulders and tenderly licked one eyelid and then the other, mopping my tears with his tongue. I pulled him into me and he nestled his muzzle into my neck. We held each other for a long while, until B came upstairs and looked in on us.

'Are you crying?'

'Yes.'

'Why?'

'Why does Mummy cry?'

'Because you miss Daddy?'

'Yes.'

She paused for a moment. 'Is it Mark's birthday today?'

'Yes, it's Mark's birthday today,' I replied. I reached for her and she came to my side. 'Who is Mark?'

A smile broke across her face. 'Daddy!'

'That's right. Daddy.'

Mother arrived with a cake mix and suggested it might be nice if she and B made Daddy a birthday cake while I was out.

'Can I blow the candle out?' B asked.

'Of course,' Mother replied. Her attention turned to me. 'Are you all right this morning?'

I shrugged my shoulders and pulled on my boots. 'I'll take Brucie out before I head off to John's, if that's all right,' I said.

Mother nodded. 'It's miserable out there, but you do whatever you need to do.'

The dog and I stepped out into the drizzle and began a long walk, past the derelict farmstead which overlooks the village, over the marshy, tufted fields to where the views extend to the A1 and the Cleveland Hills far into the distance. I searched along the horizon for the radio mast that Mark and I would pass on the way home to our old village in North Yorkshire, a marker between the hills denoting our arrival, or our departure.

A couple of dog-walking friends approached and greeted us with the vim of those in the throes of post-Christmas renewal.

'I don't mean to be rude, but I can't talk today,' I said, marching on. 'It's Mark's birthday... I just can't talk today.'

Brucie and I padded through the mud-stricken tracks back up into the village, and got back to the house to find that nothing had changed. It was a Saturday in January, and B was playing on the iPad, and Mother was unloading the dishwasher, wondering where we'd got to as we'd been longer than she'd thought.

I showered, dressed, gathered up the sky lantern in preparation for the evening and asked Mother for her house keys.

'What do you need?' she asked.

'I'm going to take Mark's Guinness up for the lads,' I said. 'Might as well, it's not doing any good where it is.'

Mother raised her eyebrows. 'Whatever you want, love.'

But when I pulled up outside Mother's house to pick up the Guinness, I became less sure that I wanted to give them up. They were still tucked away on the shelf in the porch where they'd been since the night He died. I approached them with the caution of a bomb disposal expert. I lifted them off the shelf and checked them for fingerprints. None. I would take them anyway, I thought, even if I ended up bringing them back. But something stopped me. I put them back on the shelf and left the house.

Our plan was to release a sky lantern over the North Sea at Whitley Bay on the north-east coast. Storms were forecast, but nonetheless we would go ahead, even if the damn thing ended up plummeting into the sea. I had alerted the coastguard that we would be releasing it at 5 p.m. John, Neil, Paul, Fran and I wrapped ourselves up again the bitter chill and headed down to the beach.

It was black by now, the only thing delineating land from sea was a string of coastal lights. We walked down the steps to where the sea roiled against the promenade and looked out at a solitary ship illuminated on the horizon. St Mary's Lighthouse, clothed in rings of coloured light, thrust up into the blackness on the far promontory. There were no stars, and no moon. There was also no storm – only the sound of the sea against a wintry breeze.

We unfurled the lantern – a huge, flaccid sack – and lit the fuel pad. I held it as it grew bigger and tussled to be free. I let go of it, and for a moment it seemed as if the breeze might take it inland, but then it drifted up and out over the water, towards Norway, Denmark, ever higher into the moonless night. We stood, agape, watching it – Him – as He lit up the sky, a solitary fiery light, flickering. Gradually, the light dimmed and then disappeared altogether.

As we climbed back up the steps to the pub there were no words. Just a tacit understanding that no matter what, He would always be part of us.

It is 11 February 2014; exactly two years since Mark died.

We woke up this morning to a thin mist. I walked my child to school down the usual route, passing old Alf toddling back home after an early walk with his rangy red setter, and the girl with the endless legs striding forth with her son. We dodged the same potholes in the pavements, the same piles of dog shit, now with a dusting of frost. Curlews picked their way noisily over one of the fields. Today the Women's Institute hosted their Annual Winter Luncheon in the village hall. It was a day, much like any other.

Everything has changed in the time He has been gone. My daughter has grown from a toddler into a little girl, with a level of emotional intelligence and compassion incommensurate with her years. She has lost her daddy, yet become aware of the weighty anchor of support available to her from family and loving friends.

I have a new house in a new place, with new friends and a new dog, and the potential of a new relationship. These new things are my armoury. They don't bring to mind a smile or a throwaway line to remind me of what is lost.

And with the new things comes a 'new me': tougher, more rough-hewn than the old one, yet still fragile as spun sugar. This 'new me' continues to confound the old one at every turn, adding to the sense of life's sudden and ongoing volatility.

As for Mark, He is still in His ornate, lacquered box at the bottom of my wardrobe. I remain undecided what to do with Him. I may buy a small parcel of land nearby and plant Him in it, along with some native trees of the type He liked to ramble between on autumnal Sundays. It would become a wood, of sorts, a death-to-life dell, and would be named in His honour. It's impossible to think of a worthy ending for the love of your life, but this, I think, may be the best I can do.

Jupiter glows bright above the Earth like a sky lantern tonight; a solitary light in a crisp, navy sky. It burned there exactly two years ago, alongside Venus, and I looked up at it then, as I do now, thinking of Him.

And I feel like His sky lantern, tussling to be free. The trauma and the grief have taken enough. I want to live.

I believe that Mark would want us to be happy.

Acknowledgements

THANKS GO TO:

Kate Moore and the whole team at Virgin for believing so passionately in me and this book, and for nurturing us with generosity, sensitivity and skill.

My agent Jemima Hunt for her unwavering faith in me and my writing.

Mother, Dad, my brother and my sister, without whom...

The Cavalry – old and new, you know who you are.

My nieces M and G, and my nephew, T.

My daughter. This is what happened, B. When you are old enough to read it, I hope it'll help you to understand.

And finally, thanks go to the love of my life, Mark – the most courageous man I've ever known. Wherever you are, I miss you, pet.